the series on ⌐

Patricia A. Wasley	Ann Lieberman	Joseph P. McDonald
University of Washington	Carnegie Foundation for the Advancement of Teaching	New York University

SERIES EDITORS

(Continued)

the series on school reform, *continued*

SCHOOLS Within SCHOOLS

Possibilities and Pitfalls
of
High School Reform

Valerie E. Lee & Douglas D. Ready

Teachers College
Columbia University
New York and London

Published by Teachers College Press, 1234 Amsterdam Avenue, New York, NY 10027

Library of Congress Cataloging-in-Publication Data

Lee, Valerie E.
    Schools within schools : possibilities and pitfalls of high school reform /
Valerie E. Lee and Douglas D. Ready.
        p.   cm. — (The series on school reform)
    Includes bibliographical references and index.
    ISBN-13: 978-0-8077-4752-0 (pbk. : alk. paper)
        1. School improvement programs—United States—Case studies.   2. High schools—United States—Administration.   3. School size.   I. Ready, Douglas D.
II. Title.

    LB2822.82.L44 2006
    373.12—dc22   2006025554

ISBN: 978-0-8077-4752-0 (paper)

Printed on acid-free paper
Manufactured in the United States of America

14   13   12   11   10   09   08   07   8   7   6   5   4   3   2   1

■ ■ ■

Contents

■ ■ ■

Acknowledgments

THE LAST DECADE has seen an enormous amount of interest in high school reform. Although many flaws have been identified, one of the major concerns about high schools is their large size. How to "fix" this problem is vexing; it would be difficult and costly to close down our nation's large high schools and open many small stand-alone schools. Perhaps a more reasonable approach— and one that has expanded substantially over the last few years—is to divide large high schools (usually those that are quite troubled) into a set of schools within schools. How this reform plays out in a few high schools is the subject of this book.

Our interest in schools within schools grew out of our shared and fundamental interest in how the form and structure of high schools influence the students who are educated in them and the adults who work there. The idea for this particular study, which began in 1998 at the School of Education at the University of Michigan, grew out of a difficult question regarding high school reform: "If small schools facilitate student learning (as our earlier studies had indicated), how can high schools actually be made smaller?" When we began this study, the schools-within-schools reform was far from widespread. Thus, we decided that it made sense to study a few such schools in depth to learn how they worked. We are enormously grateful to the Spencer Foundation for agreeing with us about the importance and timeliness of this topic, manifested through their generous support for this work. This support first took the form of a 3-year major grant starting in 1998, and subsequently continued with a smaller grant in 2001. Because so much of our previous research had been focused on large-scale samples and quantitative methods, the Foundation's support for and confidence in us to conduct field research was especially important and appreciated.

Besides financial support, research requires human support. Many people participated in the research activities that eventually led to this book. Two groups of people were invaluable: (a) those who helped us collect and analyze our data, and (b) those who worked in the schools we studied and who, in effect, played the central roles in these stories. Fortunately, we are able to recognize those in the first group by name. We assembled a large research team to develop what we wanted to know and how we might best find out these things. Ultimately our research team was divided into two- or three-member teams assigned to the same school for the duration of the study. Each team was headed by a lead researcher, who was assisted by one or two research assistants. We are deeply indebted to our very talented team, which included, as lead researchers, Bob Croninger, Diana Oxley (who headed the team for two schools), and Shana Pribesh. Our dedicated and skilled team of research assistants included Françoise Boudon, Erika Brumfield, Eddie Fergus, David Johnson, Laura LoGerfo, and Francisco Osuna-Currea. We included a talented qualitative researcher on our team—Elisabeth DeGroot—who guided us toward the best methods to collect and analyze field-based data.

Unfortunately, we are unable to acknowledge by name those in the second group, whose efforts helped us so much. Our promise of anonymity to the schools that participated in our study precludes us from publicly thanking these people who were so crucial in our work. This school-based group includes people in many roles. First and foremost, we thank the principals and other administrators who were responsible for inviting us into their schools, who seemed very interested in what we were up to, and who were willing to put their schools up for scrutiny. Each principal and most subunit heads spent countless hours talking with us, showing us their schools, and arranging our work. The type of research we conducted was time-intensive and surely disruptive.

Invaluable also were the teacher coordinators in each school. These were the people with whom we kept in close contact, who arranged our interviews, and who collected permission slips from parents so that we could interview students. These people helped make our time in their schools flow smoothly and proceed efficiently. In some cases we also met with district-level administrators and superintendents. We spent many hours speaking with teachers, individually and in focus groups, and occasionally observing their practice in classrooms. We are very grateful to them for sharing their valuable time in helping us to understand their schools, their intentions, their ideas, and sometimes their students. To the many students with whom we spoke, mostly in focus groups, we are grateful for their time, their frank opinions, and to their teachers, who sometimes released them from class to meet with us. Although we tried hard to conduct our student focus groups at lunchtime over pizza, this was not always possible. Other help on the project at the University of Michigan came from Byron Coleman, whose word processing skills are very much appreciated.

When Doug was a doctoral student at the University of Michigan, ready to embark on his dissertation, he intended to pursue a topic unrelated to schools within schools. However, a rather short conversation together led us both to recognize the obvious—that our work together on this project was something that we were both deeply committed to. Doug's dissertation ultimately crystallized the ideas in this book for both of us, and this book is an obvious extension of that work. We have worked together as a productive team for almost a decade now. Although this book represents an important part of that work, we believe that this is just the beginning of a fruitful collaboration.

Valerie E. Lee   Douglas D. Ready
Ann Arbor, Michigan   *New York, New York*

■ ■ ■

Prologue

ZACHARY TAYLOR HIGH SCHOOL is located in the southeastern corner of a mid-Atlantic city, quite near the state's major north–south interstate highway and two blocks from one of the city's busiest east–west highways. The somber gray, two-story structure housing the school is surrounded by somewhat decrepit rowhouses to the west, several aging factories and a railroad track to the east, and a Catholic elementary school to the north. Taylor's 2,300 students, drawn from a 14.2-square-mile catchment area that includes several central-city neighborhoods, make it the largest public high school in the city. The history of Zachary Taylor High School, both rich and varied, includes a decade-long experiment with schools within schools.

TAYLOR HIGH SCHOOL

For more than 60 years, generations of families in the mostly eastern European working-class neighborhoods in the southeastern corner of the city have sent their children to Taylor High School. Almost entirely White as late as 1975, the school's enrollment in 1998 was 75% African American, 20% White, with small numbers of Hispanic, Asian, and Native American students. In the mid-1970s, federal court orders required the city to desegregate its public schools. As a result, the school district designated two types of high schools: citywide magnet schools with selective admissions criteria and zoned high schools that were required to enroll students from particular residential areas that were purposely redrawn to include several neighborhoods with different racial compositions. Although southeastern city residents were not happy with the court-ordered desegregation plan, they grudgingly complied.

The expanded catchment area, its designation as a zoned high school, as well as social and economic changes throughout the city, all combined to change the academic and demographic composition of Taylor High School's students. It now enrolls high proportions of economically disadvantaged and minority students, and it is also the city's most racially diverse high school. Taylor is now the high school that students from a wide area of the city attend if they cannot gain entrance to (or subsequently succeed in) one of the city's many selective magnet high schools.

TAYLOR HITS BOTTOM

Although Taylor High School's reputation had been solid until the 1980s, by the early 1990s it was widely known as a school in trouble. Delinquency and drug use were endemic, contempt shown toward teachers reached crisis proportions, and attendance was sporadic. Many staff and students who were part of Taylor during that period described the school as seriously "out of control." For example, an African American student who attended the school between 1994 and 1998 described her early years at Taylor: "You just roamed the halls, and some of the teachers didn't even know who you were . . . because you never went to class. You just passed because they wanted to pass you." A teacher on the Taylor staff during that period concurred: "It was difficult. I went home every night exhausted, wondering what I had done wrong that God has punished me, to put me in such an environment. I felt as if I was dropped down in a war zone. And that is what it was like, literally!"

In 1994, the State Board of Education designated two city high schools, one of which was Taylor High, as "eligible for reconstitution," based on both declining test scores and continuing failure to show substantial and sustained progress in meeting state standards. Many faculty and students who were part of Taylor during this period confirmed the state's assessment that the school had very serious problems. Less than two-thirds of students showed up for any class on a particular day. About a third of Taylor's 11th graders failed the state basic skills test. Annual dropout rates approached 16%. Even those who graduated had not earned sufficient credits to enroll in any of the state's colleges and universities. Violence was endemic, both between students and against teachers. Many students came to school but never attended class.

A MODEL OF URBAN SCHOOL REFORM

Under reconstitution, the State Board would monitor the designated schools for improvement, typically to be accomplished within 5 years. If a reconstituted school was unable to document sufficient progress, it could face dramatic sanctions—including state takeover, privatization of school operations, or even permanent closure. As part of its reconstitution plan, Taylor appointed new administrators, transferred many faculty and hired many new teachers, and restructured many of its academic programs. Central to the reconstitution plan was the implementation of a schools-within-schools (SWS) design, under the guidance of the new Talent Development High School reform program. These changes, particularly the division of the school into smaller learning communities (which in this book we call "subunits"), led Taylor to be the subject a large volume of local, state, and national publicity. It was trumpeted as an exemplar of urban school reform and "turnaround."

By most accounts, the early results of the initial reforms were impressive. The morale of remaining staff rebounded, and student discipline improved dramatically. As students and staff coalesced around the new Talent Development subunit models, identity and purpose were rekindled. Most notable was the new sense of control and order at Taylor High School. A school administrator crowed: "First year, I think it was 100% turn around . . . overall the school was in much better control. In [my subunit], it was very, very tight. You knew those kids. I mean, they were under control." A teacher in the same subunit concurred: "With the subunit model, staff who remained had a vision and felt supported. [We] came in and decided that we were going to go ahead and give it another shot. We reached down within ourselves . . . we were a force, we were united, and we were supported!" A student who attended the school before and after reconstitution added: "I used to cut a lot, didn't come to school sometimes or when I did come, I would just come for lunch and then leave. Nobody knew you, nobody cared, that's just the way it was. It's different now . . . you can learn more because you don't have to cakewalk in the hallway. I think that [now] it is more like, not necessarily family, but it's more like everybody knows everybody, so you know if you do something, your teacher will know, a lot of people will know what you did because you are in the subunit."

The environment at Taylor High School changed dramatically as a result of reconstitution. The new principal was able to institute "zero-based staffing," in which no staff positions were guaranteed and the principal could hire and fire faculty at will. As a result, there were dramatic staff changes during the first few years. All faculty who were not supportive of the new organizational form were asked to leave or take early retirement, and many new and eager faculty were recruited. The school, following the Talent Development model and with considerable professional development from that organization in its early years, was reorganized into schools within schools. These included a separate 9th-grade subunit and four upper-grade subunits that students entered by choice, each organized around a career theme. Within each subunit, staff were grouped into cross-disciplinary teams that together taught smaller groups of students. The school followed a block schedule with four 90-minute classes per day. The traditional academic departments were disbanded, and the locus of decision making moved to the subunits, each of which had a full-time administrator and an instructional leader. Subunit staff were allowed to develop new courses and order new materials. Taylor also instituted a quarterly grading system, whereby students received more frequent feedback about academic progress on four report cards per semester, eight per year.

STEPPING BACK FROM REFORM

Although there is near-universal agreement on the dramatic improvements in Taylor's social environment as a result of its reconstitution into an SWS organizational design, improvements in academic indicators have not followed suit. Consistently since adoption of the SWS design, 9th graders have represented 40% of the student body, due to continuing high dropout rates and 9th-grade retentions. Staff members disagree about what should happen to the relatively large numbers of 9th graders who do not accumulate sufficient credits to move to 10th grade. Although daily attendance improved—attendance was a priority within the reform—it remained relatively low when our study began, averaging 74% (compared with the city average of 82% and the state average of 92%). In 1998–1999, 71% of Taylor students missed more than 20 days out of the 180-day school year. Moreover, very few Taylor students who persisted to graduation entered any form of higher education. Administrative turnover was high: between 1995 and 1998, the school had four principals. Fortunately the current principal, who began in 1998, is leading the school to this day. In the last few years, this principal has taken a firm grasp on the school and has moved away from fully embracing the SWS design. Although Talent Development still includes Taylor High School on its membership list, the reform organization is now much more active in other high schools in this and other cities.

It may be useful to think of change at Taylor High School as occurring in several phases. Phase One would encompass the school's early history, as a predominantly White working-class high school with a very positive reputation in the neighborhood and across the city. Phase Two arrived with court-ordered desegregation in the mid-1960s, when the school began to enroll higher proportions of low-income and minority students drawn from a much larger area in the city. Within Phase Two, Taylor High became a zoned high school that enrolled students uninterested in or unable to be admitted to one of the city's several selective magnet high schools. Phase Two continued into the early 1990s—as the school's reputation, performance, and social environment slid into crisis. Phase Three began in 1994, when the school was designated as reconstitution-eligible by the state. Because the school embraced the SWS reform as a major element of its response to its mandated need to change, Taylor High School is particularly interesting within the context of this book. Although we describe Taylor High during Phase Three in more detail later in the book, we emphasize that there is also a Phase Four in this story. In this phase—which encompasses Zachary Taylor High School today—the school has reformulated (but not abandoned) its SWS design and in some ways backed away from its full embrace of that reform.

THIS BOOK TELLS the "reform stories" of five public high schools that have adopted the SWS reform, and Zachary Taylor High School is one of them. Each high school is different in many ways—whom it is charged with educating, how it is organized, how the school arrived at this particular structural reform, and how the reform has played out in each setting. We have introduced our book with a brief journey through the recent history of one of these schools—Taylor High School—because it seems to be quite representative of the particular type of school (and the special circumstances) where the SWS high school reform is seen as especially useful within today's educational environment. We recognize that this reform is sometimes viewed as a solution for many of the problems that our most troubled urban high schools currently experience. The story of the decline of Taylor High School is an all-too-familiar story, and the arrival of the SWS reform a not entirely unique suggestion for "salvation."

As we describe throughout the book, not only did the reform play out differently in each of the five schools we studied, but to some degree each school backed away from the reform after an initial period of enthusiasm. Although there is no "typical" high school in the United States, Taylor High School, perhaps more than others we describe in the book, seems to exemplify the type of school—and the type of problems—that the SWS reform strategy is seen as targeting.

1

The Challenge of Large High Schools and the Promise of Schools Within Schools

COMPREHENSIVE HIGH SCHOOLS, as we know them, began to emerge about a century ago. Almost from their inception, writers have portrayed them as failing institutions (Bobbitt, 1924; Hollingshead, 1975; National Education Association, 1918; Thorndike, 1906; Warner, Havighurst, & Loeb, 1944). Today, indictments come from many quarters: researchers, pundits, and politicians all disparage the state of American education in general and the public high school in particular (see, for example, Angus & Mirel, 1999; Boyer, 1983; Goodlad, 1984; Hammack, 2004; National Association of Secondary School Principals, 1996; National Commission on Excellence in Education, 1983; Newmann, 1981; Oakes, 1985; Powell, Farrar, & Cohen, 1985; Sizer, 1984, 1992). Although the specific targets of criticism of high schools have evolved somewhat over time, two facets have come under continual attack. First, many high school students are unknown by their teachers and "fall through the cracks" as they move anonymously through school. Second, few students—particularly minority and low-income students—engage the rigorous academic coursework that leads to high levels of academic performance.

FOCUSING ON SCHOOL SIZE

High Schools Became Larger

Over the last decade, critics have increasingly pointed to one structural feature of high schools to explain these undesirable social and academic characteris-

6

tics: their large size. Almost 50% of students currently attend high schools that enroll more than 1,500 students (U.S. Department of Education, 2006a). The development of such large public high schools can be traced to three related educational phenomena: consolidation, persistence, and specialization.

Consolidation. During the 1900s tens of thousands of small school districts were combined to form larger districts. Although over 119,000 local school districts operated in 1937, fewer than 15,000 districts exist today (National Center for Education Statistics [NCES], 2002). The powerful consolidation movement reduced substantially the number of secondary schools, as many small high schools merged to serve many more students and more diversified clienteles. For example, between 1910 and 1960 the number of one-room schools (many of which included high-school students) declined by 90% (Tyack, 1974, p. 25). This necessarily increased enrollments in the remaining schools. A striking comparison exemplifies this trend. Since 1930 U.S. public high school enrollments have grown by over 700% (NCES, 2004). During this same period, however, the number of public high schools increased by only 8% (NCES, 2002). Underlying district consolidation was a belief that cost savings would accrue through economies of scale. However, the cost of increased transportation and burgeoning administrative layers have tended to offset any savings (Fox, 1981).

Persistence. Increasing high school size was also due to growth in the number and proportion of adolescents entering high school and persisting to graduation. This expansion reflected both increasing numbers of high school aged adolescents (due to immigration and population growth) and growth in the proportion of this age-group attending high school (due to economic forces and a push for universal attendance). For example, in 1890 few states required attendance in secondary schools, and U.S. public high schools enrolled only 203,000 students—barely 6% of the 14–17-year-old population. By 1920, however, states had increased mandatory attendance ages, and one third of the eligible age-group was enrolled (NCES, 2001). All states now require students to attend through the age of 16, and 14 states require attendance through age 18. Today, public high schools enroll almost 15 million students—over 95% of the eligible age-group (NCES, 2004).

Specialization. The least complicated and perhaps the most calculated reason that the size of high schools has expanded is that, historically, many school districts and communities simply wanted larger schools. In the minds of many, small high schools became obsolete—incapable of providing the wide array of specialized curricular offerings students, parents, teachers, and communities came to expect. The consolidation figures cited earlier exemplify this trend. The modern "comprehensive high school"—in the early decades of the 20th century, a new design intended to meet the needs of increasingly diverse groups of students under a single roof—required sufficient enrollments to offer the myriad vocational and academic programs the new configuration required (Angus & Mirel, 1999; Grant, 1988; Kliebard, 1995; Lee, 2000). Not only did schools need large numbers of students to offer an extensive and specialized curriculum, the desire to sustain performing arts programs and competitive sports teams also fueled the demand for larger high schools.

A Counter-Trend Toward Smaller Schools

Opposing the historical trend toward large high schools is a more recent movement that has coalesced around the belief that smaller schools are more beneficial for both students and teachers (Bryk, Lee, & Holland, 1993; Lee, 2000; Lee & Smith, 1997). The arguments behind the movement toward smaller high schools fall roughly into two explanatory frameworks. One stresses the social climates commonly found in smaller high schools; the other focuses on the academic and curricular structures that characterize smaller schools.

We distinguish here between two types of writing about smaller schools. One type is composed of empirical studies about school size. Although that research has generally demonstrated that smaller high schools produce more favorable outcomes than larger schools, there is some evidence that the relationship between size and outcomes is not linear (i.e., schools can be *too* small). The second type of writings relies less on empirical evidence and seems to resemble advocacy more than objective research. The current advocacy movement for small schools relies largely on case studies of very special small schools. A complicating factor in writings about this topic is the issue of selectivity bias—that is, which kinds of students attend such schools and how to account for this phenomenon in conducting such studies. We return to this topic later in this section, when we distinguish two types of small schools.

School Size and Social Organization. Size is an ecological feature of organizations that influences social interactions. According to classic sociological theory, as organizations grow larger, social relations become increasingly hierarchical and formal (Weber, [1922] 1978). Sociologists of education have applied these ideas to schools, concluding that as schools grow larger, positive and sustained personal relations are more difficult (Bidwell, 1965; Bryk & Driscoll, 1988; Bryk et al., 1993; Newmann, 1981). The influence of school size on social relations flows largely through formal and informal opportunities students and teachers have to interact. Instead of identifying with the whole school, teachers in larger high schools tend to be "specialists" who associate with small subgroups of teachers and only the students they teach. These subgroups are often defined (and limited) by departmental structures (Newmann, 1981; Siskin, 1994b).

Compared with teachers in larger high schools, teachers in smaller schools typically play more diffuse, multifaceted roles in their students' lives. For example, a math teacher in a small high school may also teach driver's education, be the softball or basketball coach, direct the debate team, and serve as the senior-class advisor. This expanded set of roles results from the fact that smaller schools try to provide numbers of extra- and co-curricular offerings comparable to their larger counterpart schools. As a result, opportunities for student and teacher interaction are increased (Barker & Gump, 1964; Raywid, 1996; Schoggen & Schoggen, 1988). These diverse settings, where teachers and students are more likely to interact both formally and informally, help to weaken the hierarchical social structures often found in larger schools.

School-based social networks are crucial for adolescents, many of whom begin high school at a time of considerable psychological growth and social uncertainty. Peer networks established in elementary and middle school are often interrupted, and new social ties are forged. Familial relations are transformed, as parents become less involved in their children's daily activities and take a more "hands-off" approach to managing their social and academic lives (Stevenson & Barker, 1987; Useem, 1992). Conflicts and tensions with family members sometimes arise as autonomy increases and students develop unique identities outside the family (Buchanan, Eccles, & Becker, 1992; Steinberg, 1990). Thus, school-based social relations become a crucial medium through which students receive the support that enables them to succeed (Lee & Smith, 1999).

However, an important strand of research developed by Eccles and her colleagues suggests that young adolescents' developmental needs are misaligned with the school environments in which they are placed (Eccles & Midgley, 1989; Eccles et al., 1993). Beginning in middle school and extending into high school, many adolescents experience their education in large, anonymous, and bureaucratic schools that do not meet well their social, psychological, and developmental needs (Bryk & Driscoll, 1988). Optimal educational environments should offer both cognitive challenges and psychosocial supports that match students' developmental needs (Eccles et al., 1993). However, the new freedoms to choose friends, courses, and levels of academic effort that characterize many larger high schools provide opportunities for adolescents to remain anonymous or to embrace school cultures not characterized by academic motivation and effort.

School Size and Academic Organization. Another line of research suggests that the academic benefits of small high schools—and the disadvantages of large high schools—accrue through features of their academic rather than social organizations. Larger high schools typically offer a more differentiated curriculum—different courses intended for different students, depending on students' academic backgrounds and their occupational and educational futures. Tailoring specialized programs to particular groups of students is often seen as a necessary response to students' social and academic diversity (Bryk et al., 1993; Lee, 2000, 2001). Unfortunately, this approach fosters inequitable academic environments. A substantial body of research concludes that a differentiated curriculum produces learning that is strongly linked with students' social background (i.e., race, ethnicity, and social class; Bryk et al., 1993; Lee & Bryk, 1988, 1989). In racially and ethnically diverse high schools, a differentiated curriculum typically results in within-school social segregation, as minority and low-income students are less likely to be placed in (or choose) advanced academic classes (Lee, Burkam, Chow-Hoy, Smerdon, & Geverdt, 1998; Tyson, Darity, & Castellino, 2005; Wells & Crain, 1997; Yonezawa, Wells, & Serna, 2002).

Unlike large high schools, smaller schools must direct resources to core programs, because their resource bases are limited. Thus, students at either end of the ability distribution have more common academic experiences. Not only is a constrained academic curriculum associated with higher achievement, it also has a more equitable social distribution of student learning by race/ethnicity and social class (Lee et al., 1998; Lee & Bryk, 1989). However, the degree to which all small schools offer constrained academic curricula is unclear.

James Bryant Conant, often called the father of the comprehensive high school, was an early advocate for larger (not necessarily *large*) high schools. Conant (1959) actually claimed that high schools enrolling as few as 400 students—quite small by today's standards—could offer an appropriate curriculum to serve a diverse group of students. Conant's real concern was that very small (often rural) high schools offered very limited academic programs. His unease has been confirmed by contemporary research suggesting that many small schools offer a disjointed curriculum that is driven more by students' tastes than by thoughtful consideration of their academic needs (Lee, Smerdon, Alfeld-Liro, & Brown, 2000). In terms of a specific size, students learn more (and learning is more equitably distributed by race and class) in medium-sized high schools—those that enroll between 600 and 900 students (Lee & Smith, 1997). High schools of this size are large enough to provide a solid curriculum, yet small enough to foster positive social relations.

Two Types of Small Schools

These conclusions raise a question rarely discussed by advocates of small schools. Why do some small high schools work better than others? Some high schools (public and private) have small enrollments because they wish to consciously limit the numbers of students they serve (and also the types of students they enroll). However, the vast majority of small high schools are public, and must enroll all students in their catchment areas. Even with the powerful trend toward consolidation, many high schools have small enrollments because there are simply not many students in the community (especially in rural areas and those with declining populations). It seems quite inappropriate to confuse these two types of small schools. Some are "small by design" and others are "small by default." The first group of schools inherently possesses many advantages not shared by the latter group. Interesting as they are, such small schools as New York's Urban Academy or Central Park East Secondary School (Cook, 2000; Meier, 1995) are incredibly different from the majority of small, rural high schools.

Our own and others' research has led us to wonder whether "smallness" by itself is the inherently valuable characteristic of high schools that many advocates claim. In the large-scale quantitative study by Lee and Smith (1997), students in the smallest schools (fewer than 600 students) learned less than those in the schools enrolling 600–900 students. Smallness accompanied by the ability to organize a school around a special theme or ideology; to enroll only students, families, and faculty to whom this theme appeals; and to select among applicants is a special kind of smallness. This is very different from smallness experienced by the large majority of small high schools that are small by default. Many small high schools would prefer to be larger, partly because resources flow to most public schools based on head counts (Lee et al., 2000). But more often this desire arises from the belief that their small size (and correspondingly limited resource base) does not permit them to offer the wide array of courses and extracurricular activities that many parents, teachers, and communities see as a defining and desirable feature of comprehensive high schools.

THE SCHOOLS-WITHIN-SCHOOLS REFORM

The generally undesirable social and academic outcomes associated with large public high schools led researcher John Goodlad (1984) to state that he "would not want to face the challenge of justifying a senior high school of more than 500 to 600 students" (p. 310). Regardless of how "small" or "large" is defined, virtually no contemporary writer suggests that high schools should be larger than most currently are. Despite the consistent calls for smaller high schools, it seems quite unlikely that taxpayers would support constructing many new small high schools and abandoning buildings that currently house large public high schools. In some locations, particularly our nation's urban areas, even maintaining existing schools is a financial challenge. Building new schools would be a fiscal impossibility.

In this sense, the conclusion that smaller high schools are generally better for students collides with the public's ability (or willingness) to increase spending on public education. The reality is that most school districts must "make do" with their existing facilities (Raywid, 1996). With the perceived advantages of smaller high school enrollments in mind, what policy options are available to reduce the size of large high schools? How might large public high schools reproduce the environments typically associated with smaller schools without substantially increasing costs?

Alternatives to the Comprehensive High School Model

A logical (and seemingly inexpensive) alternative to constructing new schools is to divide large high schools into several smaller schools that inhabit the original building. This increasingly popular design, often referred to as "schools within schools" (SWS), seeks a balance—to reduce the social and academic shortcomings associated with large public high schools without incurring the cost of constructing new buildings. A fundamental notion underlying the SWS model is that by dividing into smaller units, large high schools can reproduce the more positive social environments typically found in small schools. There is an implicit connection within this idea: positive social ties between students and teachers will improve student engagement and commitment, which might ultimately lead students to higher achievement. In Chapter 3, we spell out this idea in more detail, conceptualizing how schools within schools might improve student outcomes.

Historical Evolution of Schools Within Schools. Enthusiasm for schools within schools seems quite new, but the philosophy behind it claims a longer history.

Almost a half-century ago, Barker and Gump (1964) suggested a "campus model" for high schools. In such schools,

> students are grouped in semiautonomous units for most of their studies, but are usually provided a schoolwide extracurricular program. The campus school provides for repeated contacts between the same teachers and students; this continuity of associates probably leads to closer social bonds. A common-sense theory is that the campus school welds together the facility advantages of the large school and the social values of the small school. (pp. 201–202)

In the late 1960s and early 1970s, many high schools implemented "house plans" incorporating elements of the structure suggested by Barker and Gump. In this period, a few new high schools were constructed with house plans in mind (Oxley, 1993). However, the idea of house plans in many restructured schools faded over time, and some schools built to accommodate house plans never used the facilities as originally intended.

More than a decade later, Goodlad (1984) revived the notion of smaller organizational units, advocating a high school structure that incorporated "houses organized vertically, so that each contains students from all secondary grade levels" (p. 311). More recently, the first recommendation in *Breaking Ranks,* an influential report about secondary schools issued jointly by the Carnegie Foundation and the National Association of Secondary School Principals (NASSP), was that "Schools must break into units of no more than 600 students, so that teachers and students can get to know each other" (NASSP, 1996, p. 5). Early in the study on which this book is based, we drew a similar conclusion: "We believe that the 'school-within-a-school' reform . . . is a feasible and cost-effective way to accomplish this structural reform and to facilitate other useful changes" (Lee & Smith, 1995, p. 262).

Increasing Interest, Support, and Implementation. Over the past decade, substantial federal and foundation support has been directed to the SWS reform. Although the majority of this support has targeted urban schools enrolling substantial proportions of socially disadvantaged students, the SWS model is also becoming increasingly popular in suburban areas. The U.S. Department of Education has awarded over $100 million through its Smaller Learning Communities Grants program for schools seeking to divide themselves into smaller units (U.S. Department of Education, 2006b). Foundations have provided even more substantial support for the idea. In less than a decade, the Bill and Melinda Gates Foundation has invested over a billion dollars in its initiatives to encourage smaller high schools. The Annenberg and Carnegie Foundations and the Pew Charitable Trust have also directed substantial resources toward implementing schools within schools, especially in Chicago and Philadelphia. The first school district to take a systemic approach to creating schools within schools was Philadelphia, with major support from the superintendent (Raywid & Schmerler, 2003). By 1995, Philadelphia had 132 "small learning communities" in 22 high schools. Today, most high school students in Philadelphia attend SWS schools, although support has waned somewhat with a new superintendent.

Different Schools-Within-Schools Models. Even more than other educational reforms, the schools-within-schools (SWS) movement is neither standardized nor unified. Multiple SWS models exist, with no central organization governing implementation or monitoring the status and prevalence of the reform. However, a few reform organizations have made the SWS design a central element of their efforts, helping hundreds of schools to adopt their models.

The "Talent Development" SWS model was designed by researchers at the Center for Research on the Education of Students Placed At Risk (CRESPAR) at Johns Hopkins University (Jordan, McPartland, Letgers, & Balfanz, 2000; McPartland, Legters, Jordan, & McDill, 1996). First implemented in Baltimore in 1994, this design now operates in 83 high schools in 32 districts in 20 states (Kemple, Herlihy, & Smith, 2005). Important elements in all Talent Development (TD) schools are separate 9th-grade "freshman academies" and upper-grade "career academies." TD schools also implement block scheduling, freshman seminar/advisories, "double doses" of specially designed skill-building courses for struggling 9th and 10th graders, and substantial professional development. Although several Baltimore and Philadelphia high schools employ the TD design, the model is sanctioned but not financially supported by these districts.

Another important organization offering professional development around schools within schools is "First Things First" (FTF), created by the Philadelphia-based Institute for Research and Reform in Education (IRRE). Although originally implemented throughout the schools in Kansas City, Kansas, the FTF model currently operates nationally in 22 high schools in eight districts. Within the FTF model, all students are organized into smaller educational units that enroll students in 9th through 12th grade. Within these smaller units, students take 75% of their coursework—all core courses and one thematic elective per year. Other specifics of the FTF model are one-to-one student/ teacher mentorships, instructional reform, and strong professional development (IRRE, 2006; Quint, Bloom, Black, & Stephens, 2005).

By far the largest and most visible organization currently advocating the SWS structure is the Bill and Melinda Gates Foundation, which has made small high schools (including the schools-within-school model) the centerpiece of its reform agenda. To date the Gates Foundation has supported restructuring over 2,000 schools in 41 states. Whereas the Talent Development and First Things First groups offer specific guidelines and extensive professional development to member schools, the Gates Foundation does not advocate a particular comprehensive school reform model. Rather, it provides extensive financial support to encourage schools to create small schools themselves, as a platform for fostering a broader set of school characteristics—the Gates Foundation's "three Rs of rigor, relevance and relationships" (AIR & SRI, 2005). Although Gates began with a focus on converting preexisting high schools into several smaller organizational units, more recently it has begun shifting its funding toward new small stand-alone high schools. In New York City, the Foundation has directed over 100 million dollars to implement autonomous small high schools (Herszenhorn, 2005). This shift in emphasis seems to result from early evaluations of Gates-funded schools, which report more positive results from small stand-alone schools than from comprehensive high schools that convert to the SWS model (see below).

Defining Schools-Within-Schools Models

Not only has the SWS movement not coalesced around a single model, the terminology SWS high schools use to describe their smaller units also differs from district to district and school to school. Such labels as "houses," "academies," "blocks," "small learning communities," and "subschools" all refer to smaller organizational groups within larger schools. To avoid confusion, we use a more generic term—"subunits"—to describe these smaller educational groupings.

The most common SWS design organizes subunits around curricular, pedagogical, or (most often) career themes such as the fine arts, cooperative learning, or careers in health or business (Lee, Ready, & Johnson, 2001; Oxley, 1989, 1994; Raywid, 1996; Wallach & Lear, 2005). Subunits with vocational themes sometimes award state certifications and endorsements in such fields as child development, health care, or auto mechanics. We define these many SWS designs along three dimensions, based on (a) whether all students in the school are organized into subunits, (b) the degree of subunit autonomy, and (c) the extent to which the reform facilitates change in the school's technical core of teaching and learning. We describe these distinctions below.

Full- and Partial-Model Designs. Dividing large comprehensive high schools into smaller units is a deceptively simple notion. In practice, however, there are multiple ways to "downsize" large high schools. Our first distinction identifies whether all students in a school participate in the reform. In "full-model" SWS structures, all students and most faculty are members of one of several smaller subunits. This structure is distinguished from the more common (and less comprehensive) "partial-model," in which one or a small number of subunits are offered, but most students remain in the regular high school program (Lee et al., 2001). These partial SWS structures sometimes involve one or two vocationally oriented "career academies" within a larger public high school (Kemple & Rock, 1996; Kemple & Snipes, 2000; Stern, Raby, & Dayton, 1992). Other schools provide an alternative subunit that groups together students who are disaffected, low-performing, or at risk of dropping out. Likewise, Muncie and McQuillan (1996) investigated the implementation of several Coalition of Essential Schools programs that were implemented as self-contained subunits within larger high schools. None of these models are whole-school reforms, which is how we would label full-model SWS structures. In fact, Muncie and McQuillan concluded that implementing such partial-model SWS structures was a poor idea, because it led to animosity between members of "special" subunits and the remainder of the school.

The large majority of full-model SWS schools permit students to select among theme-based subunits. However, other SWS schools organize subunits around grade levels or implement 9th- to 12th-grade subunits to which students are randomly assigned (Allen, 2001). These alternative SWS structures do not allow students to choose subunits. In some models, student choice is limited to the upper grades. For example, subunits can be created for the school's youngest students (usually 9th graders), who then select upper-grade subunits at the completion of 9th grade. This is the Talent Development approach, wherein 9th graders are assigned to one or more "freshman academies" but subsequently choose among "career academies" beginning with 10th grade (Jordan et al., 2000; McPartland et al., 1996).

Subunit Autonomy. The second distinction we make among SWS models is the degree to which individual subunits are fiscally and administratively autonomous. An important issue—which we discuss repeatedly in the book—is the extent to which subunits are dependent on their larger "host" schools. The degree of independence strongly influences other governance structures and processes. Recognizing the importance of autonomy for SWS schools, Raywid (1996) created a taxonomy in which she divided full-model SWS structures into four broad types:

- *House Plans.* The least involved SWS model, house plans randomly assign students to themeless, nondescript subunits. These administrative units coordinate guidance counseling, homeroom assignments, and other bureaucratic tasks. Students may or may not take most of their coursework within their subunit. Co- and extracurricular activities remain organized at the school level. Subunits have virtually no autonomy from the larger school.
- *Minischools.* Minischools are usually themed subunits that create instructional programs distinct from others in the building. To match student interest to subunit themes, students generally select their subunit. As with houses, minischools are dependent on the larger building for staffing and resources, although minischools have somewhat more autonomy in crafting curricula and specialized programs.
- *Schools Within a School.* According to Raywid's taxonomy, schools within schools are fully autonomous small schools that report directly to district superintendents and school boards. They have their own budgets and complete responsibility for hiring staff. Subunits may have little contact with other subunits in the building beyond negotiating shared spaces such as gymnasiums and cafeterias. These schools within schools buildings are "reconstitutions" in which the original school is reorganized into new small schools in the same building.
- *Small Schools.* Unlike schools within schools, small schools are new schools that hire new staff that are assigned to a new building. These "multischool sites" are not reorganizations of preexisting high schools. For example, New York City's Julia Richman High School was organizationally replaced with the Julia Richman Education Complex. The building currently accommodates several fully autonomous small schools and programs. These include four distinct small high schools; a pre-K–8 elementary school; a center for infants and toddlers; a program for high school seniors; and a program for junior high children with autism (see Cook, 2000).

Raywid reserves the label "schools within schools" for subunits that are fully autonomous and report directly to district-level administrators. She acknowledges that this model is actually quite rare in practice. Indeed, our nationwide search for SWS high schools identified very few examples of this model (Lee et al., 2001). Those we located were in New York City, where Raywid has conducted much of her research. Although Raywid would use the label "minischools," we use the more common term "schools within schools" throughout this book.

Transforming the Technical Core. Our third dimension for defining SWS schools asks how deeply the adoption of this structure transforms the daily work of teachers and students. Comprehensive high school reform requires a fundamental look at the purposes of secondary education and how daily life in schools should be organized. Although the SWS design seems to suggest considerable structural reorganization, the reality is often otherwise. Schools adopting the SWS design often remain "grounded in a set of beliefs and practices drawn largely from comprehensive high schools," with subunits designed and implemented as "miniature comprehensive high schools" (Wallach & Lear, 2005, p. 17). Studies of such schools report considerable variability in how willing (or able) they are to use the SWS structure to develop new instructional practices and to limit their comprehensive scope. The depth of change that accompanies the SWS structure can vary from "minimal additions to and departures from conventional comprehensive high school organizational arrangements [to] total organizational restructuring" (Raywid, 1996, p. 16).

Pondering the results of one comprehensive high school that converted to an SWS design, McQuillan (2004) queried, "If the schools continue to do what they have always done, why would the outcomes change?" (p. 48). Transforming deeply entrenched cultural norms and practices is no easy feat. Schools adopting the SWS structure face different challenges from stand-alone small schools or even newly created SWS high schools (McQuillan, 2004; Oxley, 1993; Raywid, 1996; Wallach & Lear, 2005). For example, teachers in comprehensive high schools converting to the SWS design often fear losing school unity, their common vision, or the familiarity of preexisting departmental structures (Allen, 2001). In short, existing high schools that convert to an SWS structure often find themselves caught between "two worlds—the 'old world' of comprehensive high schools and the 'new world' of small schools" (Wallach & Lear, 2005, p. 1).

We suggest that our three defining characteristics for SWS schools—whether all students are organized into subunits, the degree to which subunits are autonomous, and the extent to which teaching and learning are transformed— are important indicators of whether an SWS high school has used the new structure as a springboard to reform. There is solid evidence and general agreement that smaller high schools typically provide social benefits (through increased personalization) and some hope that they also induce academic benefits (through a more constrained curriculum). However, evidence about the degree to which SWS high schools actually replicate the social and academic climates that have been demonstrated to accrue in small stand-alone high schools is scant. One measure of the effectiveness of individual SWS high schools is the extent to which they depart socially and academically from traditional comprehensive high schools. This is crucial, because the distinctions between small and comprehensive high schools are empirically linked to student outcomes.

EVALUATING THE SCHOOLS-WITHIN-SCHOOLS REFORM AND STUDENT OUTCOMES

Similar to many other educational reforms, the SWS reform has been promoted and implemented without a solid base of empirical evidence to support it. Over the past decade, dozens of strong studies have examined the separate issues of high school size and small schools. However, very little research has been specifically directed toward evaluating the efficacy of full-model SWS structures. Moreover, methodologically sound studies—particularly those that examine student learning—have only recently appeared (for example, AIR & SRI, 2005; Kemple et al., 2005; Quint et al., 2005). By "methodologically sound" we mean that the analyses have taken into account the types of students who attend different schools. Two major issues in quantitative research of this type are also important to consider: (a) whether or not the analyses have made use of multilevel methods (as the research questions are inherently multilevel), and (b) whether the studies have strong experimental designs to strengthen causal inferences about effectiveness. The studies we describe here fall (at least in part) into these categories, although even they examine relatively small numbers of schools.

The Difficulty of Separating Components

Several challenges face evaluators of the SWS reform. First, there are multiple ways to create smaller units within a larger comprehensive high school; evaluators must be clear about the details of the designs being evaluated. Second, SWS structures are often implemented alongside other reform strategies. For example, the Talent Development (TD) and First Things First (FTF) models include student/teacher advisories, compensatory coursework for students who are at risk of school failure, and substantial professional development activities. Due to the multifaceted nature of these intervention models, it is impossible to isolate the benefits attributed to the SWS design per se; these reform models include multiple components. In other words, the auxiliary strategies implemented by these reform groups—block scheduling, advisories, professional development, and the like—might have engendered similar results even if the schools had not had the SWS structure. Indeed, the TD and FTF organizations themselves stress that the SWS organizational structure is only one element of their larger and more comprehensive reform strategy. The evaluations we summarize here were meant to assess the reform models in their entirety, not simply their SWS components.

Social Relations and Social Climate

One area of almost universal agreement is that, compared with traditional comprehensive high schools, social relations in SWS high schools are more positive; relationships among subunit members are more often built upon notions of trust (AIR & SRI, 2004; Jordan et al., 2000; Sporte, Correa, & Kahne, 2003). Social relations improve because students are likely to encounter teachers in multiple courses across several years, thereby increasing opportunities to deepen positive social bonds (Oxley, 1989). Activities that are subunit-specific, such as trips, cross-disciplinary projects, and community-based career activities, increase student interest and motivation (Allen, 2001).

Compared with teachers in traditional high schools, those working in SWS high schools report improved social and learning environments (Jordan et al., 2000), increased opportunities for staff to share information about their students, and greater willingness to take responsibility for student learning (Wallach & Lear, 2005). Some studies suggest that teachers in SWS schools experience stronger professional communities, more collegial atmospheres, more democratic organizational structures, and higher career satisfaction (Holland, 2002). Despite the positive influence of the SWS structure on social relations, authors have questioned whether increased personal relations are ends in themselves; they wonder whether these more positive social environments necessarily lead to improved student performance. As small-schools advocate Michele Fine argued, "Small is simply a vehicle for doing other rigorous, accountable work. [Small schools] will produce a sense of belonging almost immediately, but hugging is not the same as algebra" (quoted in Gewertz, 2001, p. 16).

Academic Outcomes

Compared with demographically comparable comprehensive high schools, evaluations of FTF schools (Quint et al., 2005) and TD schools (Jordan et al., 2000; Kemple et al., 2005) suggest improved student attendance. Matched against other Philadelphia high schools, students in TD schools averaged nine fewer absences per year. Although these are hopeful findings, "improvements" in such large, urban high schools must be seen in context: the average 9th grader attending a TD high school still missed 40 days of school—almost one quarter of the school year (Kemple et al., 2005). Unlike the positive findings of FTF and TD high schools in terms of improved attendance, Gates Foundation SWS-conversion high schools actually had less favorable attendance rates than non-SWS schools in the same districts (AIR & SRI, 2005).

Beyond improved attendance, students in Philadelphia's TD high schools earned more course credits and experienced fewer course failures than did students in comparable non-TD high schools in that city (Kemple & Herlihy, 2004; Kemple et al., 2005). Both TD and FTF high schools also had somewhat higher graduation rates (Kemple et al., 2005; Quint et al., 2005). Despite relatively promising findings for attendance and graduation rates, links between the SWS design and student achievement were more mixed. Although the FTF evaluation suggested improvements in reading and math achievement, evaluators reported only slight improvements in achievement in mathematics for TD schools, and none in reading (Kemple et al., 2005).

The recent evaluation of Gates-supported SWS-conversion high schools (i.e., comprehensive high schools that adopted SWS designs) reported slight improvement in reading achievement but none in math (AIR & SRI, 2005). Compared with the conversion schools, Gates-supported newly created small high schools and SWS high schools had somewhat more success in implementing small-school cultures and practices that might lead to improvement of student outcomes (AIR & SRI, 2004, 2005). On average, the newly created small stand-alone high schools demonstrated more beneficial social and academic climates than existing schools that were converted to SWS schools. The evaluators concluded that SWS-conversion high schools face challenges replicating small-school social and academic climates that stand-alone small schools may not. In this sense, research on small schools and on school size may not be relevant to SWS-conversion high schools. Raywid's (1996) earlier appraisal seems prescient: "Restructuring a school is almost impossible: starting over holds far more promise" (p. 7). Raywid offers three conjectures for why comprehensive high schools converting themselves to the SWS design may produce limited results: (a) conversions are often unfaithful to small-schools concepts, (b) subunits are rarely afforded sufficient autonomy, and (c) cultural change does not automatically follow structural change.

ORGANIZATION OF THE BOOK

The study we present in this book differs from the evaluations described above in several ways. First, we studied in depth a relatively small number of schools that had been operating under a SWS structure for several years. All but one were the "conversion" type that the Gates evaluation found less promising. Well before the misgivings that have emerged from these recent evaluations, we began our research with the belief that the SWS design offers a promising high school reform. We still hold this belief. When we began our study of schools with this design in 1998, these evaluations were unavailable, and the reform strategy had generated more interest than implementation.

Implementation of the SWS reform strategy has grown rapidly over the years since we began our study. Once targeted to urban schools that enrolled large numbers of minority, low-income, and low-achieving students, the SWS model is now being implemented increasingly in suburban schools and districts. Indeed, the SWS structure has attracted considerable interest from many of the same practitioners, researchers, foundations, and government agencies that earlier touted small schools. Despite this groundswell of support, the empirical base on schools within schools remains quite sparse, beyond the very recent evaluations of schools supported by particular reform organizations.

In this book we describe what we learned from the five schools we studied and the reform they shared—particularly how the design influenced the daily work of those who experienced it. We approach this work neither as detractors nor as advocates of the SWS reform, but rather as policy analysts. Considering the groundswell of enthusiasm for the SWS model, the substantial political and financial support it has received, and the almost one million students who currently experience it, it is sometimes difficult to encourage funders to support research about it or for policymakers to step back and ask, "Do these schools really work?" or, more important, "*How* do these schools work?" Our in-depth exploration of how the reform plays out in a few settings is intended to be helpful to practitioners considering adopting the SWS model or engaged in its implementation, policymakers involved more broadly in high school reform, and researchers interested in how school structure plays out among students and faculty.

In Chapter 1 we have offered a theoretical and policy context for our study. Chapter 2 provides portraits of the five SWS high schools we studied and their local contexts. The schools differed from each other in many ways—their histories, their local contexts, the students they served, their SWS designs, and numerous additional organizational features. Chapter 2 also offers information about how we located and selected the schools. The variability between and within the five schools, combined with the expansive qualitative database resulting from this multisite and multiyear study, allowed us to explore how the social and structural processes that accompany the SWS structure influence students' experiences.

In Chapter 3 we present an explicit causal model for how the SWS design might improve the social and academic climates of large high schools, something that seems implicit in the discussions of this reform strategy. Here we also explore the extent to which these theoretical benefits actually accrued to students and teachers in the five schools we studied. We offer brief case studies of two subunits that demonstrate the reform's potential to fundamentally transform the "givens" of comprehensive public high schools. Chapter 3 also examines how the SWS structure influences social relations in these schools. We consider student behavior, attendance, commitment, safety and discipline, and teachers' satisfaction and self-efficacy. These social benefits lie at the very heart of advocacy and support for the SWS reform.

Chapter 4 explores governance structures within these five schools. By definition, the SWS design imposes an additional layer of bureaucracy. We describe the tensions we observed between academic departments, schoolwide administrators, and individual subunits. These disparate administrative levels vied for control over staffing, curriculum, budget, the use of time and space, student discipline, guidance counseling, and special and bilingual education. We found that the autonomy afforded (or denied) subunits deeply influenced the extent to which they could create and sustain the unique identities and personalized environments that constitute this reform's raison d'être.

One of the potential benefits of the SWS reform is its ability to stimulate alternative approaches to teaching and learning. In Chapter 5 we discuss how the SWS design influenced what was learned and who learned what—the core mission of secondary schools. Each school was a hybrid organization, part small school and part comprehensive high school. Although these schools differed from regular high schools in many ways, their academic programs were quite traditional. Each school sought to reap the benefits of smaller schools while retaining the perceived benefits of large, comprehensive high schools. We discuss how these remnants of the comprehensive high school collided with the practical and conceptual underpinnings of the SWS structure.

Chapter 6 describes how students were matched to subunits. Authors advocating the SWS reform typically suggest that schools create subunits organized around different themes and allow students to choose their subunits—and this is exactly what we found. Theoretical benefits of matching students' interests to subunit themes include more engagement and the ability to better meet students' needs. All five SWS high schools we studied functioned as choice-driven educational marketplaces. Students were consumers whom the schools believed selected their subunits rationally, based on their current interests and future plans. We explore the rationales students actually offered for their subunit selections; the links they made between their interests, motivations, academic abilities, and subunit choices; and how their selections were influenced by their social and academic backgrounds and institutional processes.

Chapter 7 explores the implications of the SWS reform for equity and access. We focus on how the free-market mechanisms within each school shaped students' experiences, based largely on their social and academic backgrounds. We are particularly concerned with the extent to which the SWS structure exacerbated or alleviated the social and academic stratification common in most comprehensive high schools. Choice in almost any context increases variation in the actions and decisions of groups and individuals. How did choice play out in these five high schools? To what extent did the themes around which subunits were organized influence the types of students each subunit attracted and the quality of instruction they subsequently received?

In Chapter 8, we explore the implications of our findings in the larger context of American secondary schooling. Is the SWS structure a solution to the problems of large high schools? We draw several conclusions and recommendations about this reform that we hope are relevant to practitioners who are considering implementing the SWS design, as well as to those who have already done so. In this final chapter we expand on the hopeful trends we have observed in these five schools with cautions that we feel are warranted, based on careful study of how the reform has played out in these five settings.

Because the initial research we conducted in these five schools ended in 2000, we also provide an Epilogue. Here we describe what has happened in the schools in the ensuing years, and what we learned during our more recent visits to and contacts with these complex educational settings. Most high schools weather constant change. We were interested to see the changes these schools had experienced, and how those changes had influenced their SWS structures.

2

Five High Schools Divided into Schools Within Schools

INFORMATION ABOUT HIGH SCHOOLS divided into schools within schools was scarce when we decided to undertake this study in 1997. In a few cities that had created such schools, especially Philadelphia and Baltimore, researchers had studied the reform. However, no one had attempted to gauge the prevalence or impact of the reform on a national scale. Today, dozens of local, state, and national organizations promote and monitor the reform, but when we began our study these networks had not been created. Even in school districts that were considering reforming their high schools, typically the schools-within-schools (SWS) structure was developed as a "bottom-up" movement initiated by parents, teachers, and administrators. We open this chapter with a brief explanation of how we learned about the universe of SWS high schools, what it looked like, and how we chose the schools we ultimately studied. The remainder of the chapter provides descriptive "portraits" of the five SWS high schools we studied.

THE SEARCH FOR AND SELECTION OF SCHOOLS

Our search for appropriate SWS high schools to study turned out to be much more difficult than we had originally thought. Because the SWS model was often mentioned as a possible (and relatively low-cost) way to improve public high schools, we assumed that there were many of them and that they would be quite simple to locate. We began our national search by trying to get some basic information about the prevalence and location of the reform. Three purposes drove our original search: (a) to compile an extensive list of SWS high schools; (b) to identify the various SWS models; and (c) to create a relatively short list of SWS high schools that might serve as fruitful sites for our research. We began by contacting organizations and individuals whom we thought might know about SWS high schools: state departments of education, schools of education, the National Association of Secondary School Principals (NASSP), U.S. Department of Education regional laboratories, and administrators of school districts where we had heard such schools were located. We also made extensive use of the Internet. We searched Web sites of hundreds of school districts, many of which had links to their individual high schools.

At the conclusion of our conversations with informants at the schools suggested to us by our initial contacts, we always asked if they knew about any other SWS high schools. Our list of actual and potential schools quickly "snowballed" (Patton, 2002). In a sense, we were detectives following leads, many of which were dead ends. We made over 600 phone calls, sent dozens of e-mail requests, and spent hundreds of hours on the Internet. We ultimately cataloged phone interviews with 163 high schools we were led to believe might have schools within schools. We asked our informants to describe their subunit structures, the extent to which students took courses within their subunit, and how students and teachers were allocated to subunits. We also asked about the themes around which subunits were organized and how the school's physical layout accommodated the SWS structure.

Of the potential SWS high schools we contacted, only about a third (55 out of 163) had actually implemented full-model SWS structures. We decided that it was only full-model SWS high schools we wanted to study in depth, although we were somewhat surprised by how few full-model SWS schools we located. Our many telephone conversations and e-mail exchanges with knowledgeable informants made clear that local educators adapt and modify the SWS structure to fit the political realities and social and economic constraints associated with their local contexts.

Once we had constituted a complete research team, we met to decide on a subset of the 55 SWS high schools that we might want to study in depth. We established two criteria that all schools we studied would share: they would all be full-model SWS high schools, and they must have been operating with this structure for at least 3 years. We applied the latter criterion to avoid the problems of start-up; we wanted to study schools where this reform was mature and (relatively) stable. Another objective was to maximize variability (Patton, 2002) by selecting schools that differed across several dimensions: (a) the types of students they enrolled, (b) their histories with the SWS structure, (c) the themes around which their smaller organizational units were organized, (d) the manner in which students were allocated to these units, and (e) their locations. We ultimately met this objective for all but the first dimension. Despite concerted efforts, we were unable to locate a single U.S. full-model SWS high school that served a relatively affluent or high-achieving clientele. This in itself was an important finding, one to which we return throughout this book. We refer readers interested in learning more about how our selection process and our procedures for conducting the study to Appendix A of this book and to Lee et al. (2001).

SCHOOL PORTRAITS

Like all high schools, these five SWS schools were unique in terms of their histories and traditions, the types of students and communities they served, and the roles they played in the lives of their students and staff. Considerable variability also existed in their subunits' themes, how deeply the subunit structure guided the schools' operations, the methods used to allocate students to subunits, and the reasons why they originally adopted the SWS structure. In this chapter we offer portraits of the five schools that describe their local contexts and the components, processes, and histories of their SWS structures. As we discuss in subsequent chapters, these histories both reflected and influenced students' experiences with the SWS reform. Throughout this book we use pseudonyms for individuals, subunits, and schools to protect informants' confidentiality.

These portraits are based on the schools as they were during our earliest encounters in 1999. Because some have longer and richer histories than others, the portraits are not equally comprehensive. Much about the schools has changed since our initial visits, including their personnel and SWS structures. Rather than including such changes in our portraits, we describe them in an Epilogue at the end of the book. To help readers remember something about these five schools and their subunits, we summarize a few important characteristics. In Table 2.1, the schools are described. In Table 2.2, we provide a few details about the subunits within each school. It may be helpful to refer back to these tables as the schools and subunits are discussed in subsequent chapters. In Appendix B we provide more detailed descriptions of the subunits.

TABLE 2.1. School Descriptions, as of 1999

School	Enroll-ment	Number of subunits	Minority enroll-ment	Free/reduced-price lunch eligible	Location
John Quincy Adams	1,900	6	61%	21%	New England, inner-ring suburb
Ulysses S. Grant	2,600	5	99%	87%	Mid-Atlantic, inner-city
Benjamin Harrison	1,300	4	30%	35%	Northwest, working-class suburban
James Monroe	1,400	4	87%	52%	Southwest, large-city outskirts
Zachary Taylor	2,300	5	69%	48%	Mid-Atlantic, inner-city

John Quincy Adams High School

A century of renovations and reincarnations explains Adams High School's patchwork of architectural styles; Corinthian columns from the 1800s compete with modernist, poured-concrete additions. Adams's structural mélange seemed to fit its diverse New England city well. The only public high school in its district, Adams High was situated in the midst of a vibrant and cosmopolitan educational and commercial center. Its mixed-use neighborhood bustled with pedestrian and vehicle traffic heading to and from the cafes, small shops, hotels, subway stops, and bed and breakfasts that served the city's nearby universities and business communities.

The Population. Of the five schools in our study, Adams enrolled the most racially, economically, and academically diverse student body. The 1,900 students at Adams included substantial numbers of Caribbean, European, and Central American immigrants, as well as American-born Blacks, Whites, Asians, and Hispanics. The flags of 62 countries hung from the rafters of the main gymnasium, each representing a nation in which a current Adams student was born. Coupled with the considerable racial and ethnic diversity was substantial socioeconomic diversity; students came both from affluent professional families and from families on government assistance who resided in public

TABLE 2.2. Subunit Descriptions, as of 1999

School and subunit	Enrollment	Status and selectivity	Year developed	Selected by students?
Adams				
Alternative	240	High	1969	Yes
College Prep	400	High	1989	Yes
Community	370	Low	1989	Yes
Core Curriculum	360	Medium	1976	Yes
International/Cooperative				
Learning (ICL)	450	Medium	1989	Yes
Vocational	250	Low	1978	Yes
Grant				
Arts	350	Medium–Low	1990	Yes
Business	470	High	1981	Yes
Communications	350	Medium–High	1981	Yes
Health	339	High	1990	Yes
African American Studies (AAS)	300	Low	1993	Yes
Harrison				
Arts/Communications (AC)	300	Medium–High	1991	Yes
Business	250	Medium	1991	Yes
Health/Human Services (HHS)	350	High	1990	Yes
Science/Technology (ST)	275	Low	1991	Yes
Monroe				
Generic 1	425	Low	1996	No
Generic 2	425	Low	1996	No
International Business				
Magnet (IBM)	225	Medium	1996	Yes
Math/Science Magnet (MSM)	225	High	1996	Yes
Taylor				
Arts/Humanities (AH)	340	High	1995	Yes
Business	340	Medium	1995	Yes
First-Year 1	380	Low	1995	No
First-Year 2	380	Low	1999	No
Health/Human Services (HHS)	250	Medium	1995	Yes
Mechanical	250	Low	1995	Yes

housing. Every year dozens of Adams graduates attended selective colleges and universities; equal numbers left Adams (and formal education) after 9th grade.

The History. The economic and cultural gulf between these populations was widening as middle-class families increasingly abandoned the city and the school district. When voters eliminated citywide rent control in the mid-1990s, many middle-income families fled the district as rents skyrocketed. The proportion of housing the city deemed "affordable" dropped from over half to 14% in just a few years. Public housing remained an option for very low-income residents, but only affluent families could afford homes or condos priced at $500,000 or more. As the middle class departed, Adams was challenged to serve a student clientele with very disparate social, economic, and educational backgrounds. An administrator lamented, "We're becoming more and more the haves and have-nots."

Although Adams was among the first SWS high schools in the nation, its SWS structure evolved slowly over several decades and was not intentionally designed. The city operated two public high schools through the late 1970s. One provided traditional vocational education; the other offered a college preparatory focus. In 1969, a group of teachers and parents coalesced around the belief that the pedagogies and curricula employed by the district's high schools constrained students' social and intellectual development. Assisted by like-minded faculty from the nearby university, this coalition created a stand-alone "Alternative School" that operated within the vocational high school. Launched as a program of choice for both teachers and students, Alternative provided a 1960s take on progressive education. Social relations were informal; students called teachers by their first names and entered and exited the building and classes as they pleased. The Alternative School attracted politically liberal students and families—the "antiestablishment crowd," as a veteran Adams teacher described them.

Partly in response to Alternative, in 1976 another group of parents and teachers developed the "Core Curriculum School," organized around a narrow set of academically oriented and tracked courses, a dress code, and teacher-centered approaches to instruction. At the beginning, the fact that Core Curriculum was housed in a vacant Catholic elementary school seemed appropriate, as its academic and behavioral climate reflected that in Catholic schools. Alternative and Core Curriculum remained stand-alone schools of choice through the 1970s, each enrolling 200–300 students. Although their students could access academic and extracurricular offerings in the regular high schools, their programs were distinct and separate.

Over time, enrollment in the district's vocational high school became disproportionately minority and low-income, whereas the college preparatory school's students were mostly White and affluent. By the 1970s, the district faced declining enrollments and a looming desegregation court order. In response, the district closed (and demolished) the aging academic high school and transferred its students into the newly renovated and expanded vocational school. John Quincy Adams High School was born. The superintendent at the time felt that the SWS structure would produce a more secure school environment, which he saw as important for a large high school in a city experiencing considerable racial tension. As one long-time Adams teacher put it, the district (and many staff) felt that through the SWS structure they could "divide and conquer." In justifying the initial adoption of schools within schools, most staff acknowledged that teaching and learning were secondary to "keeping the lid on."

The Subunit Structure. When the two schools were combined, students were randomly assigned to one of four nondescript administrative subunits (Subunits 1, 2, 3, and 4). Although Alternative and Core Curriculum remained programs of choice, they joined Adams from their off-campus locations. To assist the maintenance of their unique identities, each was provided a separate floor of the main building. An additional subunit of choice was also created—Vocational—which served students interested in traditional career education. When the dust settled, Adams was operating seven subunits: three thematic subunits of choice and four randomly composed subunits without themes. Students who applied to Vocational were always admitted, but a lottery decided which students were admitted to the oversubscribed Alternative and Core Curriculum subunits.

Two factors pushed Adams toward a full-model SWS structure. First, Alternative and Core Curriculum's popularity created a supply and demand problem. By the mid-1980s, three quarters of incoming 9th graders were applying to Alternative, Core Curriculum, or both. The fact that students would apply to both subunits is interesting, because their philosophies were completely antithetical. Veteran Adams teachers explained that many students (or their parents) felt that Alternative and Core Curriculum offered identifiable values and goals—they *stood* for something. With the aim of relieving pressure on Alternative and Core Curriculum, the district suggested (but did not require) that Adams extend choice to the four nondescript subunits. Subunits 1 through 4 were encouraged to develop distinct themes so that students could chose among them.

A second factor leading Adams toward a full-model SWS structure emerged in 1989, as the district closed Subunit 2 due to declining enrollment. Rumors circulated that another subunit might also be closed, and the remaining subunits felt their odds of survival would increas if they developed clear themes like those of Alternative, Core Curriculum, and Vocational, as the district had suggested. An Adams teacher recalled, "Everybody said, 'Well, how do we justify who we are?'" In short, Adams opted for the choice-driven, full-model SWS structure in the interest of survival.

Subunit 1—although randomly composed and themeless—had developed a reputation for traditional academics. It was often requested by high-achieving students who had been denied admission to Alternative or Core Curriculum by the lottery process. Subunit 1 decided to further this reputation and became "College Prep." Its first director told us, "We weren't into the touchy feely, sit around, 'How are you doing, we want to be your buddy' kind of stuff." Subunit 3 adopted the name "Community" and a theme involving community service and leadership. Subunit 4, into which Adams's non-English-speaking students were automatically placed, sought to capitalize on its multicultural identity. It developed a curriculum that emphasized cooperative learning and team teaching, and became "International/Cooperative Learning" (ICL). By 1989, Adams's full-model, choice-driven SWS structure was in place.

Ulysses S. Grant High School

Situated on a once-thriving residential and commercial boulevard, by 1998 Grant High School was an island of activity in a sea of neglected storefronts, abandoned homes, and graffiti-covered buildings. As often happens in blighted urban neighborhoods, the large mid-Atlantic city that was home to Grant had renamed several local streets after famous African American figures. Solidly working and middle class 50 years before, Grant's neighborhood offered scant employment except in the underground economy, and crime was widespread. Grant's imposing silver and black metal detectors sought to keep these environs outside the school. Uniformed security guards and city police officers inspected visitors' bags and purses. Security was even tighter for students, whose identification cards were scanned by a machine that determined if they were skipping a class, suspended or expelled from school, or wanted by law enforcement.

Grant was one of many high schools constructed in the district in the early 1970s with schools within schools in mind. To serve an original planned enrollment of 1,000, a central stairwell divided the two floors into two wings, each of which was designed to accommodate about 250 students. Each wing contained two clusters of four classrooms and a common area on one side of the corridor; student lockers, study carrels, and teacher offices were on the other side. The classroom clusters were designed as open spaces that were divided into four classrooms by folding partitions—the "open school" plan popular at the time. Although designed for small learning communities and open class-rooms, the facilities were never actually used for these purposes. The mostly concrete building was acoustically challenged, and many of its classrooms lacked solid doors and walls. For almost two decades, neither students nor teachers were organized into subunits, nor were the partitions ever opened to accommodate communal activities. Instead, the wings were organized largely around academic departments, and the school operated as a traditional com-prehensive high school. Reportedly, Grant's original administrators never solved an administrative dilemma we discuss more fully in Chapter 4: What type of governance structure affords subunit autonomy, yet constrains that autonomy within the confines of buildingwide administration?

The Population. Given the contextual conditions surrounding the school, it is unsurprising that Grant's students have historically been among the nation's most socially, economically, and academically disadvantaged. The exodus of manufacturing jobs from the city and decades of White and middle-class flight left Grant with a demographically homogeneous student body. Among the five schools in our study, Grant had the least diversity in terms of race/ethnicity, social class, academic achievement, and future educational plans.

During the period we studied the school, virtually all of its students were Black, and close to 90% were eligible for meal subsidies. Each year the school enrolled over 900 ninth graders but graduated fewer than 250 seniors. Course failure rates approached 40%, and attendance for many students was erratic. Barely 20% of Grant's students scored at even "basic" levels on the reading por-tion of the district's standardized assessment; fewer than 5% met minimal standards in mathematics and science. Although school district records indi-cate Grant enrolled 2,600 students in 1998–1999, only 2,100 students actually received report cards, suggesting the challenges of documenting this highly mobile population.

The Subunit Structure. The construction of a large classroom wing in the late 1970s more than doubled Grant's capacity and enrollment. In 1981, the school offered two selective and choice-based subunits—Business and Communi-cations—housed in the new classroom wing. Students who selected these mag-net programs often lived outside of Grant's catchment area. They also tended to be higher achieving and socioeconomically more advantaged than students from the surrounding neighborhood. Although students in these two subunits took many of their classes schoolwide, their separate space, magnet status, and a few unique classes set them apart.

In 1988, the entire district (with the assistance of a local philanthropic foundation) launched a major initiative to restructure all of the city's middle and high schools into schools within schools. A nationally prominent superintendent who supported the SWS model was hired, accelerating the movement toward small schools. District directives about the reform stressed the value of subunit autonomy. A district publication at the time stated: "[Subunits] will be accountable for student outcomes and will have decision-making authority commensurate with that responsibility." In 1990, as part of this initiative, Grant organized two more subunits: Health and Arts. A few years later Grant opened an additional subunit, African American Studies. By the early 1990s, all Grant students were part of its choice-driven, full-model SWS structure.

Grant was required to enroll all "local" students who applied, but students who applied from outside the neighborhood could be rejected. Although entry to subunits was choice-based, there was considerable controversy during the years before our study about how selective subunits could be (and which criteria could be used for selection). Application rates were consistently higher (and acceptance rates thus lower) for the Business and Health subunits than for the others. Due largely to these two highly sought-after subunits and an energetic and well-known new principal, Grant's reputation improved dramatically throughout the 1990s. Enrollment swelled from 1,800 to 2,600 students, and the number of motivated students increased substantially. By 1998, about two thirds of entering 9th graders lived outside of Grant's catchment area. Although lagging far behind the city's highly regarded selective high schools, many students and families viewed Grant as superior to their regular neighborhood school. Explaining why she chose Grant over her neighborhood school, one student claimed that a friend had told her, " 'Grant was more advanced than the other schools and that I'd learn better here.' I just came here to get out of my neighborhood school." A Grant subunit head echoed these beliefs:

> Part of the pitch is that if you're looking for an alternative to the neighborhood high school and you aren't quite certain that you're going to get into [one of the city's competitive high schools], then we're the alternative. We would be a big step up from going to the neighborhood school.

Students in the district could apply directly to any public high school or subunit. At Grant, the fact that applications went directly to subunits exaggerated differences among them. Recruitment, reputation, and ratios of applicants to spaces became important. The district had previously permitted subunits to adopt their own criteria for selecting students from outside the school's catchment area, which allowed the Business and Communications subunits to enroll more committed students. However, by 1999, the district required all schools (and subunits) to use the same admissions criteria for incoming eighth graders: at least a "D" average, no failing grades for behavior, and less than 49 absences in the previous year. These criteria may not seem very rigorous, but relative to the neighborhood high schools in this large urban school district, even these criteria helped Grant to attract a somewhat more selective clientele than if it had enrolled only neighborhood students. However, 8th graders from Grant's two feeder middle schools were guaranteed admission to any Grant subunit to which they applied, even if they did not meet the admissions criteria for outsiders. Students from these middle schools, however, constituted less than one third of Grant's enrollment in 1999.

Benjamin Harrison High School

Harrison High School opened in the 1950s as the sole secondary school in a newly consolidated school district. Photographs of the dedication ceremony show the school surrounded by the rolling fields and farms common to this area of the Pacific Northwest during that period. Proud students, parents, and staff posed in front of their modern facility. Almost rural at the time, the social and political differences separating Harrison from the large urban area 20 miles to the north soon evaporated. Explosive growth transformed the community into a major residential and commercial center in its own right.

The demographic shifts that left Grant an island of social and economic despair fueled growth and prosperity in Harrison's neighborhood for almost three decades. However, these same social forces, propelled by the American penchant for novelty and change, soon worked against Harrison. As the community expanded, developers constructed newer and more expensive residential neighborhoods. Over the next several decades, three new high schools were constructed with facilities rivaling or surpassing Harrison's. These neighborhoods and schools soon attracted more affluent families away from Harrison and its environs, which experienced gradually declining growth and prestige. As a result, Harrison High began to serve increasing proportions of lower achieving, lower income students.

The Population. In 1998, Harrison High School enrolled 1,300 students in Grades 10 through 12. Among the district's four high schools, Harrison students had the lowest test scores and were the most socially and racially diverse, contributing to its reputation as the district's "urban school." Harrison's catchment area contained 90% of the city's rental housing, and proportional growth in Harrison's minority enrollment was double the district average. Interestingly, this "urban" reputation belied the fact that Harrison's enrollment was two thirds White. Its students were aware of their school's reputation in the community. "We're sort of the ghetto of high schools," remarked one student, "and if you come from [Harrison] you're obviously a hoodlum." Another student added that when he told others he attended Harrison, they responded, "Dang, you go to [Harrison]? Haven't you got beat up yet?"

The History. Harrison's enthusiasm for schools within schools developed largely in response to its changing demographics. In the mid-1980s a group of teachers sought a design that would serve the growing number of disadvantaged students as well as their more advantaged college-bound peers. A veteran teacher recalled the guiding question: "How do we make a high school more personal, more intimate, and more effective?" Staff considered the writings of John Goodlad (1984) and Theodore Sizer (1984), both of whom advocated high schools with smaller and more personalized learning environments. Several teachers traveled to SWS high schools in other states, and they returned convinced that the SWS structure would help Harrison accomplish its goal. A small group of these teachers started one subunit in 1990: Health/Human Services (HHS). With considerable teacher buy-in, Harrison implemented a choice-driven full-model SWS structure the following year with three new subunits: Arts/Communications, Business, and Science/Technology. From their inception, certain subunits (especially HHS, but also Business) were chosen by more motivated students, whereas others (Arts/Communications, Science/Technology) attracted students whose interests lay outside traditional academics.

Subunit Structure in Trouble. Although a core of strong SWS supporters remained among Harrison staff as we began our research, broader enthusiasm for the reform was on the wane. After a decade's experience with the design, some Harrison teachers, administrators, and community members began to argue that the SWS structure actually harmed the school's reputation. Harrison served the district's least-advantaged clientele and was the only school with the SWS design. In their minds, the two were linked, because the original argument in favor of the SWS structure was its value in serving struggling student populations well. As an alternative, parents of some Harrison high-achieving students and district administrators were encouraging the school to add an International Baccalaureate (IB) program as an autonomous subunit. Their hope was that Harrison's test scores (and reputation) would improve because the IB program would attract higher-achieving students from outside Harrison's catchment area.

A long-time SWS faculty supporter wistfully explained, "We've had a 62% turnover of teachers in the last 5 years, and a lot of the teachers that started the whole thing have bailed out of here." The challenge to sustain staff-initiated reforms amidst teacher retirement and relocation is a theme we found across several of the SWS high schools we studied. Harrison's SWS structure was also threatened on other fronts. The principal seemed to exhibit only tepid support for the reform. Some district administrators were almost antagonistic to the SWS design, which they saw as incapable of improving (and possibly accounting for) Harrison's lagging test scores. One Harrison assistant principal lamented, "We're always measured against test scores." Central to administrative resistance was a belief that the SWS structure in itself could alter neither classroom instruction nor student learning. As we completed our initial rounds of data collection, the SWS structure at Harrison seemed severely threatened, and we thought that it might not survive.

James Monroe High School

The events surrounding the "birth" of James Monroe High School were common throughout the desert Southwest during the 1990s: unbridled residential and commercial development, an abundance of inexpensive arid land, and an explosion in local populations. Driving through the area on our first visit to the school, the sights and sounds of construction were everywhere in the dry desert air. Freshly paved roads often ended into the nothingness of the desert, waiting to welcome the residents who were already on their way. New neighborhoods blossomed between our several visits to the school from 1998 to 2001, rendering our original map more irrelevant with each trip. The area's proximity to the Mexican border, NAFTA, and a global economy had fueled the "maquila" industry; products were assembled in nearby Mexico, trucked over the border, then distributed from U.S. warehouses. Despite the expansion in this sector of the Southwest region's economy, the local unemployment rate was twice the national average, and many of the newly created jobs paid low wages, offered no benefits, and were held by illegal immigrants.

The History. Bordered by mountains, rivers, and state and international borders, growth in the metropolitan area surrounding this large city was channeled directly through Monroe's school district. Suburban and urban sprawl had increased school enrollments tremendously since the early 1970s, when the entire district served only 1,000 students and a single high school enrolled only 150. By the mid-1990s, the district served more than 23,000 students, including 6,000 crowded into two high schools. To address this burgeoning school population, in 1994 local voters approved a bond issue to fund the construction and operation of two elementary schools, three middle schools, and a high school: James Monroe.

There was strong and broad commitment to the small-schools movement among the superintendent, the principal who would open Monroe, and numerous teachers and administrators assigned to Monroe. Similar to a group of Harrison teachers, Monroe staff-to-be took their theoretical grounding from Goodlad (1984) and Sizer (1984), and they discussed these books at length. With a physical layout for schools within schools in mind, district personnel worked closely with architects in designing the new school. The building was organized into four classroom "pods," each connected to a central area housing facilities the whole school would share: the library, computer lab, and administrative offices. Each pod contained its own classrooms and teacher work areas, a multipurpose area, lecture hall, and science labs.

The beautiful new James Monroe High School opened in 1996 with 1,050 students in Grades 7–9. In subsequent years those students advanced, so that in 1999–2000 the school enrolled Grades 9–12. In that year (and during our study), Monroe added its first class of new 9th graders and graduated its first class. This unusual "rolling start" approach had two advantages: (a) it allowed students already enrolled in the district's other high schools to graduate with their peers (and not change into an SWS program midway through high school), and (b) it created an initial core of students with up to 6 years' experience with the SWS model.

The Population. The large majority (over 80%) of Monroe's 1,400 students were Hispanic. Spanish was almost as common in the hallways as English. Half of Monroe's staff was also Hispanic (as was the principal), and their conversations with students and each other casually maneuvered between English and Spanish. Although Monroe was ethnically quite homogeneous, its students were socially quite diverse. Some came from professional families living in elegant and expensive homes surrounding the school. At the other extreme were students from poor families living in "colonias" located in the surrounding desert, where homes often had dirt floors and no electricity or running water. Monroe's gleaming new facilities and upper middle-class neighborhood obscured the fact that over half of its students were eligible for free or reduced-price lunches. Although there was a stable core of long-time students, Monroe's enrollment also grew as many new students arrived (some mid-year, some directly from Mexico).

The Subunit Structure. Before Monroe was constructed, one of the district's existing high schools offered two individual schools within schools as districtwide business and math/science magnet programs. Although the high school did not offer a full-model SWS structure, the perceived success of these small, stand-alone magnets suggested a broader, full-model SWS structure as a logical next step. Monroe's new principal, who had been an administrator at that school, convinced several teachers from the magnet subunits to join him in the new Monroe venture. Their charge was to recreate their programs as subunits within the new school's full-model SWS structure. Math/Science Magnet (MSM) and International Business Magnet (IBM) were launched at Monroe as districtwide magnet programs.

But what should happen to the majority of Monroe students, who did not see themselves pursuing careers in math, science, or business? Monroe's response represents the most unusual aspect of its subunit structure. In contrast to its specialized magnet subunits, students who did not select MSM or IBM were randomly placed into one of two nonthematic subunits. These "Generics" (as students and staff labeled them) were regular high school programs— no explicit themes, no organizing rationales, and no choice. Monroe's principal acknowledged, "There's no concept to really hold them [the Generic subunits] together just yet." Moreover, the IBM and MSM subunits (especially the latter) could select their students from among applicants, whereas the generic subunits enrolled all who were assigned.

The presence of selective, districtwide magnet subunits alongside generic subunits engendered tension and resentment among students and faculty. The hierarchical nature of Monroe's SWS structure and the resulting social divisions were not accidental; certain subunits were designed to attract better students. Thus, the stratification we found between subunits came as no surprise. Monroe High School's unusual subunit structure is a stark example of a common theme running throughout this book: the challenge of creating subunits that attract students with similar interests but varied social and academic backgrounds.

Zachary Taylor High School

As we noted in the Prologue, Taylor High School in many ways exemplifies the types of schools that have adopted the SWS structure over the past decade. Built in the late 1960s, Taylor High School resembled the factory buildings surrounding it. Its gray exterior was encased in row upon row of Plexiglas windows, many clouded and yellowed with age, some cobbled together with duct tape and cardboard. Although both Grant and Taylor were inner-city high schools in large mid-Atlantic cities, Taylor's neighborhood was farther from its city center than Grant's. The exodus of the city's manufacturing sector left a residue of abandoned factories, glass-strewn parking lots, and aging rowhouses. In this postindustrial landscape, unionized employment in the automotive and shipping industries had yielded to service sector jobs offering low wages and few benefits. Many long-time working-class neighborhood residents followed the good jobs to the suburbs; between 1950 and 2000 the city lost a third of its residents. Beyond a nearby strip of fast food restaurants, Taylor's community had witnessed little social or economic reinvestment. As we began our study there, Taylor was a "zoned" (i.e., neighborhood) high school that enrolled 2,300 students who were not admitted to (or did not choose) one of the city's several selective public high schools.

The Population. Taylor students were among the lowest-achieving and least-motivated in the city and district. "My basic approach to every kid who walks through the door at Taylor is that they're a student at risk," a teacher commented. "They're at this school because they didn't go to a citywide school." A quarter of Taylor's students were absent on any given day, and almost three quarters missed more than 20 days of school annually. Dropout rates were high: only 40% of incoming 9th graders made it to 12th grade. Taylor publications suggested that it prepared students for either college or work, but very few students entered college. Among the roughly 250 annual graduates, less than a dozen would enroll in a 4-year college or university the following fall.

Taylor's enrollment was two thirds Black and one quarter White, with small numbers of Asian and Native American students. This made it the most racially diverse regular public high school in a district where enrollments were overwhelmingly Black. As recently as 1975, however, Taylor had been almost all White, when it enjoyed a reputation as one of the district's better schools. White and middle-class flight resulted in Taylor serving increasing proportions of students from minority and low-income families. A large parking lot originally built for students generally went unused; few could afford their own cars and most took pubic transportation to school.

The History. Changes in Taylor's demographic composition over the previous two decades had resulted in a steady decline in both reputation and community support. "Things have really changed since I went to school here," a White parent told us. "All [the neighborhood residents] know about the students is that they're a different color. When there is a problem in the community, it's 'Those Black kids.'" By the early 1990s, students' scores on state assessments distinguished Taylor as the state's second to lowest performing high school. Serious student misbehavior was rampant, and teachers focused on classroom management often to the exclusion of teaching and learning. By 1994, Taylor had hit "rock bottom"; staff and students alike described the school at that time as "out of control." Roughly a third of students were absent each day, and strangers frequently wandered the hallways.

As we described in detail in the Prologue, in 1994 the state deemed Taylor "eligible for reconstitution" for academic reasons: low test scores, poor student attendance, and very low graduation rates. In return for considerable freedom to restructure the school, the state mandated that reconstitution-eligible schools like Taylor make serious improvements or face teacher dismissal, state takeover or privatization, or even permanent closure. Clearly, the stakes were high. The district was required to submit an extensive proposal detailing the reform strategies they planned for Taylor. As part of its efforts to help the school avoid even more serious reconstitution, the district appointed new administrators, transferred faculty, created new academic programs, and hired an outside reform group to help restructure the school.

The Subunit Structure. The most substantial element of Taylor's reform involved the adoption of the SWS structure in 1995. With major assistance from the local university-based school reform group, Taylor created five subunits, four of which were upper-grade "career academies": Business, Arts/Humanities, Health/Human Services, and Mechanical. A unique component of Taylor's SWS structure was that 9th graders did not participate in the career academies but were instead enrolled in a separate "freshman academy" (First-Year 1). Although this subunit had no career theme, 9th graders and faculty were grouped into several cross-disciplinary teams. Only after successfully completing 9th grade were students permitted to select among the four career subunits. Due to growing numbers of 9th grade repetitions each year, a second freshman subunit (First-Year 2) was opened by 1999.

Despite many dramatic improvements in the climate of Zachary Taylor High School as a result of its conversion into an SWS school, the school's academic performance continued to lag behind the state average and even behind its peer schools in the district. State test scores remained low, and the school experienced constant turnover of central administrators. Thus, as we began our study at Taylor, the threat of severe sanctions loomed again. In 1998, the district appointed yet another principal. This veteran and locally well-respected woman would challenge the autonomy of Taylor's subunits and question the legitimacy of Taylor's SWS structure.

CONCLUSION

Although these five high schools all shared an organization that reflected the full-model SWS design, there was considerable diversity both within and among them. As the summary information in Table 2.1 suggests, the schools varied considerably in terms of their locations, histories, student populations, subunit structures, and other organizational features. There were also clear differences in how each school's SWS structure was implemented: some evolved over time, whereas others were intentionally created. The 20-year development of Adams's subunits, for example, differs markedly from the concurrent implementation of Monroe's and Taylor's full-model structures.

Overall, these five schools serve greater proportions of low-income and non-White students than does the average public high school. As pointed out earlier, we were unable to locate a single affluent high school with the full-model SWS structure (although we did locate one that had recently abandoned a weak SWS design). Moreover, although we sought schools that represented regional diversity across the nation, we chose to study no schools in rural areas, in the Midwest, or in the South. How our findings might differ had we not studied these particular schools and communities, or if we had studied schools of this type more recently, is unclear. Nevertheless, the SWS designs implemented within these schools do represent considerable variation.

Although we do not claim that this sample of SWS schools is representative of the population from which it was drawn, we argue that our sampling criteria—which captured considerable diversity among schools that share this organizational form—allow us to describe schools of this type quite well. We argue that deep study of a few schools that are similar in one respect but quite different in several others is valuable. Studying these full-model SWS high schools provides the opportunity to explore an educational reform that has been afforded considerable publicity and advocacy but subjected to little empirical scrutiny. Rather than selecting a few schools to study that represent "the best of the lot," we chose to study SWS schools that differed substantially from one another. Such an analytic approach seems especially warranted, considering the rapidity with which U.S. high schools are embracing the SWS model, the hundreds of thousands of students who will experience the reform, and the advocacy tone of much writing about it.

Now that we have familiarized readers with the actual SWS schools we studied, we move to explaining their functioning in more detail. In the next chapter we explore the reform somewhat more conceptually. What challenges did these schools face in trying to foster small-school climates via the SWS model? What beliefs and rationales brought these schools to this reform, and to their own particular ways of implementing it? How did students and teachers ultimately benefit from participating in high schools divided into schools within schools?

3

Benefits of the
Schools-Within-Schools Design

HOW MIGHT THE schools-within-schools (SWS) reform fundamentally improve U.S. secondary schools? Our conversations with staff in the five SWS high schools we studied often began with such questions as, "Why did you implement schools within schools?" "What benefits did you expect?" "How has the SWS structure influenced teaching and learning?" In this chapter we combine our knowledge of secondary schools with what we learned during this study to describe the theoretical and actual benefits of the SWS reform. We used what we read in the literature and what we saw and heard in these schools to develop a conceptual model that spells out the mechanisms through which the SWS organizational design might improve student outcomes.

Before discussing particular benefits of the SWS design, we offer mini–case studies of two subunits (in different schools) that we felt were functioning well. Our first week-long visit to each school included in-depth scrutiny of two subunits: one that the school felt functioned well and another that experienced some problems. In some schools, the "strong" subunits that were recommended to us seemed to function well because they enrolled a disproportionately high number of motivated students. The two subunits we highlight here are not of this type; neither necessarily enrolls its school's socially or academically elite students. Our rationale was to focus on subunits where *organizational* or *instructional* procedures explained why they seemed to work well, rather than the fact that they served better students. After presenting the case studies, the remainder of the chapter spells out more general benefits that we observed resulting from the SWS design. Although these benefits would accrue largely to students, we also discuss the benefits that teachers might experience from working in SWS high schools. We highlight some approaches implemented in one or two schools that flowed from the SWS design that we think would be promising if incorporated in other schools.

Our aim in the book is to provide a balanced examination of the SWS reform based on the evidence we gathered in these five schools. We are enthusiastic about this design, but we stress our stance as neither supporters nor detractors. Because the reform has grown in popularity, we want schools considering the SWS model to be aware of both the benefits and the challenges that accompany such fundamental restructuring. With this goal in mind, the remainder of the book examines the extent to which our conceptual model of the reform's potential benefits actually holds true for the five SWS high schools we studied.

CONCEPTUAL MODEL LINKING THE SCHOOLS-WITHIN-SCHOOLS DESIGN TO STUDENT OUTCOMES

All educational reforms rest on some theoretical conceptualization about how the reform should lead, directly or indirectly, to improved student outcomes. Although not every educational reform aims to directly improve how much (or what) students learn, at least implicitly, changes in schools should ultimately improve student learning. Our study sought to examine how the SWS reform actually played out in several contexts. In the course of our work, we began to hear from school staff that they too thought the SWS structure should result in positive changes in student attitudes, behavior, and learning. Although no school had a conceptual model (at least not one they shared with us), they all seemed to base their actions on a similar causal mechanism.

Figure 3.1 presents our effort to infuse some theory into how the SWS reform might work more generally, beyond just the schools we studied. There surely is no solid empirical support for every linkage in the model; however, our experiences in these schools and our knowledge about secondary schools suggest that such linkages are reasonable. We highlight two boxes in the model: "Implement Reform" at the top left and "Student Academic Outcomes" in the bottom right corner. The boxes between these two constructs represent our ideas about the mechanisms and processes by which the SWS reform leads, at least in theory, to positive student academic outcomes.

Subunits within SWS high schools are generally organized around themes, which are meant to attract students (and sometimes teachers) whose interests

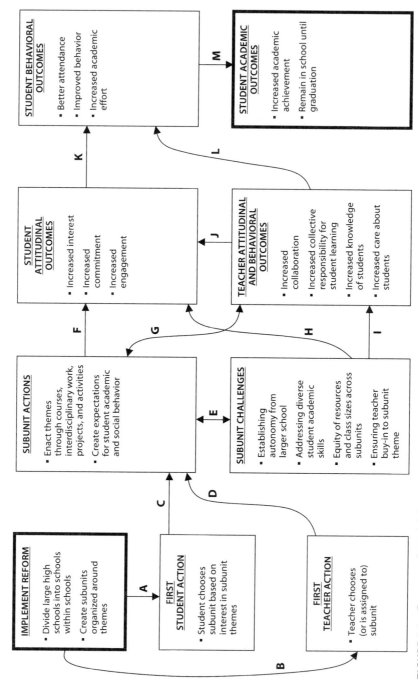

FIGURE 3.1. Conceptual Model for How the Schools-Within-Schools Design Influences Student Outcomes

align with the subunits' academic or pedagogical focus. Throughout the book we discuss student choice, the central mechanism by which student interests are meant to match subunit themes. The process through which choice operates is captured in Paths A and B in Figure 3.1. For both students and teachers, the "action" occurs within subunits, indicated in Paths C and D. But what happens inside the subunits? First, they create and offer courses and projects, many of which are meant to reflect their themes. Of course, they must also offer more general courses that together comprise a student's high school education. Although some academic and behavioral standards are dictated by the school (even the district or state), subunits may also set standards in certain areas for their members.

Subunits also confront several challenges (double-headed Path E). How much autonomy are they actually afforded in creating and implementing their missions? How much of a student's coursework (or time) should be subunit specific? Subunits typically want considerable autonomy, but other schoolwide pressures and responsibilities encroach on their ability to operate as independent entities. If individual subunits devise curricula for their members, how can the school ensure that all students are challenged and that all students find success? Given that some classes are required for everyone (e.g., 9th-grade English) but others serve small numbers of students (e.g., French IV or AP Physics), how can specialized classes with very low enrollments be offered within subunits? Another important challenge is how (or whether) resources are distributed equitably between (and even within) subunits.

Our conceptual model is mostly speculative; however, the most important links describe how subunits' actions and challenges affect subunit members. Here we highlight students' attitudes as intermediate outcomes (linked to subunit processes through Paths F and H) and teachers' attitudes and behaviors (linked to subunit processes through Paths G and I). Which student attitudes might improve as a result of subunit membership? We highlight three. Membership in subunits that reflect students' interests should increase their engagement with and commitment to school and to the subunits' missions. Among those who advocate the SWS design, there would be wide agreement about these theoretical linkages and outcomes.

Beyond increased student interest, engagement, and commitment, working in subunits should also change teachers' attitudes and behaviors. Sustained contact with fewer students might result in teachers knowing and caring more about their students. Related to caring is collective responsibility, wherein teachers commit themselves to the success of all students in the subunit. We also expect that subunit membership would facilitate greater collaboration among teachers, either directly in course planning and co-teaching or indirectly in developing and strengthening the subunit's broader social and academic mission. These changes in teachers' attitudes and behaviors should also improve student attitudes, captured in Path J.

We suggest that behavioral outcomes precede—but should lead to—academic outcomes (Path M). However, students' behaviors are also influenced by teachers' attitudes and behaviors (Path L). Which student behaviors should the SWS design improve, in theory? Students who attend SWS high schools should show improved attendance (in both school and classes) and exhibit less antisocial behavior (e.g., less fighting, fewer suspensions and expulsions; Path K). Perhaps even closer to academic success than attendance and pro-social behavior would be regular completion of homework and assignments. It seems reasonable that if teachers care about them more, know them better, and feel responsible for their success, students will respond with positive social and academic behaviors. Although such behaviors are themselves intermediate (and important) outcomes, they should also lead to improved academic outcomes, including increased learning and ultimately graduation (Path M). Research has documented empirical links between these student behaviors and student learning.

Figure 3.1 addresses two rhetorical questions surrounding this reform: "Does the SWS model lead to better academic outcomes for students?" and "If so, how?" The complexity of the model indicates that our responses to these questions are not simple. Moreover, the mechanisms spelled out in Figure 3.1 rest on several implicit assumptions about social interactions, many of which remain untested empirically. For sure, broad areas of education theory have not been subjected to empirical scrutiny. Moreover, studies that might validate all the links shown in this model would be very complex. Despite these caveats, we suggest that any educational (or social) reform should rest on logic models of how the reform might lead to the proposed outcomes. Figure 3.1 represents our own attempt to spell out these processes.

PORTRAITS OF WELL-FUNCTIONING SUBUNITS

Within these five SWS high schools 25 separate subunits were in operation (each described briefly in Table 2.2 and Appendix B). Most subunits were organized around themes. Many of these themes centered on careers or disciplines (e.g., Business, Health, Arts, Law, Math/Science, Mechanical), a few focused on ideologies or pedagogies (e.g., most subunits at Adams High), and a few highlighted organizational features (First-Year or Generic subunits). Because allowing students to select their subunits was so widespread, we decided to provide portraits of subunits whose students had selected to enroll in them. However, we wanted to avoid subunits that might function well because they enrolled a select or elite group of students. Thus, we sought subunits that seemed to work well for average students. This reduced the potential sample to 14 relatively nonselective, theme-based subunits. Among these 14, we considered such positive characteristics as inclusiveness, cooperation among subunit staff, curriculum integration, and other approaches that distinguish students' experiences from those in comprehensive high schools. We also did not want to describe two subunits in the same school, nor two with similar themes. Although there were many more than two subunits that worked well, the two we chose for these small case studies provide some indications about the benefits of the SWS design that we describe more generally later in the chapter.

Harrison's Arts/Communications Subunit

Students. Known for its emphasis on artistic and aesthetic values, Harrison's Arts/Communications (AC) subunit enrolled many students whom others described as "at-risk," "lower socioeconomic," "from broken homes," "outsiders," or just plain "weird." A teacher in one of Harrison's more traditional subunits told us she thought of AC students as "potheads, skateboarders . . . glad that they can wear their dog collars and have their noses pierced." To some extent, AC teachers agreed with these characterizations. When asked to describe her students, one AC teacher laughingly claimed that "if there's a nose ring and purple hair, they're in Arts and Communication . . . automatically." However, AC teachers also described their students as "really nice to one another" and "more creative than those in other subunits." Importantly, AC teachers embraced their students' unique personalities. As another AC teacher put it, her students were "different, to the point of weirdness—but that's OK." Responding to a query about why Harrison students might choose AC, another subunit staff member told us: "because we do more hands-on activities, close to their interests and abilities." Our own observations led us to agree; creativity and diversity, in terms of personalities and styles, appeared to thrive in AC. We saw also (and heard about) considerable tolerance and sensitivity to difference.

Faculty. A core group of AC faculty were among those who introduced the SWS design to Harrison, and more recent AC faculty recruits generally shared enthusiasm for the reform. However, these teachers' continuing support put them at odds with many school and district administrators. Among that core group was AC's subunit head, a veteran English teacher and published author who also chaired Harrison's English department. Although several students described him as an inspirational teacher, his leadership of the district teachers' union furthered his confrontational reputation among administrators. Despite tensions between the administration and the AC subunit, AC faculty worked unusually well together as a team. They spent time in and out of school planning classroom activities, integrating their courses, and deciding on common approaches to serve problematic students. We were told by AC faculty that interacting with students in multiple courses over several years was very beneficial. As one teacher asserted, "The kids tend to be in a lot of the same classes, so they tend to feel more comfortable with one another . . . to express their opinions or feelings . . . you get a lot more open discussion." Such a high degree of familiarity with students allowed teachers to "bug them, call them at home and say: 'Come to school!'" Across the many subunits in these five SWS high schools, the AC faculty's commitment to their collective mission was quite remarkable.

The Academic Program. Beyond social interactions, AC faculty described their subunit as "totally production-oriented." As instruction in the arts was incorporated into many academic activities, most subunit classes were taught in art studios located in a separate arts building; thus, they were often isolated from the rest of the school. Whenever we visited the arts building or AC classes, we saw students actively involved in art projects, which were displayed everywhere. Most students seemed very engaged and productive; in some classrooms, music played softly. According to a recruiting brochure distributed to students in middle school, the AC subunit

> is designed to integrate English (including drama and journalism), history, art, music, business, home and family life. It emphasizes effective and imaginative communication, aesthetic experience, the process of creating, independence and cooperation, and it aims to prepare students for any possibility after graduation.

There was considerable structural variation across Harrison's subunits. The AC school day was organized so that students had a contiguous three-period daily block of AC classes that included English, social studies, and one

AC-specific elective. Electives were organized by grade, so that course choice was somewhat constrained within grade levels. The subunit organized its core courses in English and social studies around the arts theme, with writing emphasized in most classes.

Another distinguishing feature was AC's use of conceptual themes that ran through its courses. The theme in 10th grade was "Identity." Within this broad theme were separate subthemes for each quarter: Dignity, Value of the Other, Struggle for Common Ground, and Value of the Circle. The 11th-grade theme was "The Journey," containing such subthemes as Unfolding the Map, On the Road, Destinations, and Coming Home. The senior-year theme was "Transformation," with subthemes of What Work Is, Social Change, Passages, and Synthesis. Subunit faculty went to considerable lengths to integrate these themes into the content of the three AC-specific courses. According to an AC English teacher,

> The first year we all sit down and talk about "Dignity"—the dignity of yourself, and showing other people dignity. Don't tell someone to "Shut up!" Don't make fun of others, don't cut each other down, help each other, we're all in this together. I had them do family totems, where they sat and wrote down all the characteristics and mannerisms of their family members. We transposed that into an animal that would represent those characteristics. And then they sculpted it into a totem, a family totem. And they loved it, you know. "Hey, I get to make my sister a snake! I've been waiting to make her a snake all these years!" I asked them: "So tell me about this!" . . . and there was a tremendous amount of insight.

For two reasons, AC faculty put more emphasis on themes and integrated curriculum in 10th grade than in subsequent grades: (a) they were allowed more common planning time to integrate the curriculum for 10th grade, and; (b) they sought to familiarize new students with the SWS design and the AC subunit (recall that Harrison enrolled grades 10–12). Teachers were articulate and specific in explaining how they integrated themes into their courses, suggesting that they had expended considerable time and energy. Although most students we interviewed recognized the value of these interconnected themes, a few felt that the themes sometimes resulted in repetitiveness. Dignity became "that D word!" in one focus-group discussion. However, an older student in that focus group was quite reflective and supportive of the thematic approach; despite a bit of grumbling, many students valued the cross-cutting themes.

Beyond the high degree of cooperation among AC faculty and considerable curriculum integration across classes (especially around themes), other aspects of the AC program also motivated us to single it out. One was the focus on community service. Although community service is a rather common feature of high schools, this activity worked especially well in AC, which organized a service-learning class to coordinate students' community service activities. Although all Harrison students had a community service requirement to graduate, only for AC students was the experience combined with a service-learning course. Many AC community service projects were tied to the subunit theme, and they brought arts into the school from the larger community. Another interesting endeavor was AC's annual publication of work by its students, which was collaboratively organized by two AC teachers. This publication included student writing, photography, painting, poetry, and book abstracts. The publication's quality was high, and the students' pride in the public display of their work was obvious.

Another impressive AC activity involved career exploration. AC 12th graders contacted local professionals with occupations loosely connected to the subunit's arts and communications theme. Several of these individuals spent a day at the school, and students had an opportunity to sign up for extended conversations with poets, potters, journalists, painters, and even a stand-up comedian. AC students described these sessions very positively; they allowed students to interact with role models who combined artistic, intellectual, and business abilities. Speaking with these practicing professionals allowed AC students a window into what they might themselves become as they looked beyond high school.

Summing Up. What especially struck us about Harrison's AC subunit were the positive statements students made about their school experiences. AC students, who recognized themselves as different, appreciated that AC faculty valued their "differentness." AC offered a highly interactive form of education in which students and teachers knew one another well and learned from one another both formally and informally. Guidelines and criteria for success were developed collaboratively, and standards were high. AC students recognized that they were treated with respect and pushed to do their best, and they worked hard to live up to the high standards teachers set for them (and they subsequently set for one another). Teachers were also proud of their work in AC, especially about keeping students in school who might otherwise drop out. "We hold on to our kids," one teacher told us, "even if their test scores are lower!" The constant pressure to raise test scores at Harrison was especially troubling to AC teachers. They felt such pressures undermined the success they were having with academically nontraditional students. AC faculty were committed to the SWS reform, and they made the design work well for their students. The integrated curriculum, deep thematic approaches, extended activities outside the school, and collaboration among faculty suggest how deeply the SWS structure had influenced AC's social and academic environments.

International/Cooperative Learning (ICL) Subunit at Adams

Students. Adams High School's largest subunit, International/Cooperative Learning (ICL), was also its most racially and ethnically diverse. English language learners (ELLs) were automatically placed in ICL, as was Adams's ELL staff. Adams's ELL population was sizable, and English was a second language for almost half of ICL's students. Although Alternative and College Prep remained at the top of Adams's subunit status hierarchy, more students were designating ICL as their first choice, and it was attracting higher-achieving students. As a result, ICL's test scores had risen above the school's average, and it was no longer viewed as a subunit of last resort. Given its large proportion of ELL students, ICL's academic performance was all the more remarkable.

Why would non-ELL students choose to enroll in a subunit where half of the students had limited English skills? In two important respects, ICL students resembled those in Harrison's AC: (a) their embrace of diversity, and (b) their openness to cooperative learning. Although many of Adams's nontraditional students selected Alternative, ICL's multicultural environment had become increasingly attractive to students seeking a more diverse experience. For some, membership entailed immersion into ICL's multicultural community, representing a welcome opportunity to learn from students whose life experiences differed from their own. A non-ELL student described what ICL membership meant to him:

> To be present. You know, to talk to people and not just say, "OK, they're part of that group, so I'll just move to the side over there. Let them do their thing." I'm not like that. Around my locker there are many cultures. Some guys from Bangladesh [are] right next to me; some Spanish-speaking people. There's Haitians two lockers down. I mean, I communicate with everybody. And I try to at least learn how to say "hello" in each one of their languages. Like I can say "How ya doin'?" in Ethiopian. "How ya doin'?" in Somali. And you just . . . you have to take advantage of that. That's what an ICL person is.

Similar to AC, ICL's climate of inclusion developed in relative seclusion, as the subunit was housed in a building separate from the main school building. Connected by an enclosed second floor walkway, ICL's building also housed Adams's auditorium and gymnasium. We saw this isolation as having both positive and negative consequences. Unlike subunits in the main building, whose hallways were often congested with students passing through to other subunits, the cafeteria, or the media center, non-ICL students had little reason to be in ICL's remote hallways. Teachers therefore found it easier to identify students who did not belong; they also felt comfortable confronting disruptive students (who were likely to be "theirs"). This increased familiarity between ICL teachers and students produced communal areas that seemed quieter and more orderly than those in other subunits.

This physical isolation, however, added to the sense that ICL was somehow "different" from the other subunits. Not only did it enroll students who looked, talked, and dressed differently, it was hard not to notice that Adams relegated these students to a separate building. Despite ICL's efforts to move beyond its reputation for enrolling only ELL students, many community members still saw ICL as the "immigrant subunit." For example, ICL was derisively known among many Adams students as the "Haitian Station" because of its large Haitian enrollment. Moreover, some ICL teachers were questioned by colleagues about why they willingly chose to work in ICL. One teacher recounted, "When I was at the elementary school and was asked to come up to the ICL, every teacher said, 'Do you want to be in a subunit where no one's going to be able to speak English to you?' I was shocked."

Faculty. With the exception of Monroe High School, the SWS structures within these five schools had been implemented within preexisting comprehensive schools. This had important implications for teachers' subunit loyalties at Adams. Although some teachers were able to choose their subunit when the school converted to schools within schools, many teachers were simply "absorbed" at random by subunits. For example, several Adams teachers declared that their subunit affiliations were mainly logistical: they chose the subunit that would permit them to remain in the same classroom and avoid moving decades' worth of classroom materials. As such, individual teachers' enthusiasm for their subunit's theme (and the SWS reform in general) varied greatly both within and across subunits.

This sense of "membership by default" was less frequent among ICL teachers. Many expressly selected ICL because they valued both its educational philosophy and its pedagogical approach. One ICL teacher asserted that specific subunits suited certain teachers; since the late 1980s, some teachers had slowly migrated to subunits that fit their personalities and beliefs: "I like ICL because it really has its act together—really feels like a place. A certain kind of person/ teacher/student wants to be in Alternative, and certain kinds of teachers wind up in other subunits." Another ICL teacher declared, "I'm an Adams teacher that has become an ICL teacher, because it's a democratic, diverse kind of a subunit where teachers are committed to helping each other and not shutting their doors." Reflecting an organizing rationale that focused on equity and democracy, the ICL faculty had developed a nonhierarchical administrative structure that was unique across the schools we studied. ICL faculty elected two codirectors who served 4-year "terms" and simultaneously taught at least one class. As we discuss in more detail in Chapter 4, subunit administrative structures varied widely among and even within these five schools. However, only ICL had elected and rotating leadership.

The Academic Program. Our major reason for highlighting Harrison's AC and Adams's ICL subunits is that they had crafted innovative instructional and curricular structures. Although considerable research supports the value of such structures, they would have been quite difficult to implement within a traditional comprehensive high school. Adams's course catalog described ICL's emphasis as "collaborative learning through team-teaching, heterogeneous class groupings, and integrated studies." ICL's promotional and recruiting materials underlined this emphasis in more detail by listing six "core values": cooperative learning, team teaching, challenging integrated curriculum, democratic decision-making, cross-cultural education, and a strong sense of community.

ICL implemented these core values mostly in the lower grades. All ICL classes in 9th- and 10th-grade English and World History were team-taught and organized around interdisciplinary approaches. Two-person teams— composed of an English and a World History teacher—worked in contiguous classrooms that were separated by movable dividers. Ninth- and 10th-grade English and World History classes were also scheduled back-to-back, with enrollments capped at 15 students (much smaller than the Adams norm). The structure of these classes—small enrollment, sequential scheduling, and teachers' physical proximity—permitted a 90-minute block of instructional time during which teachers assigned group projects and interdisciplinary activities. This structure echoed the thematic approaches employed in Harrison's AC subunit. ICL faculty were considering expanding the integrated theme to a wider core curriculum that would include mathematics. Such explicit attention to integrating coursework in this format, together with the team teaching and longer time blocks, reflected ICL faculty's dedication to the subunit's central themes.

Several students described ICL's focus on cooperative learning and group work as the subunit's best quality. A student from Romania spoke slowly in broken English while other ICL students in the focus group waited patiently. He explained that collaborative work habits defined ICL students:

> ICL gets the "human" out of you, not the "machine" that studies a lot. It's sociable. It's based on discussions. Our core classes, for example, are based on discussions—not writing a lot or a lot of tests. It's about doing group work. Meeting friends and helping each other.

Other students contrasted ICL's cooperativeness with the more traditional academic climates and students in Adams's other subunits. Another ICL student differentiated the subunits this way:

> College Prep's got this philosophy of really hard work, really academic. And, like, do stuff primarily by yourself as opposed to more group work, like ICL does. So it [College Prep] is really kind of independent and less community-oriented than ICL. And so . . . judging from that, it's the type of person who'd get there: someone who want to do everything by themselves.

Summing Up. These case studies of the AC and ICL subunits are intended to serve as examples of subunits that capitalized well on the SWS design. Neither enrolled their schools' academically or socially elite students, although they also did not enroll the very weakest students. Our judgment of them as "successful" rests on two shared attributes. First, both subunits had fundamentally transformed the nature of teaching and learning. Unlike many other subunits we observed, these two functioned as much more than organizational or bureaucratic entities. Although all the schools we studied had schools within schools, teachers' daily activities in some subunits seemed virtually unaffected by the SWS structure: classes were indistinguishable from those commonly found in regular comprehensive high schools. In both the AC and ICL subunits, however, teachers capitalized on the flexibility of the SWS structure to develop new physical arrangements, different instructional strategies, more collaborative activities, and some innovative curricular approaches. Several Harrison and

Adams teachers mentioned that not all faculty would be comfortable teaching in AC's or ICL's somewhat unusual academic environments. Teaching in AC or ICL had a distinctive meaning, and such "specialness" was transmitted to their students.

Beyond curricular innovation, another reason for highlighting AC and ICL is their more personalized and welcoming social environments. This is also especially achievable—but far from inevitable—within the SWS structure. A stroll down the hallways in other subunits within the same schools would afford little evidence that they actually functioned as small learning communities. Within AC and ICL, however, social interactions among students and teachers differed from those often decried in comprehensive high schools. In these subunits, faculty and students often approached academic endeavors as joint efforts. Subunit members generally saw their own cultural or linguistic diversity as a strength rather than an obstacle to be overcome.

Although advocates of the SWS structure argue that organizing students into smaller subunits will inevitably and positively impact teaching, learning, and social relations, this is not what we observed in these five schools. We suggest that those who favor the design temper their statements somewhat. Schools within schools create the *conditions* under which innovation and change can flourish, but such advances do not arise automatically. In the two subunits we have highlighted, creating and sustaining these environments required substantial faculty time and effort—and also some serious compromising. Moreover, in some cases these efforts met lukewarm support or even active hostility from other faculty and administrators, even in the same school. We showcased AC and ICL because they provide clear evidence of the promise and possibilities of the SWS reform. In short, AC and ICL faculty were able to create environments in which students from disparate backgrounds shared meaningful social and intellectual experiences.

PROMISING INITIATIVES FOR STUDENT LEARNING

Although social benefits deriving from the SWS structure were very common across these five schools, the benefits we observed flowing from innovative academic activities or classroom instruction were surprisingly rare. Here we describe some promising academic initiatives we encountered within individual subunits. We also mention some logistical and structural obstacles that may hamper the universal adoption of these initiatives.

Extended Periods of Instructional Time

Block scheduling is now quite common in U.S. public and private high schools. However, examples of teachers making productive use of the longer class time are more elusive. The extended instructional segments we discuss here go above and beyond simple block scheduling, which typically involves longer class periods to study single subjects. We instead focus on subunits' efforts to block out several periods to teach core subjects only to subunit members. That is, such classes were "pure" in that the blocked classes contained only that subunit's students. Different subjects could be taught, but typically to the same students, usually (but not always) at the same grade level. This approach permitted faculty to organize other initiatives, which we explore below. As we discussed, Harrison's AC and Adams's ICL made especially good use of such instructional blocks.

Given the SWS structure, there is no reason why all subunits in any school must follow the same schedule. However, the schools we studied did use school-wide schedules. Scheduling all students in a particular subunit into a single block of time makes it difficult to organize advanced courses with small enrollments (e.g., AP Physics or French IV) or "singleton" courses with larger enrollments (e.g., band or choir). Thus, courses outside the subunit structure create serious pressure not to tie up long blocks of subunit-specific instructional time. Schools need to decide which of these options is more important. Unfortunately, most of the schools we studied found that schoolwide courses were an insurmountable barrier to subunit-specific time blocks.

Core Courses Organized Around Subunit Themes

In several schools, some subunits created courses reflecting their themes. This was easier in subunits whose themes coincided with traditional departments (e.g., Business at Grant, Harrison, and Monroe; Math/Science at Monroe; Vocational at Adams; vocationally oriented Science/Technology at Harrison), because such courses required no special curriculum development. It was also less difficult to keep courses pure in such subunits because students from other subunits were rarely interested in their courses. In contrast, art classes in subunits with arts themes at Grant, Harrison, and Taylor typically attracted students from other subunits. A unique situation was found at Monroe. Math and science courses in MSM were generally closed to students from other subunits, meaning that MSM faculty had the freedom (and responsibility) to organize courses in these core areas. It also meant that Monroe's other subunits had to organize other math and science courses that were rarely pure and sometimes difficult to staff.

This issue may be clarified by a comparison between the Health subunits at Grant and Harrison. Both subunits tended to enroll many of their school's academically motivated students. Grant's Health subunit required its students to enroll in one subunit-specific (and pure) course each year (Health Science I and II in 9th and 10th grade, Health Seminar I and II in 11th and 12th grade), courses that subunit faculty had designed themselves, were very committed to, and worked constantly to improve. On the other hand, Harrison's HHS subunit lacked a coherent focus, instead relying on its traditional college preparatory program to attract the school's strongest students. HHS in fact offered only one special course: Health Careers. However, this course was open to students from other subunits. The subunit advised its students to take several advanced science courses (often in other subunits) to support its ostensible Health focus.

Across the five schools in our study, we were surprised that so few subunits had developed special courses that reflected their themes. However, the courses we did see that were organized around subunit themes were generally thoughtful and engaging. Given the positive implications of such initiatives, why were thematic courses and cross-cutting integrative themes so rare? Creating new courses is hard work, and it is even harder to develop a new course with colleagues. Crafting curricula acceptable to all faculty in a subunit requires substantial agreement about basic issues, as well as considerable time to forge the common understanding that would undergird such courses. The subunits in which we saw the strongest thematic efforts were those in which faculty had worked together for many years, shared ideas about what students should learn, and were willing to expend the time and effort to accomplish curricular innovation. Sadly, we conclude that this kind of fundamental agreement about what students should learn, and who should learn what, is quite unusual in U.S. public schools—even those that have collectively chosen to implement the SWS design. We return to this issue in Chapters 5 and 8.

Problem-Based Multidisciplinary Projects

Besides the commonality of coursework and time, we observed at least three subunits that required students to engage in projects that were organized across subjects, usually around particular problems. An outstanding example in this regard is Grant's Health subunit. We considered showcasing this well-functioning subunit, but decided not to because it enrolled some of Grant's strongest students. However, we believe the subunit's problem-based learning (PBL) component deserves special attention. The subunit head described it to us as follows:

> I have a PBL group in the 10th grade . . . top kids that passed everything in the 9th grade. This year they will be [scheduled] together for first, second, and third period. The teachers they have for biology, health science, and history have all been trained by [a nearby] University in problem-based learning, which is a method of learning by case study that is used in medical schools.

Although it created "a scheduling nightmare," small groups of students with good academic records would undertake a project about every second month for a week or two. Although PBL required substantial time and effort to train participating teachers, subunit faculty felt the program was worthwhile because the PBL projects focused students' activities on authentic topics concerning public health policies and issues. Grant's Health subunit head was justifiably proud of the PBL focus, although she also recognized the difficulty of sustaining the human, fiscal, and time resources necessary to offer a program to a relatively small number of the school's best students. Other examples of multidisciplinary projects were those offered within Harrison's Science/Technology (ST) subunit. Unlike Grant's Health subunit, ST enrolled many low-income male students seeking vocational careers. In cross-cutting interdisciplinary classes, ST students built houses and constructed go-carts and paddle-boats. The latter projects culminated in an annual competition with other high schools in the Northwest.

Both the benefits of multidisciplinary projects and the obstacles in undertaking them are obvious. The two Harrison subunits that engaged in this type of learning (AC and ST) involved all their students in such projects. However, Grant's Health subunit took a different approach, as their students had to earn the right to participate in PBL by accumulating a solid academic record. Moreover, teachers who led the PBL projects received the benefit of special professional development by outside experts from a local university. Not only does such an approach require considerable resources in terms of time, expertise, and materials, it also requires considerable agreement on the part of a subunit's entire faculty that this type of learning (which takes students away from traditional coursework) is worthwhile. Moreover, the issue of whether such multidisciplinary projects should be available to all students in a subunit or only to a special group is unlikely to find agreement among faculty, in either a subunit or a school.

Integrated and Interdisciplinary Teaching

As we stated at the beginning of this chapter, the social benefits of the SWS design are well established and close to universal. Our concentration here has been on academic benefits, some of which have a social component or accrue ancillary social benefits. We have chosen to focus on a relatively small number of promising academic initiatives. These initiatives were not completely independent of one another, as some subunits adopted several initiatives together. The subunits we chose to describe in case studies—Adams's ICL and Harrison's AC—did not attract their school's best students, but they were among the most promising locations for integrated and interdisciplinary teaching we observed. Harrison's ST subunit, where we also observed some interesting interdisciplinary projects, actually enrolled the fewest of its school's elite students. Clearly, such initiatives do not require elite students to make them successful.

We argue that interdisciplinary teaching is especially possible in SWS high schools due to the smaller number of students and teachers who work together over sustained periods and who often share interests and aims. We do not want to underestimate the fact that teaching this way is extremely demanding for faculty. It requires considerable and sustained planning and deep discussions about the purpose and value of cooperatively developed courses. Contiguous and extended blocks of instructional time are crucial, which confronts a basic issue driving almost all high schools: the schedule. They also require teachers to open their practice to outside scrutiny, an undertaking that flies in the face of another cherished characteristic of secondary schools: teacher autonomy. Such crucial requirements of time and effort are above and beyond the regular time necessary for instruction, tutoring, and informal consulting with students in which nearly all teachers already engage.

Although we were gratified to observe examples of this type of teaching in some of the subunits in these five schools, we were also discouraged that it was not more widespread. We believe that the SWS organizational design can facilitate the best instructional approaches and the most promising innovations, but these do not occur just because a school chooses the SWS structure. After spending so much time in these schools, we recognize that such practices will not arise automatically—no matter what organizational structure a school adopts. Only through the hard work of administrators and teachers will innovations develop and take hold.

OUTCOMES FOR TEACHERS

As described so far, the benefits of the initiatives enumerated in this chapter would accrue largely to students. However, the same initiatives could probably generate substantial benefits for teachers. A common feature across these five SWS high schools is that students were allocated to subunits almost entirely through the mechanism of choice. As Figure 3.1 suggests, students theoretically benefit from the SWS design by way of increased interest, commitment, and engagement (Paths F, H, and J). However, our theoretical model also posits some benefits for teachers, including the ability to engage in collaborative activities and to develop meaningful relationships with students and colleagues (the reciprocal relationships: Paths G and I in Figure 3.1).

Improved Work Lives

Many of the writers who have focused on high schools have advocated improving social relations, which is especially difficult but also especially important in large schools that serve disadvantaged clienteles. Staff members in the schools we studied unanimously agreed that the SWS structure fostered more positive student–teacher interactions and that such relationships often rested on a foundation of trust. Beyond positive social relations, long-term staff listed additional improvements in student behavior, attendance, and commitment to school. Importantly, faculty told us that they felt more satisfied with their work and more efficacious as a result of their schools' transition to the SWS model. Such benefits have also been described by small-school advocates over several decades.

Improvements along these lines surely help make teachers' daily work lives more engaging. As we have described throughout this chapter, the SWS structure facilitates innovative instructional practices, and experiencing such instruction would probably help students become more engaged in complex learning. Observing such results would surely provide intrinsic intellectual satisfaction in secondary school teaching. The typical isolation and autonomy of the teaching profession have been well documented, qualities that some teachers value and many more do not. The instructional innovations we have documented would move teachers away from isolation, especially when teachers who share beliefs about teaching and learning come together to act on those beliefs. However, teaching in this way is unlikely to be appreciated by every-one. Moreover, many practicing teachers would be reluctant to expend the effort needed to bring some of these innovations to fruition.

Potential Drawbacks for Teachers

Even in this chapter, where our focus is on the benefits and promises of the SWS design, we recognize some potential drawbacks for teachers who work within this reform. First—and we heard this from many, many teachers—truly collaborative teaching requires enormous amounts of time and effort outside the classroom. Many teachers simply do not want to (or cannot) devote much out-of-class and out-of-school time to collaborative planning. Second, teaching in this way moves teachers away from something that many value highly: autonomy. Collaboration requires that teachers open their practice to the scrutiny of their colleagues. Third, teaching this way (at least in these settings) means that faculty maintain sustained contact with a relatively small number of students and faculty colleagues. What if a teacher and student simply do not hit it off? In a comprehensive high school, that teacher and student may team up only for a single course. In the SWS organizational design, they could be forced to interact year after year in course after course.

An important affective domain of high school teaching is professional loy-alty. Many individuals choose secondary school teaching because of their strong interest and skill in a particular discipline (e.g., chemistry, English, or mathe-matics). In traditional high schools, teachers interact often with colleagues in the same department with whom they share a professional and intellectual affinity. In SWS schools, teachers work in small teams that explicitly run *across* disciplines; an individual teacher may be the only team member in a particu-lar discipline. Such an organizational form makes it harder to maintain con-tact with and loyalty to departments and disciplines. Ideally, the SWS design requires that teachers' major loyalties be to the subunit rather than the disci-pline, and that teachers be team players with colleagues with whom there is sometimes little shared vision. In Chapter 4 we provide more detail about administrative and organizational conflicts between departments and sub-units, some of which are not trivial. This type of conflict might very well apply to individual teachers. We argue that the benefits—defined in terms of collab-oration and teamwork—are extensive but probably do not accrue equally to all faculty. Teaching in a school organized into subunits may require a special type of faculty member, one who is committed to the learning of all students and who feels his or her practice would benefit from working collaboratively.

CONCLUSION

Both the SWS organizational structure and the theoretical model introduced in this chapter rest on an assumption: "smaller is better." The basic idea underlying the SWS reform is that when teachers interact with fewer students more frequently, the quality of teacher–student relationships will deepen, becoming more positive and more meaningful. Again, it is assumed that these enhanced relationships increase students' engagement with and commitment to school—perhaps because they feel that teachers who know them better are more concerned with their well-being as individuals (rather than simply as producers of academic work). Students' increased commitment may be behaviorally manifested, through attending school and class regularly, exhibiting fewer antisocial actions, being more engaged and attentive in class, and spending more time on homework and studying. According to the causal sequence in this model (Path M in Figure 3.1), such improved behaviors should ultimately result in increased academic achievement.

Even though this sequence is logical, rational, and appealing, it is important to recognize that not all links in this causal chain have solid empirical support. Supporters of the SWS reform model often cite research on school size, assuming that the benefits associated with small schools automatically accrue to the smaller subunits found within larger SWS high schools. As we argued in Chapter 1, the knowledge base about small schools itself rests on shaky empirical ground. Moreover, it is unclear whether such research is directly applicable to the SWS reform. In subsequent chapters we explore more deeply other parts of this conceptual model.

Our focus in this chapter has been on describing the benefits flowing from the SWS design. In general, we were very impressed by these five SWS high schools. We observed some examples of innovative programs, collaborative and integrated teaching, and methods that engaged students in authentic academic work that would be difficult to reproduce in traditional high schools. Across all the schools, what impressed us most was their willingness to engage in fundamental structural reform. Breaking up an existing (and often poorly functioning) comprehensive public high school into schools within schools is a difficult enterprise, requiring faculty and administrators to reexamine virtually everything they know about high schools. For example, these transformations required new governance structures and substantial changes in staffing (which we describe in Chapter 4). Questions about the fundamental purposes of public high schools arose in each school, and virtually every aspect of the comprehensive high school was reconsidered:

- What courses should be offered (and to whom)?
- What schedules are most productive for this new structure, and how many periods per day should the school have?
- Where should classrooms, labs, and schoolwide facilities be located?
- How should schoolwide activities such as band, choir, newspaper, and yearbook be accommodated within this structure?
- What about such compensatory programs as special education or bilingual education?
- Should rules and disciplinary standards be consistent across subunits, or should these organizational units be allowed to devise their own operating procedures?

Beyond the need for fundamental consideration of the everyday issues that constitute "high school," these schools were forced to consider how the SWS design would affect the school's basic mission of teaching and learning:

- What should all students know?
- Who should know what?
- Who should make decisions about what courses to offer, what demands should be made on students, and how students should engage with academic work?
- How should adolescents' lives in school should be organized?

We saw some of these questions being addressed in some subunits, through some activities, and among some faculty. In one sense we wish we could report more consistency in how schools and faculty confronted these important issues. In another sense, however, the very devolution of decision making from the central administration to the subunit level suggests the inconsistency with which such issues would be addressed. Clearly, the dialogues in which these schools engaged as they implemented this unusual structure were valuable in themselves—regardless of their resolution. Each school was forced to confront the "givens." For us, this is a primary advantage of the SWS reform: it requires staff to look critically at virtually every aspect of the traditional comprehensive high school. Any reform that forces people to reexamine the everyday features of high schools is good, in and of itself. We laud the school staffs we met for having examined—and considered changing—these fundamental (and seemingly intractable) elements of the traditional high school.

4

Governance and Leadership in Schools-Within-Schools High Schools

REGARDLESS OF THE NUMBERS and types of students they enroll, and the special purposes they may serve, public U.S. secondary schools typically are organized as bureaucracies with rather similar hierarchical governance structures. The leadership team is usually composed of a single principal and one or more assistant principals. These individuals are responsible for the overall operation of the school, including complying with federal and state policy, record-keeping, maintaining order and discipline, and fostering positive relationships between the school and the community it serves. Other members of the schoolwide leadership team are charged with such specialized functions as guidance counseling, assessment, bilingual education, and special education. Although some schools have an assistant principal responsible for the technical core (i.e., curriculum, teaching, and learning), the academic functions of public secondary schools usually are not the major responsibility of the overall school leadership team. Academic leadership more commonly rests within subject-matter departments, each of which has a chair.

As described in Chapter 2, the five schools-within-schools (SWS) high schools we studied were relatively large public institutions serving diverse clienteles. They all had leadership teams to perform the several schoolwide functions just described. However, the organizational structures of these SWS high schools included, by design, an additional administrative layer: the subunit. This did not preclude the need for whole-school governance. But how were the necessary (and sometimes competing) governance functions of these complex multilevel secondary schools organized?

Because we studied only five such schools over only two years, it is hard to separate the schools' governance structures from the personalities and leadership styles of the individuals who filled these administrative roles. One school's very visible principal decided almost every aspect of the operation of his school and its subunits. By contrast, another principal saw her major role as negotiating with the district office to bring resources to support relatively autonomous subunits. Two schools had new principals with mandates to lead their schools through major reorganization while also maintaining their subunit structures. Yet another principal, close to retirement, experienced active conflicts with many teachers who were strongly committed to the school's SWS structure; to him, the SWS structure hindered school improvement. The intertwined nature of these principals and the governance structures within their schools creates some analytic challenges. Any inquiry that focuses on schools within schools would seem incomplete without addressing issues of governance and leadership. However, it is difficult to separate the issues from the context in which we study them. Which facets of the governance structures we observed in these schools would endure without the particular people in these roles is hard to say.

We begin this chapter with a brief description of relevant theory and research about school governance. The majority of the chapter describes how—and by whom—these five SWS high schools were led. We include an interpretive section with short portraits of the major administrators. Reflecting the dozens of disparate SWS designs, governance structures vary widely across and even within SWS high schools (see Allen, 2001; Oxley, 1993; Wallach & Lear, 2005), particularly the degree of autonomy afforded each subunit. Indeed, the extent to which subunits required additional governance depended largely on the autonomy they had been granted. We also explore academic departments and how their efforts either supported or frustrated subunit goals. In keeping with our term "subunit," we describe "subunit heads." Across the schools, we encountered various labels for these individuals: assistant principals, coordinators, deans, directors, leaders. Our term, subunit head, is intended to describe the role similarly across all the schools, without conveying additional meaning. The responsibilities of these administrators, and how they differed across our five schools, is an important part of the governance story.

UNDERSTANDING SCHOOL GOVERNANCE

Until recently, research on school administration and leadership has used the theoretical lens of individual agency to study principals and what they do. This lens is located within a conceptual framework of school institutional structure known as "loose coupling" (Rowan, 1990; Weick, 1976). Under this model, the technical core of education—what should be taught at any given time, how and to whom it should be taught, what students should be expected to learn, and how they should demonstrate that learning—is implemented by teachers in classrooms and is not typically seen as a major concern of the school. Moreover, knowledge about the technical core in loosely coupled schools is seen as uncertain, difficult to evaluate, and reliant on the judgment of individuals. The loose coupling model is especially prevalent in research on secondary school administration. Under this model, a major responsibility of school leaders is "buffering" the technical core from outside forces (Bidwell, 1965; Lortie, 1975), leaving teachers free to do what they do in their classrooms. If schools are actually loosely coupled organizations, it is easy to understand why reform of the technical core would be hard to implement and even harder to sustain.

The loose coupling theory may not fit well in schools with the SWS design, because they require leadership at several organizational levels, rather than solely from the principal at the top. A more useful theory in these settings is a newer theoretical framework: distributed leadership (Spillane, Halverson, & Diamond, 2001). The general theory of distributed leadership locates human activity within the context where it occurs, where actors hold common understandings that draw on social, cultural, and historical norms. Although the context where Spillane and his colleagues first explicated their model was urban elementary schools, it seems to characterize secondary schools that require leadership at several levels. Authors have suggested that this governance style is particularly well suited for SWS high schools, which are administratively quite complex (see Allen, 2001). Indeed, SWS advocates have explicitly argued for a distributive approach: "If small units are to realize their full potential for permitting staff to respond to students' needs in an immediate and flexible manner, unit staff must be granted sufficient authority to make a wide range of decisions locally" (Oxley, 1993, p. 6). In short, the SWS structure—at least in theory—rests on the notion that substantial decision-making authority should rest at the subunit level.

A major difference between the distributed leadership and loose coupling governance models is that the former connects school leadership, directly or indirectly, to the technical core of teaching and learning. The distributed leadership model includes all dimensions of management needed to help the school achieve its goals, rather than focusing only on "the man at the top" (Cuban, 1988). These managerial influences include a broadly defined set of resources that may be brought to bear on the major goal: improving teaching and learning. Contrary to traditional leadership theories, the distributed leadership lens focuses as much on leaders' activities as on their roles (Spillane et al., 2001). These activities occur at both the macro (broad organizational tasks) and micro (day-to-day work) levels. Distributed leadership means that macro- and micro-level activities are linked within a school.

Consistent with the theory of distributed leadership, but located more specifically within the contemporary educational environment of standards-based reform, Elmore (2004) highlights elements necessary for instructional leadership. His leadership perspective is relatively narrow, centering on the current imperative for school-site accountability. He defines it in terms of common and externally imposed measures of student performance, an imperative evident in several of the SWS schools we studied. He writes:

> In a knowledge-intensive enterprise like teaching and learning, there is no way to perform these complex tasks without widely distributing the responsibility for leadership ... among roles in the organization, and without working hard at creating a common culture.... Distributed leadership means multiple sources of guidance and direction [joined by] the "glue" of a common task or goal—improvement of instruction. (p. 59)

Another complementary view of administration is also applicable to SWS schools: the perspective of schools as professional communities, in which leadership is viewed "from the center" rather than the traditional "from the top" (Louis, Marks, & Kruse, 1996). Professional school communities are "supportive and facilitative of expertise and initiative distributed widely across that school" (Smylie & Hart, 1999, p. 430). At the same time, good leaders in such schools are assertive about the school's collective vision. This perspective calls for a balance between autonomy of teachers, on one hand, and the school's common organizational needs, on the other. In the SWS context, leaders who function effectively must pay attention to the reciprocal influences between individuals and groups (here, teachers and subunits; subunits and the school). Smylie and Hart (1999) conclude, "efforts to develop one to the neglect of the other will be insufficient to significantly improve teaching, and hopefully, student learning" (p. 437).

SCHOOLWIDE GOVERNANCE

With many administrative responsibilities devolved to the subunits in these SWS high schools, what did their principals actually do? In some ways, the overall organization of these high schools was even more loosely coupled than in most public high schools (Rowan, 1990; Weick, 1976). The principal performed the traditional role of buffering the school from outsiders. When the community, the district office, or the superintendent was unhappy with the school, the complaints went to the principal. Another traditional role performed by the principal and central office staff was to draw resources to the school. All of the schools we studied served students and families with diverse academic and social backgrounds, and it was the principal to whom the subunits turned for needed resources. In most cases, distribution of resources to subunits seemed quite even-handed, relying either on the subunit's enrollment or simply on its existence. In only one school, Monroe, did we hear complaints about unequal distribution of resources.

Another traditional responsibility of principals is to staff their schools. Across schools, principals reported special problems of staffing subunits because, like all public schools, the size of the faculty is based on the school's total enrollment rather than the enrollment of individual subunits. In these schools, efforts to keep subunits "pure" often resulted in smaller classes in some subunits (e.g., MSM at Monroe). However, the districts in which these schools were located were unwilling to allocate additional faculty to the schools because of such scheduling problems. When enrollment dropped from one year to another (as was the case in some schools), the number of faculty was reduced—so principals had to make hard decisions about which subunits would lose teachers. Whereas in some schools (e.g., Grant), faculty recruitment was by subunit, more typically a subunit head would inform the principal about staffing needs, and it was the principal's responsibility to locate a teacher to fill the need. Some principals, especially Monroe's Hernandez, were particularly careful to hire only faculty who expressed commitment to the SWS idea.

Portraits of Principals

All five schools had building-level principals, three women and two men. Leadership at Adams and Grant may be contrasted with two other schools, Monroe and Harrison, where the same principals had led the schools since the implementation of schools within schools. Monroe's principal was largely responsible for organizing and staffing the new SWS school. Taylor High School suffered the greatest administrative instability, with five different principals in as many years. One conclusion we drew is that the SWS reform, at least in schools where the structure had been in place for several years, was sufficiently entrenched to survive leadership changes.

Although all these principals assumed buildingwide macro-level roles that made them the "voices" of their schools (e.g., liaison with the community, district, and state; ultimate authority over staffing, schedules, record-keeping, and reporting), the roles they played in directing such micro-level activities as curriculum and learning varied considerably. Because we studied only five SWS high schools, it was difficult to completely separate the roles and responsibilities of each principal from the nature and character of the people who filled the roles and assumed the responsibilities.

Adams Principal, Angela Johnson. Our study in Adams High School began in the midst of a comprehensive critique of the school's SWS design by the School Board, the superintendent, and the community. In retrospect we recognize that our access to Adams was based on our study's purpose. Insiders saw our work as one aspect of their long and hard look at the school's subunit structure. As described in Chapter 2, the school was at a crossroads. Adams in 1998–1999 had an interim principal, and the School Board had embarked on a national search for an innovative new principal who would receive a mandate to implement serious change in the school's SWS design. The search ended with Angela Johnson, a White woman in her forties selected as the best candidate to fulfill the mandate. Prior to the Adams job, for over a decade Johnson had served as a high-level administrator in a prominent national educational institute focused on high school reform. Earlier in her career, Johnson had been a social studies teacher in a nearby city; her roots were in New England.

Her choice as Adams's new principal was heralded with considerable local publicity. In an interview with the local newspaper, Johnson clearly articulated her main goal in reforming Adams High School: to intellectually challenge and hold high standards for all students. She added, almost as a shot across the bow, "I think that's hard to do in a school that is heavily tracked." In the same interview, Johnson said that she did not want to "come in and start making decisions in any realm until I get to know the school well." Most staff agreed that it took Johnson about a week to learn enough to begin changing virtually every aspect of Adams's organization and procedures. She quickly eliminated the music that poured out of loudspeakers to indicate a change of classes and the beginning and end of the school day. She also locked the school's door at 8:05 (school began at 8 A.M.); previously students had drifted into homerooms more casually.

Grant Principal, Elena Lincoln. A very dynamic and outgoing White woman in her late fifties or early sixties, Elena Lincoln had served as Grant's principal for 5 years when we began our study. She had succeeded two principals with reputations for weak leadership. Before assuming the Grant principalship, Lincoln had been an assistant superintendent for several years. Asked what drew her to the Grant principalship, she described herself as "someone who is good at leveraging money," suggesting that she knew the district well enough to devise ways to draw resources to this underfunded school. Her first quite visible actions as principal included transforming a physical plant that was run down and deteriorating into an attractive building filled with new equipment, computers, and new walls and doors. Lincoln's own office in this large school was a small corner room near the school's clerical center, the door to which was always open.

Most school staff described Lincoln in glowing terms: "unassuming," "very accessible," "extremely supportive." Explaining why she chose to teach at Grant, the English department chair stated: "Grant was desirable for a variety of reasons. Dr. Lincoln was desirable in my eyes because this was a very strong person, this was a leader, this was someone who was getting things done." With a long career in a district that was committed to schools within schools, Lincoln understood well the ideas and purposes around which the reform was organized. Under her leadership, Grant High School's poor reputation improved so much that faculty from other schools transferred in, and better students from outside Grant's catchment area applied directly to certain Grant subunits.

Midway through our study, the nationally prominent superintendent of Grant's district was replaced. Rather quickly thereafter, citywide commitment to schools within schools diminished (because it was closely associated with the ex-superintendent). Lincoln was offered and accepted an attractive retirement package (and subsequently became the principal of an affluent high school across the state line). She was replaced by a middle-aged African American male who seemed, according to many, unenthusiastic about both the SWS design and our research in the school. Although he did allow us to continue our work, he did not make himself available for an interview during our second round of data collection. In many interviews and focus groups, faculty members reported lowered morale and rumors that many of the best faculty members were planning to transfer to other high schools in the city. The brief period of Grant's improved reputation, enhanced academic program, and strengthened subunit structure began to evaporate shortly after Lincoln's departure.

Harrison Principal, Ben Miller. A tall and athletic African American man in his early sixties, Ben Miller's manner with outsiders to his school was gentle, soft-spoken, and amiable. His obvious devotion to his school, its students, and their accomplishments (especially in sports) was quite evident. His daughters had been athletic stars at the school several years before. When we began our study, Miller had been at Harrison High for eight years, the first two as an assistant principal and the last six as the principal. His tenure with the school encompassed its adoption of the SWS organizational form; the first subunit began when he was an assistant principal. He announced his plans to retire in 2000, stating strongly his desire to "walk out on my own terms." He was considerably less visible around the school during the second year of our study.

Miller's leadership style over his tenure at Harrison was not obvious; he appeared to lead the school more through informal relationships than through confrontation or vision. We learned from many Harrison sources (including Miller himself) that there was considerable conflict among staff. When we asked him about this, Miller said, "Yes, it's war!" On one side were several long-term faculty (those most supportive of SWS design and also militant members of the teachers' union); on the other was the administration, teachers with weaker commitments to schools within schools, and an African American assistant superintendent. The former group claimed that Miller was a weak academic leader who did not demonstrate active support for schools within schools. Although the controversy had many facets, it seemed to crystallize around the value of Harrison's SWS structure.

Once we learned even this short history, we understood why Miller seemed less than enthusiastic about speaking with us at length (as several other principals had done on several occasions). SWS advocates on the staff saw participation in our study as a possible means to save the reform they had worked so hard to create, and they tried to recruit our researchers as advocates (a role we declined). Consequently, Miller was less accessible during our second round of data collection than during the first. Although our conversations with him were pleasant, he was not very forthcoming about his views about the school, its problems, its future, and its SWS organization. As our research ended and Miller prepared to retire, Harrison's subunit structure was under attack. Many believed it undermined the school's need to raise its test scores.

Monroe Principal, Arthur Hernandez. In our visits to James Monroe High School, the first and last person we spoke with every day was Arthur Hernandez. A tall and outspoken Hispanic man in his forties, Hernandez was the central figure at Monroe High. His roots in the community were deep and strong. Born and raised in the city where Monroe is located, his 15-year-old son "Little Art" was a student in Monroe's MSM subunit during our research. Hernandez spent his entire professional career in this district.

He began as a guidance counselor in another high school, where he rose to assistant principal and implemented a selective math and science subunit. He was tapped in 1996 to launch a new high school. Informants disagreed about the reasons for Hernandez's success. Some believed he was simply in the right places at the right times, whereas others credited him with being the visionary force behind Monroe's SWS structure. All agreed that early in his career Hernandez caught the eye of the superintendent, an SWS advocate who ultimately selected him to design and head Monroe.

To staff the new high school, Hernandez lured many faculty from the high school where he had worked before. He chose teachers based on their buy-in to the SWS concept. Thus, the new high school opened with a staff committed to both Hernandez and schools within schools. Our conversations with many Monroe faculty and staff suggested that their commitment to the SWS concept and to Hernandez personally was still strong: "Art buys into the program"; "Bottom-line, it [SWS success] totally depends on the buy-in of the administration"; "He was the one with the vision, and he communicated it to everyone who came in." There was also strong agreement that Hernandez controlled almost every aspect of the school, including staff hiring and the budget. As our research ended, we saw Hernandez in firm control and Monroe's subunit structure strong though challenged by the school's burgeoning enrollment.

Taylor Principal, Diana D'Angelo. The fifth principal of Taylor High School in as many years, D'Angelo came to the job with 28 years' experience in the city's schools. Although she had spent over a decade as a high school administrator, this was the first time this White woman had been a principal. Her tenure at Taylor began simultaneously with our study. Although the school had been reconstituted with its SWS design 4 years earlier, much of the focus in the early years was on increasing social control—improving attendance and enforcing disciplinary standards—rather than on instruction and achievement. D'Angelo explained her mandate in coming to Taylor: "to improve our performance on [standardized] tests . . . we must do this!" Because of very low test scores, the school again faced a state takeover. D'Angelo's mandate from the district gave her leverage with staff, parents, and district officials to institute substantial changes in Taylor's programs.

On arrival, D'Angelo listed 12 explicit initiatives that together represented the most dramatic changes since Taylor's adoption of the subunit structure. The threads binding together these changes included consolidating academic control and developing consistency across subunits—in short, limiting subunit autonomy. She commented on changes she believed were needed in the subunit structure:

> Even though they [the subunits] are schools within schools, they are still part of a big school, which is Zachary Taylor. . . . I say to my staff, "You are part of the big picture . . . not autonomous entities." They [the subunits] can enhance what we are doing or what the general philosophy of the school is, but everything . . . is across the board, so everybody is on the same page. That's the only way we can make some gains and have some achievement, with everybody on the same page!

Taylor's staff gave D'Angelo mixed reviews during the first year, but they were more enthusiastic by our second visit. Some recognized the value of a strong leader who cared about the quality of education, whereas others saw her actions as "muscle-flexing" and her attitude overly concerned with numbers (test scores, graduation rates). One of her most controversial actions was to reinstitute academic departments, which had been disbanded 5 years earlier when the SWS design was implemented. Although the school under D'Angelo retained its subunit structure, subunit autonomy was diminished.

D'Angelo saw her job as improving outcomes in a school with a history of very low performance—using whatever means she thought necessary. If the subunit structure was unable to improve student performance, she would weaken it. By the end of our research, we saw D'Angelo very firmly in control at Taylor, and its subunit structure evaluated in terms of its effects on test scores and graduation rates.

Principals' Commitment to the Schools-Within-Schools Structure

Our school selection strategy, wherein we studied only schools that used the full-model SWS design and had been offering it for at least 3 years, resulted in schools where principals presided over relatively stable subunit structures. Two principals (Miller and Hernandez) had led their schools since the inception of schools within schools; one (Lincoln) improved the school considerably within an existing SWS structure that also characterized the city's other high schools. Two others (Johnson and D'Angelo) were hired with specific mandates to substantially change their schools' SWS structure.

Had we chosen schools where the SWS structure was less entrenched in terms of both history and depth of impact, the principals' inclinations toward the structure would probably be more important than was the case in the schools we studied. Zero-sum logic would see the devolution of power to sub-units and away from the top as threatening to principals. However, with the possible exception of Miller at Harrison, the principals we spoke with seemed firmly in control and unthreatened by the structure.

Although we selected these schools because of their subunit organizations, not all these principals saw schools within schools as the schools' defining character.

Long-Term Commitment. Among these principals, Art Hernandez was the most enthusiastic about schools within schools. Hernandez's enthusiasm for the structure was not consistent across subunits; rather, it centered on the magnet subunits, particularly MSM. He told us that the Generic subunits should improve themselves by selecting a theme and modeling themselves on MSM. The aspects of Adams's SWS structure that Angela Johnson was striving to change—subunit stratification and differential quality of education across subunits—Hernandez found not only acceptable but exemplary.

That Ben Miller had led Harrison High through the adoption of the SWS design might suggest that his commitment to schools within schools was high, and perhaps that was once the case. By the time we visited the school, however, he did not express much enthusiasm to us. As described in Chapter 2, Harrison High School was under considerable outside pressure to raise achievement. Many outsiders (including district office staff) felt that Harrison students' low performance was attributable, at least in part, to its SWS structure.

SWS supporters on the faculty claimed, however, that low achievement was more attributable to Harrison's less advantaged student population compared with the district's other high schools; these people believed that the SWS design served disadvantaged students particularly well. Under this pressure, Miller neither defended the school's SWS structure to outsiders nor took a strong public stand against it. Instead, he seemed to retreat from the battle, seemingly holding on until his impending retirement.

Leading *Despite* Schools Within Schools. Understanding the larger city's educational goals well, Elena Lincoln seemed to recognize that schools within schools was an important part of both Grant's structure and the superintendent's plans. As such, she was committed to improving the school within that structure and was able to bring resources to the school and subunits to do so. Even with the important and positive turnaround in Grant's reputation under Lincoln's leadership, she did not express the same high level of commitment to schools within schools as many Grant faculty and students did, describing it instead as "the lingo these days." She certainly was not opposed to the SWS design, but rather was not enamored with it as the explanation for Grant's turnaround. Despite her tepid support for the reform, she was enthusiastic about participating in our study, which she saw as a way to bring visibility to the school.

Mandates to Reform the Reform. The institute where Angela Johnson had worked took a public stance about high school reform that was consistent with a subunit structure. Johnson recognized the value of the subunit structure to Adams and its historical roots in the community; thus, she was committed to maintaining it. However, her previous work had centered on issues that were problematic at Adams. As we discuss in more detail in later chapters, Adams's subunits were quite stratified, which conflicted strongly with Johnson's stated commitment to high-quality educational programs for all students. Moreover, her ideals also clashed with subunits purposely differentiated by pedagogy and curriculum. Although choice was a bedrock quality of education in the city, Johnson was quick to notice that choice had facilitated and probably exacerbated the stratification she was committed to undoing. Not shaped by a long career as a school administrator, Johnson boldly approached reform at Adams with a firm sense of direction and without the caution or self-protection that might have constrained a career administrator. Adams's subunit structure under Johnson would surely experience big changes.

Diana D'Angelo came to Taylor with a strong mandate to improve the school's outcomes through almost any means necessary. It was clear that she thought that the subunit structure—particularly its decentralization and lack of standardization in curriculum, teaching, and learning—needed to change. Her visibility and mandate as a new principal were as important at Taylor as Johnson's were at Adams. She saw the subunit structure as part of Taylor's problem; she was willing to alter the structure as she saw fit to improve the school.

SUBUNIT GOVERNANCE

Every subunit had a designated administrator, the "subunit head," whose major responsibility was for the technical core within each subunit. Subunit heads typically led a team of teachers whose affiliations were split between their subunit and their academic department. Most schools kept subunits physically together within the building, locating the subunit head's office within that subunit space. More notable than these superficial similarities in subunit heads' role was great variation in the forms of subunit governance; in subunit heads' responsibilities; in their compensation; in the amount of teaching they were required to do; in the density of the leadership team; in the degree to which they actually controlled teaching and learning; and in how much they were valued, trusted, and empowered by the building-level administrative team.

Subunit Heads

Managing the Technical Core. The responsibility for teaching and learning in schools resided primarily in subunits in these schools, and subunit heads' main job was to coordinate their instructional programs. Weaving the subunit's theme across courses—one facet of the job—took several forms. In some subunits, integrative projects ran across several core courses. As described in Chapter 3, Harrison's Arts/Communications subunit created year-long inspirational themes (e.g., dignity) for each grade, which were integrated into subunit-specific courses and projects. The subunits profiled in Chapter 3 are examples of how subunit success depended on infusing themes into courses. Although most subunit heads with whom we spoke saw the value of integrating their themes into courses, these efforts were not always successful.

Another idea we developed in Chapter 3, subunit "purity," influenced subunit heads' ability to highlight themes. Faculty who supported the SWS structure sought to schedule as many pure classes as possible. However, subunit heads were often unable to offer classes taught by *their* teachers to only *their* students. Thus, many classes (most, really) were not pure. This difficulty increased in the upper grades, where more specialized and advanced courses were needed. To compensate, some heads developed smaller programs within their subunits to engage their themes more deeply. Recall the health-related courses and programs offered by Grant's Health subunit we described in Chapter 3.

Other Subunit Administrative Responsibilities. Beyond their academic programs, subunit heads were also responsible for gleaning resources for their programs from the central administration. This was particularly true at Monroe High School; subunit heads felt that their power to successfully administer their programs depended on maintaining a close personal relationship with Art Hernandez. The MSM subunit head and her husband (also a Monroe faculty member) had been close personal friends of the Hernandez family for several years. Much younger, the Generic 1 subunit head was appointed by Hernandez after having been his student and then his colleague in another district high school. Hernandez recruited her to Monroe. The close friendship between Hernandez and the MSM subunit head led a guidance counselor to remark: "In all fairness, Generic 1 and Generic 2 have less of an influence on the decision making (at Monroe) than the other two, especially MSM."

Although faculty recruitment was most often accomplished by the principal and central administrators, some recruitment occurred at the subunit level. Because students applied directly to subunits at Grant, in the early days of Elena's Lincoln's principalship faculty also came to Grant to work in certain subunits (and with her). When enrollment at some of our sample schools declined, the principal negotiated with subunit heads about which would lose a faculty member (and whom they would lose). At Monroe (but not other schools), we heard of several cases where one subunit (particularly MSM) would "steal" a teacher from another subunit. This practice understandably engendered resentment among faculty and contributed to strained relations between MSM and other subunits.

Subunit heads convened their staffs for frequent meetings—at least weekly—although all heads told us how difficult it was to schedule such meetings. At Grant, Monroe, and Harrison, we heard about both the value and difficulty of common planning time. Some subunit heads convened meetings after school; others refrained from this because of union rules prohibiting it. Some met in early mornings before classes began; others met over lunch. Notably, subunit faculty met together more often than departments. For several reasons—the number of faculty in subunits was small, they knew one another well, and they shared students—subunit meetings were described as quite productive. Subunit meetings also focused on critical issues seldom discussed in faculty meetings in comprehensive high schools: particular courses, coordination of courses around subunit themes, and individual student progress (particularly those having difficulty). Occasionally, the whole subunit team met with a parent.

Compensation and Motivation. Although the responsibilities of the several subunit heads in these five SWS schools were similar, how they were compensated for taking on these responsibilities varied greatly. The position of subunit head at Adams and Taylor was full-time, so heads did not teach (they often had assistants, as well). Grant's and Harrison's subunit heads taught but were released from one or two courses. A few also served as department chairs, which meant more release from teaching. Some subunit heads who taught several classes each day thought they could manage their subunits better if they had more time to do so.

Surprising to us, Monroe's subunit heads received no extra pay or release time; they taught a full course load (unless they were department chairs, as was the MSM subunit head). Although we did not inquire into the details of compensation packages that accompanied these responsibilities, we were curious about why subunit heads at Monroe would accept leadership responsibility without compensation. Their major motivation, we were told, was that the role brought them closer to the principal (the Generic 1 subunit head told us she made a point to talk with Hernandez at least once a day). At Monroe, Hernandez was the source of resources, so contact with him allowed them to argue for resources.

Subunit heads came to their positions from the faculty, albeit through a number of routes. The Adams and Harrison subunit heads were chosen democratically from the subunit's faculty. Grant's subunit heads emerged over time as natural leaders, so their appointment seemed to have come about collaboratively between subunit staff and the administration. Most Taylor subunit heads were appointed when the school was restructured into schools within schools. If a head retired or left the school, another would be appointed with some staff consultation. Taylor's Business subunit head had been appointed by central administration and did not have most subunit faculty's loyalty and support, whereas the HHS subunit head who was also appointed centrally had enormous support from her faculty. Most Monroe subunit heads were appointed by Hernandez before the school opened. Who actually led the Generic 2 subunit during our research was unclear. Hernandez said he was waiting for leadership in that subunit to emerge.

Besides being excused from teaching, having access to resources, and enjoying the respect of their faculty colleagues, a major reason why the subunit heads took on this responsibility was because the role allowed them to build something they felt positively about, to make decisions that they might see enacted without long delays, and to receive satisfaction from working within a structure they believed in. Not surprisingly, subunit heads were among the strongest supporters of the SWS structure. They were also, however, quite vocal about the frustrations and difficulties of carrying out what they felt were the requirements of successful subunits: thematic programs, pure classes, cross-disciplinary projects, and other structural features that would make their subunits run well. These people reacted particularly strongly to some residual features of comprehensive high schools they felt weakened the subunit structure.

Departments Versus Subunits

Our description of subunits as the locus of responsibility for teaching and learning is not completely accurate. In reality, subunits typically shared oversight of the instructional program with academic departments. Not always a comfortable collaboration, this relationship was notably rocky at Grant, Adams, and Taylor. Grant's district provided high school department heads with considerable status and excused them from half their course load in order to carry out their departmental duties. Across subunits, they also were responsible for deciding on and ordering instructional materials for departmental courses. Two Grant subunit heads also chaired departments (Business, Communications), providing these individuals more time for planning, recruiting, and integrating their subunits' themes than other subunit heads. The focus of the two departments coincided well with their subunits' themes; their courses were not offered in other subunits because they were not part of the school's academic core. Other subunit heads expressed some resentment of the special privileges the overlap of department and subunit produced.

In our conversations with teachers, we asked whether they tended to place their organizational loyalties with subunits or with departments. Some Adams teachers expressed divided loyalty between subunits and departments. Adams's departmental structure seemed weaker than the subunit structure, largely because department heads were districtwide (e.g., the district employed a K–12 science coordinator). The district's math coordinator, an Adams math teacher, saw great value in teachers working across disciplines with subunit colleagues. Otherwise, he told us, "you get tunnel vision about your teaching style and what you teach!" The district's English coordinator, also an Adams teacher, expressed a different view: "We have been sort of forced, over the years, to line up behind subunits." He commented on differences between subunit and departmental meetings:

> For so many years, the subunit issues were, in my opinion, very tangential. They were sort of generic issues. . . . I have always found those meetings very contrived, because you're bringing a group of teachers together who really don't have or share much more than the generic sort of aspects of teaching and learning . . . those meetings were always held at the expense of department meetings.

The tension between departments and subunits at Taylor High School became explicit during our study. Formal departments had been eliminated in

1995 when Taylor adopted the subunit design; responsibility for teaching and learning was devolved to full-time instructional leaders in each subunit (in addition to the subunit head). Diana D'Angelo's mandate in 1998 as she assumed Taylor's principalship was to strengthen the school's academic structure and to increase coordination between subunits. Among the changes she implemented the following year was elimination of the position of subunit instructional leader and reestablishment of academic departments (and chairs) that operated across subunits. Some instructional leaders became department chairs; others went back to teaching.

Although Taylor seemed to move away from distributed leadership, the principal did not become the school's instructional leader. Instead, she strengthened schoolwide academic leadership through a new administrative unit: the administrative council. This group was composed of the nine department heads, the six subunit heads, and herself. The council was responsible for schoolwide coordination and implementation of the school improvement plan, as well as for implementation of the many new policies and practices she instituted.

Academic decision-making at Monroe was shared by subunits and departments. However, the MSM subunit head (also science department chair) told us, "Most of what is done is done as a subunit rather than a department." When asked about the relative importance of subunits and departments, Art Hernandez suggested that this question might be answered by examining the frequency of meetings. Whereas faculty met with their subunit colleagues weekly, departments met only a few times a year. Some Harrison departments were stronger than others. A few years prior to our study, math courses had been moved out of the subunit structure. We were told that the structure of mathematics, where the classes students took were dependent on their existing skills and prior training, did not fit with the less differentiated subunit structure.

Guidance Counselors

These SWS high schools tried to garner from their districts sufficient numbers of guidance counselors so that each subunit could have its own. Grant accomplished this, because Elena Lincoln had worked hard to keep the subunits staffed in this way. During our second study year, Harrison's district reduced the school's guidance counseling staff due to somewhat lower enrollment, resulting in three counselors for four subunits. Rather than assigning one counselor to the two subunits with the smallest enrollment, Miller reallocated all guidance counselors so that one would serve each grade (recall that Harrison enrolled students in Grades 10–12). Several subunit faculty saw this as one more example of the principal undermining the school's SWS model.

Because a large proportion of the student body in several of these schools was economically and academically disadvantaged, guidance counselors' duties went broad. School and class attendance were recurring problems, course failure rates were high, and some students had experience with the criminal justice system. In addition, guidance counselors' typical responsibilities also included college counseling, although college attendance rates varied among subunits. For example, far more of Monroe's MSM students attended college than did those from Generic 2. This meant that the guidance counselors' roles and daily activities also varied widely across subunits.

CONCLUSION

To some degree, the governance structures in high schools divided into schools within schools are examples of distributed leadership. All of the SWS schools we studied developed intermediate-level leaders: the subunit heads. The locus of responsibility for the schools' technical core of teaching and learning rested primarily with these individuals and their subunit faculty colleagues. Building-wide principals mostly left subunits to manage the schools' academic programs, whereas the principals performed the typical buffering and resource-garnering roles. Although responsibility for academic programs rested within subunits, to some degree this responsibility was shared between subunits and departments—and such sharing was not always smooth or comfortable. Although Taylor's departments were abolished to provide more within-subunit responsibility for academic matters, over time the poor performance of Taylor's students on state tests led the district to reimpose departments and centralize academic programs. Another governance model that also applies reasonably well in SWS schools is professional community (Louis et al., 1996; Smylie & Hart, 1999), with "community" defined at the subunit rather than the school level. But if the "common vision" mentioned by these researchers must be shared by the entire school, the model would fit poorly.

To varying degrees, these schools felt the pressure of externally imposed state- and federal-level standards-based reforms. Elmore's (2004) statement on the need for new forms of governance in an era of standards-based reform reported earlier in the chapter is cautionary. Although these five SWS schools seemed to evidence one element of leadership he called for—"distributing the responsibility for leadership . . . among roles in the organization"—more illusive in these SWS schools was the second desired activity: "working hard at creating a common culture" (p. 59). Within subunits, there was considerable attention devoted to creating common cultures; however, these cultures were not the same across subunits. That means that we saw little "common school culture," and the SWS structure may make it more difficult to develop such a culture. Moreover, as is more evident in our discussion of the curriculum in these schools in Chapter 5, attention to improving teaching and learning was quite inconsistent across subunits. Thus, the schools' abilities to respond to the outside pressure to improve their students' test scores were internally varied. Herein lies a primary tension inherent in the SWS design: schoolwide efforts to standardize teaching and learning would weaken or run afoul of the ideals behind the SWS movement.

5

Curriculum and the Schools-Within-Schools Structure

HIGH SCHOOLS DIFFER from elementary schools in many ways. One important distinction is the relative weight given to curriculum and instruction across the two settings. Which courses are offered in high school typically receives more scrutiny than which instructional approaches are used to deliver them. This weighting would surely be reversed in the early grades. For example, impassioned debates rage about phonics and whole language literacy instruction in elementary schools, but virtually no controversy exists about whether all children should learn to read and write. On the other hand, much disagreement exists within high schools, the communities and districts in which they are located, and even among states about who should take chemistry and trigonometry, whether such courses should be required, and when they should be taken. But there is little discussion or disagreement about how these courses should be taught.

One explanation for differences in the relative importance of curriculum and instruction in elementary and secondary schools relates to children's developmental levels. There is considerable agreement about which basic competencies all young children should acquire and when these skills should be acquired. However, as children's developmental trajectories approach adulthood—as their parents and teachers prepare them to function within our capitalist economy—educational philosophies diverge regarding the extent to which students' future social and economic roles should determine the content and focus of their schooling. Regardless of philosophy, as children mature, the focus of schooling typically moves from child development toward a broader conceptualization of the role that schooling does (or should) play in producing the future workforce. Almost continuously over the past century, as secondary school attendance became nearly universal, public controversies have raged about the fundamental purposes of secondary education.

HISTORICAL BACKDROP FOR TODAY'S HIGH SCHOOL CURRICULUM

What should high schools teach, and to whom should they teach what? Should all students develop a common set of practical and intellectual skills, or should students be prepared more narrowly for the occupationally stratified society they will enter? If schools should prepare children for their professional futures, when should such specialized preparation begin? In a society dominated by individualism, who should participate in such important educational decisions: parents, schools, society, or the students themselves? What criteria should guide such decisions: interests, preferences, skills, motivation, intellectual ability, or societal needs?

On one end of this philosophical continuum rests a belief that all students— regardless of their academic or occupational futures—should experience intellectually challenging coursework that prepares them equally well for either college or work. This more custodial view of education holds that students' academic needs are quite similar, and their current desires or interests are secondary. The formal statement of this view came in 1893 from the Committee of Ten, a national commission studying high schools that was headed by Charles Elliot, then president of Harvard (National Education Association, 1893). The Committee advocated that students be permitted little curricular choice, and that all schools should offer a narrow academic curriculum that did not differentiate students heading for work from those heading for college.

The *Cardinal Principles of Secondary Education,* a report published in 1918, is perhaps the antithesis of the Committee of Ten's treatise (National Education Association, 1918). The underlying philosophy of the Cardinal Principles, "social efficiency," recommended that high school students' courses of study be linked to their future professions. This would require schools to offer a much wider curriculum, one that included a broad range of academic and vocational offerings with varying degrees of rigor. Supporters of social efficiency argued that offering only traditional academic courses overlooked two realities: not only did students enter high school with different academic skills, but they aspired to very disparate occupational futures. Advocates of the Cardinal Principles considered that requiring all students to complete academic courses ignored students' social realities (Ayres, 1909; Bobbitt, 1924). Psychologist Edward L. Thorndike (1906) declared that a high school should "have in mind definitely the work in life its students will have to perform and try to fit them for it" (p. 180).

Early 20th century educational reformers attacked the recommendations of the Committee of Ten—a common academic curriculum for all students—as elitist, undemocratic, and antithetical to equal educational opportunity (Angus & Mirel, 1999). Political progressives argued that their vision for the public high school was more egalitarian—more American, even—because it was meant to serve the (perceived) needs of all students. These social efficiency advocates asserted that schools had a duty to sort and match students to the social and economic hierarchies upon which U.S. society rested; for social order to be maintained, school structures should match economic structures (see Warner et al., 1944). Burton Clark (1962), for example, declared that "Sorting must take place at some point in the educational structure and . . . if it does not take place at the door [of the high school] at the time of entry, it must occur inside the doors, in the classroom and counseling office" (p. 78).

Public secondary schools clearly embraced the social efficiency model during the first half of the 20th century (Angus & Mirel, 1999; Cremin, 1961; Kliebard, 1995). Comprehensive high schools represented the "social machine" through which adolescents' diverse needs would be met. In the same buildings, college-bound students were offered academic courses, whereas students bound for work were served courses preparing them for vocations and trades. Such a "differentiated curriculum" was very broad, containing different courses for different students, who were organized into vocational, general, and academic "tracks" that determined their courses of study. The prevailing educational philosophy was that "high schools would serve democracy by offering usable studies to everyone, rather than dwelling on academic abstractions that would interest only a few" (Powell et al., 1985, p. 260). This form of curriculum organization rested on the prevailing psychological premise that increased interest and motivation resulting from such "relevant" curricula would hold more students in school until graduation.

Although differentiated curricula remain ubiquitous, public high schools have moved from formal "tracking" (e.g., placing students into predefined curricular programs) toward structures in which students select individual courses based presumably on their interests, abilities, and levels of motivation. This desire to "please their customers" has led authors to characterize public high schools as "shopping malls" (Powell et al., 1985). Although curricular choice removes the rigid determinism of traditional tracking, it addresses only the issue of ability grouping (how students are placed) and not the underlying tracking structures (what courses are offered; Yonezawa et al., 2002).

THE SCHOOLS-WITHIN-SCHOOLS STRUCTURE AND THE PURPOSES OF SECONDARY EDUCATION

These issues remain deeply embedded within schools-within-schools (SWS) high schools; the debate between the Committee of Ten and the Cardinal Principles is still relevant. However, the SWS structure raises additional questions, because it has the potential to provide another layer of differentiation not present in regular comprehensive high schools. Around what content should the subunits within each school be organized? Should some subunits be allowed to prepare students for narrow future social and economic roles, or should each subunit be expected to foster a common set of knowledge and skills?

SWS advocates have suggested that one advantage of the SWS reform is its potential to eliminate the tracking structures that typify most comprehensive high schools (e.g., Fine, 1994). Because of their smaller enrollments, it would seem to be more difficult for subunits to respond to students' social and academic diversity with a wide variety of academic programs. Thus, it seems reasonable that subunits would offer a core curriculum and create specialized courses that reflect their themes. Were this the case, the social and academic stratification resulting from differentiated curricular structures in comprehensive high schools might be reduced. A common curriculum within a single subunit, with a relatively small number of courses that are taken by almost all students, would be a logical response to the small numbers of teachers and students.

In this section, we present our findings about the curriculum and academic structures in the five SWS high schools we studied. Given the unusual nature of the SWS model, we explore these academic structures at two levels: the whole school and the subunits. Our discussion begins with the themes around which subunits were organized, noting the extent to which staff beliefs about the aims of secondary education matched the organizing rationales of the subunits. We then explore how the specific SWS designs in these schools influenced their academic programs, particularly the degree to which the curriculum departed from those in traditional comprehensive high schools. We end the section by describing the interplay between curriculum and subunit structures, and how the school's curriculum complemented or constrained the logistical and philosophical foundations on which the SWS reform rests.

Rationales for Subunit Themes

Meeting Students' Needs. In addition to creating positive social relations among school members, these five schools had another motivation for implementing schools within schools: better accommodating students' interests, academic backgrounds, and future occupational plans. With this goal in mind, each school created subunits with themes intended to attract different types of students. Support for these differentiated SWS structures was rooted in the desire to "meet the needs of the students," which required that different types of students experience different curricula and pedagogical approaches. Although these schools were engaged in fundamental structural reform, most staff retained their views regarding the value of differentiation, as well as the belief that students' intellectual needs should be tailored to their past academic performance and future occupational plans. One Monroe assistant principal described what he saw as his school's multifaceted mission:

> We need to get university-bound students ready to handle the demands of being in any university. We need to get those students who are vocational-bound geared to pursue whatever vocation they want, or those other students that are just looking to get a job, help them get a job.

A teacher in the Business subunit at Grant High School candidly expressed his opinion that the movement leading high schools away from traditional vocational education was a mistake. Proud of his students who entered the workforce with practical business skills, he was concerned that it had become "politically incorrect" to acknowledge that not all graduates would attend college:

> This is a fundamental problem. We've disavowed the notion that work is worthy. "If you're not going to college, you're worthless." We've now revamped our program so that you will be ready for any four-year college, as well as the world of work. We were [previously] clearly [geared to] the world of work, but we now have changed that around. We used to have business math. We no longer do that: everybody starts at Algebra.

A veteran Core Curriculum English teacher at Adams High School echoed the same belief, arguing against the notion that all adolescents should study academic subjects. She noted that until the late 1970s, her school district operated both a vocational and a traditional academic high school, which were later merged to create Adams High:

It was set up that way because that's where the interests are. There are people who like to work with their hands and there are people who like to work with their mind, and I think trying to make those people who work with their hands into something that they don't want to be may be impossible. There are schools for us [academics], so we have that option. Because we are academics, we think everyone should be an academic. I don't think that that's true. To tell [nonacademic students] that what they learn is going to be of practical use to them after they graduate is wrong—it *won't* be to everybody. I believe in education. I like to read, I like to learn, I like to discuss ideas. I like to do that, but not everybody does. And I don't think I should force that on people who don't.

Other teachers argued that providing only traditional academic courses denied certain students coursework that would be more relevant to their future occupations. In this view, offering vocationally themed subunits would make sense for students headed directly for work after graduation. Moreover, many teachers argued that offering both academic and vocational subunits would increase the odds that unmotivated students would remain in school and graduate (quite clearly, they were referring to the students in vocational subunits). They believed that offering only academically oriented subunits would push certain students out of high school. A teacher in Harrison's Arts/Communications subunit, which enrolled many nontraditional students, offered his opinion about the district's threat to remove the SWS structure from Harrison High: "If we drop schools within schools, we would lose those 10% of kids who are here for reasons other than straight academics or even to graduate. We have kids who flunk every class, and they love us. They say this is the greatest place in the world!"

Many students enrolled in vocational subunits supported this view, expressing the desire to "work with their hands" or "do practical work." These students—as their teachers suggested—tended to have less interest in traditional academic subjects. To explain why he selected Harrison's Science/Technology (ST) subunit, one student told us: "ST seemed to be the most appealing because I like to work with my hands. And they told us we'd get to build go-carts and stuff—that's the kind of stuff I like to do." As she was deciding which subunit to choose, another ST student recounted that students from other subunits told her, "'It's so boring. All we do is sit there and write papers.'" She was satisfied with her choice of ST, which was "better than sitting in a classroom, because you actually do hands-on things." The availability of a vocational subunit permitted some students to bridge the gulf between the adult world in which many already labored and the adolescent world they encountered in school. Some students wanted to work on their cars or become better welders—activities they often did already during their spare time for pay or for pleasure. Another Harrison ST student told us that his subunit allowed him to continue work he had been doing most of his life: "I've worked in my grandpa's shop since I was about six, on wood and stuff, so I can use all the tools. I love carpentry—that's why I took ST."

Different Learning Styles. Many teachers were anxious that their schools not be perceived as supporting tracking. Indeed, many denied that their SWS structures resembled traditional tracking, because students sorted *themselves* into subunits. "I think it's not really tracking; it's just meeting their needs," commented a Taylor teacher. "I think in education we're so afraid of saying these kids are tracked that we forget about meeting everybody's needs." Such beliefs may have been formed by the wide range of student abilities these schools accommodated; staff told us repeatedly that some students were simply less able than others. In the three schools that offered vocational subunits (Adams, Harrison, and Taylor), both teachers and subunit administrators portrayed low-achieving students—especially special education students—as being "good with their hands" and better suited for hands-on, practical work than for more intellectual activities. Teachers in Adams's feeder elementary schools steered lower achieving students toward the high school's Vocational subunit. One Adams teacher described the process: "Well, he's good with his hands, so we should probably put him in [Vocational] so he can do something. You know—shop class." Staff in Taylor's Mechanical subunit also claimed that students chose that subunit because of its "hands-on" nature: "Mechanical is not as academically oriented as the other [subunits]," remarked one Taylor teacher. "It [enrolls] students who are not interested in college; students who would have in the past been in carpentry [or] auto mechanics."

We were surprised that faculty opinions seemed to combine distaste for tracking with widespread support for subunit differentiation. This view was bolstered by the belief that students' differing needs were accompanied by varied learning styles. One reason for valuing the SWS structure was that it allowed subunits to tailor not only their content and level of academic demands, but even their pedagogical approaches. One ST teacher at Harrison posed a rhetorical question: "Why do we have to treat kids all the same, when we know that they're not? We don't have to be the same subunit, because different approaches work for different kids. I think that's what each subunit offers—a different approach." The head of Taylor's Mechanical subunit agreed; he asserted that his subunit's applied, practical approach was more appropriate for his students' learning style: "They can watch the instructor in there. He's taking apart a brake system, and these kids are watching what he's doing. They can do the same thing. But if you handed them the book and said, 'Read this,' it would be like a foreign language to them. They wouldn't be able to do it."

Echoing these sentiments, several Harrison Business students told us that their counterparts in various subunits possessed "different kinds of smarts," a typology that distinguished between academic and practical intelligence. One student remarked that the "smartest people" at Harrison were enrolled in the Health/Human Services (HHS) subunit, which focused (ostensibly) on health and medical careers. Asked why he thought HHS enrolled the most intelligent students, he replied, "Well, the type of job that you are going to be doing, you are going to have to be smart. See, like mechanics, they're smart, but they're car-smart. And people in HHS are book-smart—they know knowledge." This student's conceptualization of intelligence echoed that spelled out in the 1918 Cardinal Principles. As did the Principles' authors, he asserted that high school students were generally aware of their strengths and interests and should, therefore, be permitted to select subunits and courses of study based on this self-knowledge.

"We Rob Our Children." Although not as common as the views supporting differentiation, some staff members expressed concern about subunits with differentiated themes. A few doubted students' ability to select careers at such a young age. Others questioned the wisdom of allowing students to choose among subunits whose academic and behavioral expectations differed so widely. For example, the head of Taylor's Arts/Humanities subunit—the school's most academically traditional subunit—argued that adolescents were too young to make such important life decisions: "When you ask a 13- or 14-year-old to pick their subunit, how many people go into college not knowing what they want to do when they graduate? So, 9th graders knowing what they're going to do when they get out of high school is—sometimes ... most times, they don't think that far ahead." A Grant teacher shared the same opinion, but was more specific. She favored a narrower, academic focus for all students: "How children get that focus at the age of 14, 13, or 12, I don't know. I think it's a little ridiculous, personally. And I really do think, to some extent, that we rob our children by not continuing to offer a more liberal arts approach in high school."

A teacher in Monroe's Generic 2 subunit defended his subunit's lack of a theme. He disagreed that that all subunits in the school "needed a mantra." The teacher stated that many adolescents—himself included—changed their career interests multiple times:

> When I first went to college I wanted to be in journalism, and I wanted to do radio and TV. After a year and a half, I decided that I was going to go into teaching. I didn't really know what I wanted to do when I was 18 years old. How can a 14-year-old come into high school and say to himself, "Oh yeah! I want to go into the Math/Science Magnet because I'm going to be an engineer!" Most kids don't know that.

Staff in several schools thought there was a disconnect between their subunit's career theme and the jobs students ultimately obtained. For example, few graduates of Grant's Arts subunit became artists, dancers, or musicians; Communications graduates were not "doing newscasts for Channel Four," as its head noted. Few of his students even wanted a career in communications. He recounted his experiences in recruiting middle school students to his subunit: "If on an 8th grade recruiting tour you ask all the people who think they are going to be journalists, or broadcasters, and Web page designers [to come to the presentation], I'd have a pretty small group show up." Taylor's Health/Human Services subunit head expressed a similar concern. She told us that her subunit's sports-related career pathway had little relevance to her students' future vocations:

> They [do] coaching, officiating, and weight training, but there's nothing viable that comes out of that. There's no entry-level position that you can get when you walk out of here. Coaching and officiating—great part-time jobs, extra money—but it's not a career. As a coach you can make a lot of money, but that's after you've gone to college. I don't see our kids as defensive coaches for the Steelers or anything.

Some students also recognized the flawed logic of requiring adolescents to pick subunits based on future occupational roles. "What if you don't succeed in dancing?" asked one Grant student about his school's Arts subunit, "or what if you break your leg or a have major accident? You need to have something other than that." A Harrison student offered a hypothetical example of some-one interested in nursing, but "through fate and everything turned out to be an engineer or something. All that they learned through high school, that's use-less." This student, in Harrison's HHS subunit, was glad that she was allowed to learn more about health careers. However, she expressed some reservations: "There's a high demand for physical therapists right now, and I was thinking of being that, but then maybe in a couple of years I may not want to even be that." Her HHS focus-group colleague voiced similar qualms, admitting diffi-culty picking a subunit because, at age 14, his career plans were uncertain: "When we filled out our orientation sheet, they just told us to fill in what we wanted to do. And we were only in 9th grade going into 10th so we didn't know what we wanted to do and most of us were confused as to what to put down."

To introduce more rationality into this important choice, three of the schools we studied—Harrison, Monroe, and Taylor—administered career inventory surveys to help students select careers and the subunits that would match their preferences. Staff and students, however, questioned whether these assessments actually facilitated students' decision-making. Taylor administered such inventories to students nearing the end of their time in the 9th-grade sub-units. One student's description of taking such an assessment casts some doubt on its validity:

> You have this paper and it's like, "Do you want to draw?" or something like that. And if you want to do that, you check "yes." And then at the end of that part you write how many "yeses" you have and how many "nos." And then you do that until you get to the last page where they say, "Tally up all the yeses, and then when you finished that, you'll find out what your code is, and you'll see what you want to be when you grow up." Like, if you got "RI" it would probably mean you want to be an actress or something like that.

The Resilient Comprehensive Curriculum

In the previous section we described how the subunits within these schools were designed to serve different types of students, based on their interests and future academic and occupational plans. Despite having engaged in consider-able structural change, the curricula in these schools continued to resemble those in traditional comprehensive high schools. We don't want to paint this picture with too broad a brush, because the subunits we described in Chapter 3 were engaged in substantial deviation from this general trend. However, most subunits continued to offer a comprehensive curriculum with a broad range of courses. This included multiple levels of the same course within individual subunits, undemanding courses at the lower end of the curriculum, as well as honors and advanced placement (AP) courses at the high end.

Each of the five SWS high schools we studied recognized that they served communities that embraced such traditional visions of what high schools should be. Despite their efforts to create new organizational structures, the schools considered limiting the scope of the comprehensive high school to be politically untenable, even within their "new" form. Thus, each of these schools actually created a new layer of differentiation: the subunit. In short, the SWS structures we studied were more *additive* than *transformative.* These five high schools sought to reap the benefits of small schools (via the SWS structure), while simultaneously retaining what they saw as a crucial component of large, comprehensive high schools (curriculum differentiation). This hybrid school organization—part small school, part large comprehensive high school—created challenges and dilemmas, particularly regarding the curriculum.

Pressures Against Keeping Subunits "Pure." Despite widespread support among teachers and administrators for curricular specialization, some staff in each school reported that they recognized that maintaining the differentiated curriculum undermined the SWS structure. Many noted that the sharp distinction between regular high schools and the small autonomous schools they sought to emulate became blurred by the differentiated curriculum. The tension between "small" and "comprehensive" school structures was evident in another regard: the substantial number of academic and nonacademic courses each school situated outside the subunit structure. Such courses generally enrolled students from multiple subunits and typically did not incorporate the themes or pedagogies of the subunit in which they happened to be offered.

Even though schoolwide courses undermined the spirit of the SWS reform, two issues forced these schools to implement hybrid curriculum structures. First, schools had to deal with "singleton" courses—those that are offered only once per day and often have small enrollments. Offering singleton courses in each subunit would be prohibitively expensive. For example, providing Calculus, AP Physics, or French IV in every subunit would produce classes with very small enrollments and require substantial increases in staffing. Monroe was an exception, where the Math/Science Magnet was permitted to offer subunit-specific AP and honors courses for very few students. The resulting unequal class sizes fostered considerable resentment among students and teachers in Monroe's other subunits. A second tension involved schoolwide co-curricular courses such as band, journalism, and drama, which were offered in whatever subunit their teachers happened to be affiliated. As a result, a common, school-wide bell schedule was followed by all subunits. Moreover, as we noted in previous chapters, scheduling pure classes was difficult; students' curricular choices often trumped efforts to create subunit-specific classes. "Pureness" and "comprehensiveness" were in direct conflict, and comprehensiveness won in virtually every instance.

Teachers were conflicted about the extent to which students should take classes outside their subunits. Although most staff supported "full access" (i.e., to all courses in the school), they also recognized the dilemma it created within the SWS structure. Full access limited subunits' abilities to foster the academic and social climates championed by small-schools advocates—ideas that had drawn these schools to the SWS structure in the first place. However, many teachers had no qualms about allowing high-achieving students to take courses across subunits. For example, several Adams teachers commented that such students were generally better behaved, more motivated, and could handle complex schedules like those in regular public high schools. In this view, the SWS design was not aimed at students for whom the comprehensive high school already worked. Although intended for a particular audience, it is hard to see how the structure could be selectively applied. Hence, the conflict.

Monroe's attempts to keep subunits and courses pure while also maintaining a differentiated curriculum produced inequalities in access to curriculum resources. For example, only MSM students could enroll in MSM courses, whereas other subunits did not have such "protection." The result was that non-MSM students were systematically denied access to many honors and AP courses. Although Monroe's other subunits did offer a few AP and honors courses, such classes were offered at times that made them difficult to fit into students' schedules. In some instances, taking a particular advanced course in MSM would have solved the conflict and provided the student access. Even in such cases, neither MSM nor building administrators permitted non-MSM students to enroll in MSM classes. However, MSM students could take courses in other subunits. "What everyone is complaining about," according to Generic 1 subunit head, "is why can we take MSM kids, and why can we help this kid out, but they can never help anybody?" Monroe's International Business Magnet (IBM) subunit head echoed this complaint: "I'll be frank. We have trouble working with MSM. They've told us they don't want IBM kids, which I think is really unfair. They said, 'If your kids want to come to MSM, tough.'" Other advanced courses were offered only in MSM. Monroe's principal strongly supported this policy—he claimed that if enough students in other subunits wanted certain advanced courses, he would provide them. However, he considered that teachers had the responsibility to "beat the bushes," to market their classes well enough to fill them. If only six students were found for an AP course, that course would not be offered. His justification for this stance was that if non-MSM students wanted advanced courses, they should have selected MSM:

> Now, the concern is, "Kids in MSM are given the opportunity to take all of these advanced science and math classes." Well, excuse me! It's a math and science magnet program. They're not just given the opportunity to take these classes—they're required to take these classes. If you really encourage enough kids to sign up for these classes, you should be able to offer them across the board in the different subunits. If you want a statistics class, let's go ahead and promote it so that we can get enough kids that will take it.

Tensions Between "Small" and "Comprehensive." Nowhere in our study was this conflict more apparent than at Harrison High School. A district administrator offered a metaphor to describe Harrison's desire to sustain small subunits within a traditional comprehensive high school: "It almost reminds me of having one foot here in a little bit of glue, and one foot over here, and you don't understand why you can't be here, but you haven't let go of this foot and brought it over." She recognized that elective courses were a major obstacle to creating subunit-specific classes. She also recognized that electives were one way parents and the community judged the quality (and even legitimacy) of a high school. External perception was especially important for Harrison High, whose reputation in the district was weak. The administrator believed that if Harrison were to shed the trappings of a traditional comprehensive high school (which characterized the district's other three high schools), its image in the community might decline even further. Harrison's principal, new to the school in the year after our main study, claimed that Harrison's SWS structure had slowly "devolved" into a comprehensive high school: "The staff had come to realize that the school-within-school process had failed, was failing. It deteriorated. You're running a small-schools concept that was a bastardized form of what it was supposed to be. Then you're running a comprehensive high school, and *you can't run both.*"

As the only public high school in its district, Adams High suffered from problems of reputation only in relation to the city's several private high schools, but these comparisons produced similar tensions. Staff at Adams told us that many parents of academically successful students saw little need for reform.

In their view, a traditional comprehensive high school with a differentiated curriculum worked well for their children. An Adams administrator was aware of the source of this push to maintain a wide array of course offerings:

> The high-achieving population wants comprehensive. It works well for them in most cases. They were always the ones who could navigate the school, no matter how big. They were the ones who could read the 80-page college-like course catalog we have, and they would be able to negotiate it. They would target the teachers that they wanted [for their children], the courses that they wanted, and quite honestly, it worked well because we satisfied their needs. We looked great.

The evolution of one Adams subunit supports this view. From its creation in the 1970s through the late 1990s, Core Curriculum offered basic-level, intermediate-level, and advanced-level courses in mathematics and English. This tracked academic program appealed to many high-achieving students, the presence of whom explained Core Curriculum's reputation for academic rigor and its elite status among Adams's subunits. In the late 1990s, however, the subunit created pure and untracked 11th- and 12th-grade math and English courses that were required of all Core Curriculum students. The administrator responsible for these changes explained her decision: "The basic-level classes weren't working very well. Those kids were being written off and wouldn't pass and weren't doing well. It just didn't seem the right thing to be doing either to those kids or to the teachers that taught those courses. The kids were being labeled, and it just didn't feel right."

As a result of this new mandatory core curriculum, the subunit's juniors and seniors were denied access to schoolwide honors and AP math and English courses. Several staff members charged that this constrained curriculum had—in only a few years—led to Core Curriculum's "demise." Most high-achieving students wanted access to Adams's schoolwide academic electives and AP courses, and began selecting other subunits that had not created pure classes. The year Core Curriculum instituted this policy, applications to the College Prep subunit increased dramatically. According to many staff members, when Core Curriculum ceased offering what had been its major "marketing" tool—internally tracked classes and access to Adams's schoolwide comprehensive curriculum—students and parents began to "shop elsewhere." Core Curriculum's efforts highlight an important issue: challenging the legitimacy of the comprehensive curriculum may produce unintended and even undesirable consequences within SWS schools.

Subunit Identities. Although they were "themeless" at the outset, Monroe's Generic subunits were urged to forge distinct identities, mostly by Monroe's principal. He lamented, "I walk by and tell Generic 1 how dull their hallway looks—like a sanitarium or a hospital. They really have no concept that holds them together." Ironically, he had personally designed Monroe's SWS structure to include two nondescript and two magnet subunits. Responding to such signals from the administration, Generic 1 tried to forge an identity by adopting the acronym STARS: "Students Taking All Roads to Success." This effort seemed ineffective in fostering subunit ethos; few students or teachers could remember what the acronym stood for. "We have another subunit, Generic 1, and their name is . . . it's an acronym for something, who knows?" fumbled a teacher in another subunit. Despite Generic 1's ineffectual attempts at marketing and identity creation—which included T-shirts emblazoned with the subunit's new acronym—Generic 2 felt pressure to develop its *own* identity. "To be honest with you," explained a Generic 2 teacher, "we kind of got into this mode where everybody felt like the subunits need a mantra." Interestingly, the theme Generic 2 was considering adopting—the liberal arts—was itself rather "generic." Other than distinguishing the subunit somewhat from MSM, how this focus differed from its already ill-defined character was unclear.

The expressed themes of several subunits were virtually absent in their coursework. For example, when asked to characterize the other subunits in their school, African American students from Grant's Health subunit were able to describe most subunits, but claimed they could not describe African American Studies (AAS). One student queried, "I don't know what you do in AAS." Other students laughed in agreement, with several adding, "I don't know either." Many Monroe students and staff wondered what distinguished IBM from Generics 1 and 2. "To be honest with you," asserted a Generic 2 teacher, "I don't even know what they [IBM] are or what they do!" A Monroe special education teacher echoed these sentiments:

> To this day, as many years as I've worked here, I do not understand what makes IBM different from the other subunits. I don't understand what that program really is. I really don't. I just don't know what the difference is. And I've asked some of them several times. Even when I get an answer, I still don't understand what's different.

Adams students and staff agreed that the Community subunit had the least recognizable identity or organizing rationale. When asked about Community's philosophy, one Adams administrator bluntly replied, "I don't think it exists!" Created in the late 1980s, Community's focus was on community service and learning. A veteran teacher asserted, "[Community] was supposed to be a little like the Alternative subunit but without the crunchy granola." Alternative, however, developed a culture and reputation for using alternative pedagogies and curriculum, whereas Community had not created a distinct identity. Although it sought to forge its identity around its community service courses, these activities were offered as electives, and Community students generally chose other electives instead. As a result, the community service theme never fully developed. Rather, staff charged that Community's students had dictated its mission and philosophy. "If you don't have a vision early on," asserted one teacher, "somebody else is going to make a vision for you." Unfortunately for Community, the "vision" held by its many low-achieving students contributed to its poor reputation and position at the bottom of Adams's subunit hierarchy.

We distinguish here between the ability of students and staff to identify and articulate their own subunit's identity versus those of other subunits in their school. Clearly, subunits with themes that appeared opaque to outsiders were sometimes quite clear to subunit members. However, across all five schools, the identities of subunits enrolling academically successful students were clear to both members and nonmembers. Importantly, outsiders' views were central to the creation and maintenance of the subunit status hierarchies that emerged within each school (which we discuss in subsequent chapters).

In some schools, subunits housed programs unrelated to their themes, which created obstacles to developing curricular identities. For example, Taylor's Arts/Humanities subunit offered cosmetology classes; a component of Grant's African American Studies subunit focused on law. Some students in these and other subunits expressed dissatisfaction that their coursework was unrelated to their subunit's theme. "Biology is just biology," complained one Grant African American Studies student, whose subunit offered few courses related to its namesake. A Harrison Arts/Communications student expressed similar frustration that his subunit rarely focused on communications—part of its expressed theme: "I haven't really gotten to the communications part, I guess. I don't know if we're ever gonna do anything about that except for English, and I'm not really good at English. I want to be a sports broadcaster." In general, subunits had trouble distinguishing themselves solely through their curricular offerings. Moreover, the pressure for subunits to offer a differentiated curriculum (recall Adams's Core Curriculum subunit) weakened their ability to develop identities with unique courses.

Outside Pressures. External forces also undercut subunits' ability to make themselves distinctive. State-level demands for increased graduation requirements and the alignment of curriculum with state standards and assessments limited subunits' ability to offer specialized courses. Over the past decade, many such courses had been eliminated from the curriculum for this reason. For example, a hallmark of Adams's Alternative subunit used to be its cross-grade English curriculum, which included courses addressing a wide array of genres such as science fiction, biographies, and women and minority authors. However, facing the need to align its schoolwide English curriculum with state assessments administered at the end of 10th grade, these courses were eliminated. In their place, Adams implemented a mandatory, schoolwide English core curriculum for 9th and 10th grade. This curriculum change constrained Alternative's ability to differentiate itself via unique courses. Such external pressures were less serious for the traditional academic subunits, because their curricular requirements were (in most cases) already aligned with state requirements. For instance, the curricula within Monroe's MSM and Adams's College Prep subunits conformed well to their states' assessments and graduation requirements. As we discuss in Chapter 6, the traditional academic themes of these subunits helped them to attract a disproportionate number of high-achieving, academically motivated students.

CONCLUSION

From the curriculum vantage point, the five high schools we studied were hybrid school organizations—part small school, part comprehensive high school. Each school sought to reap the benefits of small schools and to retain what they saw as the advantages of large comprehensive high schools. These efforts to straddle very different organizational forms led to both confusion and tensions within each school. Indeed, as we see it, the comprehensive curriculum is simply incompatible with many of the practical and conceptual underpinnings of the small-schools movement. For example, most students' schedules were not subunit-specific, and subunits enjoyed little autonomy. One result was that the distinction between regular high schools and the small schools that SWS high schools sought to emulate was blurred. The major reason for this blurring was the lingering presence of a broad and diversified curriculum.

Conversely, the small autonomous high schools often praised in both academic literature and the popular press, such as New York City's Central Park

East Secondary School (Meier, 1995) and Urban Academy (Cook, 2000), have shed many trappings of the comprehensive high school. Specifically, they offer an academic curriculum taken by virtually all their students, including few AP, honors, foreign language, elective, or low-level courses. This was done both out of necessity—because their small number of students and teachers cannot support a broad curriculum—and out of a philosophical agreement among staff about what students need to know and be able to do. Because of the schools' location, in the midst of a city with excellent public libraries, museums, art galleries, and universities, these schools are not obliged to provide such experiences for their small numbers of students. Moreover, these schools enrolled students by choice, so the applicants were well informed about the type of schooling they would receive.

Although rooted in a similar philosophy, each of the five SWS high schools we studied maintained beliefs in the value of differentiation and the benefits of comprehensiveness. Indeed, the philosophical and curricular components of traditional comprehensive high schools were alive and well in these SWS high schools. This commitment to differentiation was enacted by subunits (through their varied themes) and curriculum (through courses that varied in content and rigor). Within the SWS structure, most staff expressed overarching belief in the value (and even virtue) of accommodating student differences via diverse academic and vocational offerings. Importantly, the subunits within each school provided an additional layer of stratification, delivering different skills and knowledge to different types of students separated by subunit. Staff quickly and strongly refuted suggestions that their SWS structures resembled a traditional tracked curriculum, mainly because most students *chose,* rather than were *assigned to,* subunits.

The subunits we studied existed within larger high schools that continued to offer the co- and extracurricular activities that define the comprehensive high school, so all students held "dual citizenship" in both their subunit and the larger school. Some students' affective attachments were to the school rather than the subunit, a development that SWS advocates may not support. This was largely because each school found it difficult (if not impossible) to schedule classes that enrolled only one subunit's members and simultaneously to maintain the comprehensive curriculum. Arts and academic electives were meant for students from all subunits, and subunit-specific sections of low-enrollment courses were economically and logistically impossible.

The century-old arguments framed by the Committee of Ten and the Cardinal Principles continued to play themselves out in these 21st century schools.

In each school, staff expressed wide-ranging opinions about the fundamental purposes of secondary education. Some favored common academic experiences for all students; others forged a path that led them to construct (or support) a dual obligation to prepare some students for college and others for work. Regardless of whether or not they favored curricular differentiation, most staff agreed that the SWS structure strengthened a dichotomy that separated students into academic or vocational strata; students were permitted to sort themselves into subunits based on their educational and occupational futures. Creating differentiated subunits permitted students to match their level of academic commitment to the expectations held by particular subunits. This arrangement narrowed the gap between what students were willing to do and what teachers within each subunit demanded. Many saw this system as a strength rather than a weakness.

6

Allocating Students to Subunits

ADVOCATES OF THE schools-within-schools (SWS) reform typically suggest that schools create subunits organized around different themes and permit students to choose their subunits. The motivation for this design rests on two assumptions, as reflected in Figure 3.1. First, choice will allow students to match their own interests and future plans to subunit themes and courses. Second, this matching will lead students to be more engaged with their learning and more committed to school. The goals of increased engagement and commitment are especially relevant to schools that adopt the SWS model, because many serve students with low levels of motivation and achievement.

IMPLICATIONS OF STUDENT CHOICE

Allowing student choice of subunits, although logical in the context of commitment building, raises concerns similar to those associated with educational choice in other contexts. Some authors interested in the SWS model have recognized the danger that it may be used to sort students into different subunits based on academic ability, or that such structures would permit students to sort themselves. For example, in commenting on the small-schools movement in Philadelphia high schools, McMullan (1994) warned: "The greatest concern is that [subunits] do not become thinly disguised tracks into which students are placed based on some arbitrary standard of performance or expectation" (p. 69). Moreover, some subunits may be *designed* to attract certain types of students (e.g., very able students or those especially interested in mathematics and science). Oxley (1994) recognized this potential, and cautioned that "[sub]units must not intentionally screen out particular students or inadvertently attract only certain groups of students" (p. 256).

These and other authors warn that the SWS structure may lead to stratification similar to that found within the typical comprehensive high school: the allocation of students with different social and academic backgrounds to different classes and programs. A central challenge for SWS high schools, many of which serve academically and socially diverse clienteles, is to create SWS models in which subunits attract students with similar *preferences* but varied social and academic *backgrounds.* This is not an easy task. Raywid (1996) sums this up succinctly: "The challenge is how to differentiate without tracking" (p. 12).

Choice Within Comprehensive High Schools

As we discussed in Chapter 5, these issues are at the very heart of long-standing controversies surrounding the U.S. public comprehensive high school (Hammack, 2004). Over the last century, public high schools overwhelmingly decided that students should be permitted wide latitude to design their own academic courses of study, generally through student curricular choice. The educational free markets that characterize most comprehensive high schools also provide students wide latitude in deciding how deeply they will engage the academic content of high school. Because high school curricula often contain courses with modest academic rigor, students have the option of a "path of least academic resistance." Indeed, many "adolescents care about things they have to care about, and they do not have to care about academic engagement very much" (Sedlak, Wheeler, Pullin, & Cusick, 1986, p. 13). Because high-achieving and motivated students (and/or their parents) generally seek the most demanding teachers and courses, curricular choice increases social and academic stratification in course taking (Grant, 1988).

Matching the diversity of students and courses, teachers also vary in the amount of effort *they* choose to exert or demand in the classroom. In some classes, low levels of student and teacher expectations coincide, resulting in "treaties": teachers pass students if they are not disruptive, and students cooperate if teachers demand little effort from them (Cusick, 1983; Powell et al., 1985; Sedlak et al., 1986). Sizer (1984) refers to this system as the "conspiracy for the least," meaning "the least hassle for anyone" (p. 156).

Choice Within the Schools-Within-Schools Structure

The five SWS high schools we studied functioned as choice-driven educational marketplaces. Students in each school acted as consumers who selected their subunits based (ostensibly) on their interests, abilities, and future educational and occupational plans. Such market metaphors were often literal rather than merely symbolic, as many subunits advertised, actively recruited new "clients," and discussed their missions and themes in terms of "market share" and "target audience."

Logically, we should see student choice driven by a desire to match personal interests and skills with the subunit themes and course offerings. However, only occasionally did we observe such matching. One student told us that she chose Grant's Health subunit because she wanted to be a nurse; a Harrison student who liked to draw selected Arts/Communications; a Monroe Math/Science Magnet (MSM) student planned to attend medical school and thought that "MSM would be a better way to prepare." These instances were actually rather unusual. In each school, only a few students asserted explicitly that their subunit choices were based on subunit themes or offerings. Subunit themes were only one of many factors that students told us guided their decisions. In fact, the choices made by many students were wholly unrelated to subunit themes. This lack of matching is important, because the rationales supporting the SWS structure—both in the schools we studied and in the writings about schools within schools—rest upon matching students' interests and future plans to subunit themes.

RATIONALES FOR STUDENTS' CHOICES

If not subunit themes, then what justifications *did* students offer for their subunit selections? Although students in these SWS high schools enjoyed the freedom of choice that free markets typically require, varied social and structural pressures influenced students' subunit selections. Importantly, many of these forces affected students differently, depending on their demographic and academic characteristics. In this chapter we focus on students, the rationales they offered for their subunit selections, and the links they made between their interests, motivations, academic abilities, and subunit choices. We located no studies that examined differentiated SWS structures and students' choices within them. Thus, the motivating questions that drove our research on the topic included

- How do students actually select subunits?
- Why do some students select academically challenging subunits, whereas others willingly choose low-status subunits with poor reputations?
- How are students' subunit choices influenced by their social and academic backgrounds?

The Path of Least Resistance

As some of the students with whom we spoke expressed an overall dissatisfaction with school, many reported choosing subunits they believed would place few demands on them. In all the SWS schools we studied, at least one subunit represented a path of least resistance, and many students expressed their lack of interest in academic pursuits through self-selection into such subunits. For example, although Monroe administrators claimed that Generic 1 and 2 were simply the default placements for students who did not select the two magnet subunits they offered, several students claimed to have deliberately *chosen* the Generics. As one Generic 2 student told us, "I just wanted regular classes." Other Generic students recognized that subunit choices reflected students' commitment to school; some claimed that what distinguished the magnet subunit students was their willingness to devote time and effort to schoolwork. "It's not that they are smarter than us," a Generic 1 student remarked, "they just work harder." A Generic 2 student echoed this sentiment; when she heard Math/Science Magnet (MSM) students "whining" about the extensive amount of academic effort their subunit required, she told them, "Hello! You *chose* to be in that subunit. You can get out any time you want!" She was candid in her explanation of why she did not select MSM: "I chose this subunit because I don't want to do a lot of work."

Students in the vocationally oriented subunits often expressed an interest in hands-on activities. Such interest was often coupled with a stated aversion to traditional academic coursework. Harrison's Science/Technology (ST) subunit enrolled several of these students, many of whom claimed that ST was the best of several bad (subunit) options. They were not particularly fond of school, but unlike Harrison's more academic subunits, ST permitted them to work on applied projects that reflected their current hobbies and future occupational plans. One disaffected ST student was candid about this, stating that the SWS structure permitted him to "get through high school with the least hassle":

But it's still pretty much just school. That's about it. That's mainly how I look at it. It's just school. I mean, that's about all I think of it. It's school. Got to go, got to do your stuff, and then go home. . . . I'm glad that I'm in ST and not Business, because I like to build stuff and work with my hands.

Students uninterested in academic coursework tended to select subunits known for low expectations, including the vocational and "generic" subunits. Adams's Community subunit had garnered a reputation for lax behavioral and academic standards and for enrolling many low-achieving Black students. Adams's subunits all had nicknames, and Community was called "The Ghetto." When asked why a disproportionate number of academically struggling Black students selected Community, a schoolwide administrator at Adams told us, "They choose [that subunit] to be with Black kids, and because they know its reputation: 'I don't have to get there on time. I don't have to do this. I don't have to do that.'" A Community student had internalized this reputation, characterizing others in her subunit as "thug-type people—a bunch of people who really just don't care about school."

Community's head told us that his subunit already had a negative reputation when he took the helm in the early 1990s. "We were the place where all the low-achieving kids, kids with issues, and kids with behavioral problems were going. It was supposed to be all Black and easy to get through." Reflecting on why Community continued to attract many of Adams's low-performing minority students, he claimed that many Black families saw Community as a subunit in which academically struggling students could ultimately receive a high school diploma. Moreover, he argued that teachers at four of Adams City's feeder K–8 elementary schools—all of which enrolled large numbers of disadvantaged Black children—typically recommended Community to their students by telling them, "If you go there, they'll support you and they'll keep you in school. You won't be dropping out of Community."

Students and staff at other schools also identified one or two subunits that were less demanding. Several Grant teachers claimed that African American Studies (AAS), which tended to enroll the school's weakest students, focused on students' social rather than academic needs. AAS staff and its head were known for their genuine concern for the social well-being of their students, many of whom lived in the low-income neighborhoods surrounding Grant. However, Grant students and teachers in other subunits charged that such concern for students' personal lives left little room for academics. Several Grant Business students, who tended to be among the school's more serious, doubted the integrity of AAS's thematic focus and its ability to prepare students for adulthood. As one Black Business student charged, "They teach you about your culture, but you need more than, 'We know we're Black and proud.'" A head of another Grant subunit similarly argued that AAS's weak reputation was due partly to a lack of academic press:

> AAS does wonderful things, but they're much more into the affective things. I have always told the kids, "Don't come to me if you want trips, that's not my thing. I'm trying to get you really good in science, and really good in math." My emphasis has been academic achievement, and I'm not into this other stuff. A lot of what they do in AAS, the extra efforts they put in are wonderful, and I think they do marvelous things, but it's not in making academics strong.

Subunit Hierarchies.   Across all five schools, staff consistently referred to low-status subunits as "dumping grounds." "We get a lot of the below-average type kid, because we're the dumping ground," claimed a teacher in Monroe's Generic 2 subunit. The head of Adams's Community subunit argued that status differentials were an inevitable result of the SWS structure: "There's going to be a good subunit and there's going to be a dumping ground." Adams staff and students agreed that Community was, in fact, a "dumping ground." "Community is where everyone gets put who doesn't get in somewhere else," one Adams student claimed. "Community has developed a reputation as the dummy subunit," echoed an Adams teacher.

Staff and students in low-status subunits were quite aware of their place in the school's hierarchy. Asked to describe students in each subunit, a member of Grant's African American Studies subunit responded: "Business students are the best. On a scale of one to ten, we might be a five." MSM students looked down on and even openly derided students in Monroe's Generic subunits. "They call us the idiot subunit," a Generic 2 student told us. "MSM's the place where they get the top 10 people. We're trying our hardest to prove to them that we're just as good, but it's kind of hard." Several Monroe teachers described social divisions that had developed between MSM students and those from the other subunits. "The other kids think of Generic 1 and Generic 2 kids as the dumbbells, the dummies, the ones that couldn't make it in MSM," one teacher told us. Students in other subunits redefined Generic 1's acronym ("STARS") from "Students Taking All Roads to Success" to "Stupid Teachers and Retarded Students."

These status differentials often reflected the socioeconomic status associated with particular careers and academic subjects. In 8th grade, as she was deciding which subunit to choose, an Adams student was told, "[Vocational] gets all the dumb kids who are becoming plumbers." A saying had developed among Monroe students that captured the social distance separating the career-based subunits: "MSM kids will design houses. IBM kids will sell houses. Generic 1 kids will fix things in houses. Generic 2 kids will steal things from houses." One teacher asserted that Monroe's subunit structure was a simple reflection of contemporary socioeconomic hierarchies:

> It's just like in normal society—you have your rich group, you have your middle class, and then you have your lower class. I guess that's how you can characterize the system here. MSM would be like the rich kids or the snobs, and then Generic 1 and 2 would be your lower class. You could say they're getting ready for society, because they'll all fit into the upper class or the higher echelon, the middle class, and so on.

The Search for Prestige and "High School U.S.A."

In contrast to the subunits selected by many low-achieving students, academically motivated students often chose subunits with reputations involving high expectations for student effort and performance. This search for quality differed markedly from the criteria used by many low-achieving students, who hoped to lessen the demands school placed on their lives. Students who chose challenging subunits claimed that they did so because they were "harder," "more advanced," and had environments in which they could "learn more." A Harrison student in the Health/Human Services (HHS) subunit claimed that he was initially interested in the Science/Technology (ST) subunit, which was chosen by many of his friends. However, he selected HHS out of concern that ST was not academically oriented: "What I was thinking about ST is that it's not really going to help [me]. It's more like woodworking and welding and stuff. It just seemed like it was going to be a slack-off thing. I just wanted a little more . . . a lot more academics."

Monroe's Math/Science Magnet (MSM) attracted most of that school's motivated students, many of whom claimed to have chosen MSM because of its reputation for high expectations. One student mentioned a particularly demanding MSM teacher who "wants everything perfect and really wants you to succeed. The first thing you think of [her] is, 'Oh, she's just mean to me,' but afterwards you realize instead what she was doing." Another student linked MSM's expectations to teachers' unwillingness to accept late assignments:

Well, when it's due, it's due. You can't talk your way out of it. It's like, "Turn it in." In our first semester of school in our freshman year, it was hard. It was really tough because you have tons of homework every night. The teachers are just blasting you with zeros and stuff if you don't turn stuff in.

Subunits with reputations for academic success clearly found it easier to attract able and motivated students. Moreover, subunits with poor reputations actually *repelled* such students. Several Taylor students told us that they had selected Arts/Humanities because of its positive behavioral climate. "The environment here is more pleasant than any other [subunit]," claimed one student. Another added that he had not chosen Mechanical because it enrolled students who "want to just be wild." When asked why students *did* select Mechanical, he replied, "People go to Mechanical just to have fun."

Subunit themes were not always an issue. For example, academically motivated students at Monroe chose MSM regardless of their level of interest in mathematics and science. Several Monroe students claimed that middle school guidance counselors suggested MSM to them not because they were particularly fond of math or science but because they were seen as "good students" and, at Monroe, good students belonged to MSM. Although MSM was presented in the guise of a specialized math and science magnet program, its traditional academic curriculum attracted the same types of students found in the "college prep" track in comprehensive high schools. "There's a lot of people who don't pick a [subunit] because of what they are going to do," one MSM student told us. "There are some people who do so just to get ahead, and to get more experience for college." One such student, who claimed that she was actually interested in attending law school, asserted, "A guidance counselor said to me, 'Your science and math grades are really high. Would you like to go into MSM? And I personally don't like science and math. 'Well,' she's like, 'it's advanced learning.' So that's why I selected it."

Unlike MSM's clearly identifiable focus, subunits in other schools that attracted high-achieving students actually had rather ill-defined themes. These themes did not extend much beyond that of offering a traditional academic curriculum. In fact, the identities (and allure) of these subunits were based partly on being the most traditional, "themeless" subunits in their respective schools. "College Prep is not a real philosophy, and it wasn't planned as one," remarked one Adams teacher, "but it has developed the reputation as the college-prep subunit."

Why would academically motivated students choose ill-defined subunits? The rationale offered by College Prep students for their choice was circular: they selected College Prep because other academically motivated students had selected it. College Prep students rarely mentioned either the subunit's curriculum or pedagogical approach. Rather, the primary draw of College Prep seemed to be the high academic motivation of its students. As one College Prep student put it, "It had a reputation of being an academic subunit, so it seemed like the obvious choice for me." Her counterpart added, "In the 8th grade I just figured I wanted to continue getting a good strong education. You hear things from other people, like, 'Oh, College Prep is full of brains.'" One Adams teacher claimed that students such as these had looked at the school's other subunits and concluded, "'I don't need the hippie thing [Alternative], I don't need the discipline thing [Core Curriculum]. Just let me go to school, give me the courses. I'm going to do my work. Just leave me alone. Put me in College Prep.'"

Like College Prep, the reputation of Harrison's Health/Human Services (HHS) subunit rested on the fact that it enrolled traditional, academically oriented students. Although it ostensibly focused on health and social service careers, it actually offered few courses related to these fields. "Whereas all the other subunits have a distinct flavor and classes in the curriculum that make them distinct and unique," asserted one teacher, "Health doesn't have that." An HHS student agreed: "It seems like all the rest of the subunits have something that not [necessarily] unifies them, but they'll be taking Art classes at AC. And it's like with HHS you're not taking anything that sets you aside as being in HHS." Echoing what several Adams teachers told us, an HHS teacher suggested that academically motivated students were more concerned about the types of students a subunit enrolled than about its theme or even its courses. She argued that this benefited HHS, which had never fully implemented its theme:

> I think what happens is, HHS kids don't want to go to Science and Technology, don't want to go to Arts and Humanities, and they kind of lump together by default. I mean that sounds awful. It's not that they want spaghetti with no sauce, but it kind of is. These are kids who would really probably prefer a six-period, traditional school.

Admitting that attempts by HHS to implement more courses related to health careers had failed, its head agreed that HHS's weak theme gave the impression that it was simply "high school U.S.A." According to her, this was exactly what high-achieving students and their families wanted:

Part of the draw is that HHS looks very traditional. It looks to parents like the college-bound group, because you've got your science, you've got your math, you've got your health class, you've got your language arts class. You've got all these requirements that you have to have. So I think that's part of it—it looks traditional.

Harrison and Adams staff claimed that many students who chose HHS and College Prep did so because they succeeded within didactic pedagogical contexts. Although Adams's Alternative subunit enrolled many able and motivated students, teachers described College Prep students as more *traditionally* academic: "Alternative students tend to be more intuitive and creative," declared one teacher, "[whereas] College Prep students will succeed and they'll do quite well; but they'll stay in the book—they'll color between the lines." A Harrison Arts/Communications (AC) teacher claimed that when they received assignments, HHS students wanted to know, "'How long does it have to be? Just give me the work!' They don't want to discuss it or anything, but the AC kids want to discuss it. They want to talk about it."

These stereotypes were often on target. Several HHS and College Prep students admitted proudly that they valued traditional, teacher-centered pedagogical approaches. One HHS student argued that colleges and universities were more interested in students with traditional (rather than alternative) educational backgrounds. He asserted that in evaluating students from Harrison's Arts/Communications subunit—which often employed progressive pedagogical strategies—colleges concluded, "These are creative kids, but we need some set-in-stone smart kids. We don't want creative. We want the ones that will know the material."

INFLUENCES ON STUDENTS' SUBUNIT CHOICES

As we have discussed throughout this chapter, most students were free to act as educational consumers within these SWS high schools. Differentiated SWS structures permitted students to match their level of commitment to subunits' expectations. Students' subunit choices were, however, hostage to countless outside pressures beyond their personal interests and plans. These pressures came from many sources: friends, family, school staff, and their schools' institutional policies and procedures. The extent to which these diverse pressures ultimately swayed students' subunit choices varied considerably, depending largely on their social and academic backgrounds.

Social and Familial Relationships

Unsurprisingly, students told us that their decisions were strongly influenced by those of their friends. Despite the schools' considerable efforts to create subunits with varied and easily identifiable themes and organizing rationales, many students claimed to have simply chosen the subunit their closest friends chose. "When people sign up, they try to sign up with their friends," claimed one Harrison student, "and they say, 'Hey just sign up for Business, you'll be with all of us.'" Many Monroe MSM students sought to continue friendships forged while attending the district's middle school math and science magnet program. Similarly, several K–8 schools in Adams's choice-driven district had themes that matched the high school's subunit themes. Such matching permitted like-minded students (and families) to maintain previously established social networks. Reflecting similar statements we heard from staff at other schools, the head of Taylor's Arts/Humanities subunit argued that peer influences were not always in students' best interests:

> Nine times out of ten they select subunits because that's where their friends are going. Some of them pick them for the right reasons, but a lot of the kids don't. They pick for reasons that are typical to teenagers: "Because a group of my friends are here and that's why I'm going there," or, "I can be around this person."

Similar to peer influences, several students at each school claimed that older siblings and other relatives had suggested—some rather strongly—which subunit they should join:

- My sister went to this high school and she graduated in '88 and she said, "You're going to College Prep," and that was the end of it. (Adams)
- I chose Arts and Communications because my sister was in it when she was here. (Harrison)
- My brother is in Health and he told me about it, so I went into it. (Taylor)
- My cousin used to go here [Business] and she graduated last year. (Grant)
- My sister was in ICL and she said it was cool, so I said, "OK." (Adams)

Other students reported being "denied" subunit choice by parents who chose their subunit for them. This was more common among students in subunits with reputations for high academic and behavioral standards. Students in less demanding subunits rarely mentioned their parents' involvement in their decisions—they more often chose their subunit on their own. A student in Grant's Business subunit, considered by many to be the school's strongest, asserted, "My mom sent me here—my mom made the decision for me." When we asked a group of Monroe MSM students whether their parents were involved in their subunit choices, almost in unison they replied, "Majorly . . . like . . . totally!" An Adams College Prep student jokingly lamented that her mother had *too* much information about Adams's subunits. Although she had not wanted to select College Prep, her mother declared that she "*would* be going to College Prep": "Because my mom is a teacher, she knew about the subunits already, and she was like, 'College Prep is good. You need someone there saying, "Do not do that! Stop acting up! Do this! Go to class!"'"

The implications of familial influences for the perpetuation of subunit hierarchies are important, including their broader role in social reproduction. Similar to students' curricular choices in comprehensive high schools, affluent and educated parents of students in these SWS schools tended to guide their children toward academically demanding subunits. An explanation often offered for this phenomenon is that socially disadvantaged families have less information regarding the contents of educational systems than their more affluent counterparts. As such, advocates of educational choice often argue that providing complete information about the available options will "level the playing field" and limit segregation and stratification. This assumes, however, that given access to identical information, all families—regardless of their backgrounds—will make identical choices for their children. The choice processes and outcomes we observed within these five SWS high schools lead us to question this assumption. In most instances, the various subunit reputations were well known within the schools and their broader communities. This was especially true of the most rigorous subunits. The high expectations held for student performance by Monroe's MSM and Adams's College Prep were common knowledge. It was not a lack of information about the available options that prevented low-achieving students from selecting demanding subunits.

Schools' efforts to provide information about their subunits may have actually *strengthened* the link between students' social and academic backgrounds and their subunit choices. The school district in which Adams High School was located maintained a very well-funded and well-staffed office to provide information to students and parents about the district's many educational options. A wealth of information was available—in dozens of languages—about the district's K–8 elementary schools (all of which were schools of choice), as well as the subunits within Adams's SWS structure. Each year, the district published subunit-specific standardized test scores, graduation and college acceptance rates, and other data. Many Adams staff members told us that they thought this practice *increased* stratification, because more educated and affluent parents used the information to steer their children toward the subunits with academically successful students. Even though the district publications indicated that Community's test scores were far below those of other Adams subunits, sizable numbers of Black and low-achieving students and families selected Community. Important to these students and families was the fact that Community's graduation rate was similar to other subunits, even though its test scores were lower. At Adams and at each of these five SWS high schools, different students and families appeared to seek different qualities from the subunits in their schools.

Institutional Pressures

Beyond the social pressures guiding students' subunit decisions, structural and procedural elements also influenced the types of students each subunit enrolled.

Subunits' Recruiting Efforts. Many subunits took a proactive role in subunit allocation processes, including recruiting. The extent and form of these recruiting efforts varied substantially across schools and across subunits in the same school, as did the successes of such approaches. Although Monroe administrators claimed that all who applied to MSM were admitted, only those who were high-achieving were personally encouraged to apply. "MSM staff go through students' records, and they pick the kids that they want in the seventh and eighth grade," asserted the head of IBM, Monroe's other magnet subunit. "We don't do that—we walk in cold [to recruiting sessions at the district's middle schools] and give a presentation. We tell them what we're about and hope that they want to be with us. But sometimes the very best kids have already been earmarked for MSM." Monroe's MSM had an additional recruiting advantage: the district operated a "junior" MSM program at one middle school. This helped MSM develop relationships with middle school students and teachers, many of whom suggested that their best students select MSM. One such student recounted the invitation he received from middle school staff to join MSM:

My counselor told me that some people from Monroe were going to come and give a presentation on what MSM was about. It sounded great to me. She said, "I think you'd be perfect for it. You'd have a lot of fun, and you'd like the advanced learning." She said that it was going to be way better than anything else.

Students at Monroe's magnet subunits were supposedly required to submit applications consisting of a personal statement and three letters of recommendation from their middle school teachers. The requirement of these application materials may have deterred some students from applying to those subunits, resulting in their automatic placement into either Generic 1 or 2. One MSM student, who had spent many years in the district's Gifted and Talented program asserted, "I got in without filling out an application or anything." Students and staff in other Monroe subunits recounted that MSM staff often recruited and admitted high-achieving students regardless of whether they had actually applied. MSM's application process may have served as a "filter" for less motivated, lower achieving students, but not for high-achieving students. One way or another, such students usually found their way to MSM.

Student recruitment took a somewhat different form at the other SWS schools we studied. Because Taylor's 9th graders were automatically placed into the First-Year 1 or 2 subunits and did not select subunits until the end of 9th grade, the subunit heads could recruit directly within the building. Taylor's Business subunit head sent letters to all 9th graders with grade averages of 80 or above inviting them to join her subunit. At Grant, where students throughout the city applied directly to subunits, the number of applicants to each subunit varied considerably. After previously being barred from such procedures by its district, Grant subunits were given permission to use somewhat selective admissions criteria. Oversubscribed subunits could deny students admission based on a history of very poor attendance or very low academic performance. The strong reputation of Grant's Business subunit meant that it received many more applications each year than it had openings. This demand allowed Business to set high expectations for prospective students while maintaining a large applicant pool. A Business subunit teacher told us that he "was able to look at the applications and not necessarily pick the best, but I was able to deny access to students who just had either terrible behavior or deplorable attendance."

Grant's administrative structure also facilitated certain subunits' ability to recruit students. The Communications subunit head was also the chair of the school's communications department, which was quite small. As department chair he taught only two classes per day, thus providing more time for recruiting. A similar situation occurred within the Business subunit, which had both a subunit head and a department chair. These dual-role administrators could devote considerable time to recruiting because of reduced teaching loads. In these instances, the rich clearly got richer.

Unlike the reputations of subunits that attracted substantial numbers of academically successful students, weak reputations constrained the ability of other subunits to attract motivated students. A circular conundrum resulted: low-status reputations could not improve until subunits enrolled some academically motivated students, but the importance of subunit reputation made attracting such students difficult. Taylor's 9th graders had a year to familiarize themselves with the types of students enrolled in the upper-grade subunits. It was almost impossible for subunits with poor reputations—such as Mechanical—to attract high-achieving students. At Adams, Community's subunit head tried to convince the district's 8th-grade teachers not to disparage his subunit to their students. Asked whether Community attempted to recruit academically motivated students, he replied, "We did that up until probably 5 years ago, but we stopped doing it because no matter what we were telling them, they weren't coming." No amount of "positive advertising" could overcome Community's poor reputation.

Procedural Influences. Beyond subunits' own recruiting efforts, schoolwide policies and procedures influenced the allocation of students to subunits. These further exacerbated social and academic stratification among them. Several elements of Taylor's subunit allocation process strengthened the relationship between students' backgrounds and their subunit placements. Students' subunit choices were honored on a "first come, first served" basis; students who submitted their preference early generally received their first choice. "If your attendance is good, you're going to get your choice," a Taylor subunit head reported, "but when it gets down to the end of the year and you haven't been attending for the last month of school, you're going to get pretty much what's left." A teacher explained the ramifications of such a system for Taylor students:

> The kids who aren't responsible enough to bring in their choices on time just get stuck in Mechanical. So it's not so much that there's an element that [chooses] Mechanical, it's sort of the default subunit, and the kids who obviously don't care about their academic interests get stuck there before they even make a decision. If you're not responsible, somebody else is going to choose for you.

Some students who lived in Taylor's catchment area were expelled each year from the citywide selective high schools for academic or behavioral problems, and they were automatically enrolled in Taylor. Such students were regularly placed in Arts/Humanities, the subunit considered the most similar to the academically rigorous schools from which they had been expelled. Even though these students did not succeed in the academically selective citywide schools, they were still considered among Taylor's better-prepared and more motivated students. As such, although each subunit received many transient students each year, Arts/Humanities received more than its share of those who were (relatively) higher achieving.

A related phenomenon occurred at Monroe, where students who matriculated late—after 9th grade or after the school year had started—were not permitted to select MSM or IBM. This influenced subunit compositions because transient students, many of whom migrated back and forth across the nearby Mexico border, tended to have weaker academic backgrounds and English language skills. Monroe's late enrollees also included students recently released from incarceration or expelled from other schools. These students were also automatically placed into either Generic 1 or 2, deepening the social and academic chasm that separated MSM and IBM from the Generics.

At no other school were such structural and procedural influences more evident than at Adams, perhaps because it was the city's only public high school. The lower application rates to Core Curriculum, ICL, Vocational, and Community meant that students who identified one of these subunits as their first choice were almost always admitted. On the other hand, Alternative and College Prep received twice as many applications as they had openings, leading to a lottery to decide admissions to these two subunits. Students who were denied admission to Alternative or College Prep could file a "hardship appeal," wherein they spelled out why they "must" be given their first choice of subunit.

For two reasons, the ability to appeal subunit placements resulting from the lottery process exacerbated internal segregation and stratification at Adams. First, virtually all appeals were granted, and students were admitted to their preferred subunit (often to the consternation of Alternative and College Prep staff). Second, the students and families using the appeals process were among Adams's most elite. Asked who tended to appeal subunit placements, an Adams administrator replied, "Who do you *think* appeals? It's totally predictable. It's the White, upper-middle-class population." Students and staff agreed that the parents most likely to object to unwanted lottery placements were wealthier and more educated. These were, of course, exactly the types of students *already* overrepresented in Alternative and College Prep—"the parents who always advocate strongly for their children," as one teacher described them. Another Adams teacher charged that hardship appeals were granted because of a risk-adverse school board: "Parents have threatened lawsuits. 'You put my child in subunit X, or I'll take you to court.' They give in. Once the word got out all you have to do is threaten to take the school to court you got what you wanted."

Related to the social standing of these Adams families, some parents circumvented the hardship appeals process altogether by pulling political strings. The desire to avoid low-status subunits was so strong among certain Adams families that local politicians—including the city's mayor and U.S. Congressman—were recruited to advocate the family's cause. The effect of these efforts was felt most deeply by Community, because socially advantaged children who were assigned to (but did not select) Community regularly appealed. "They've granted the appeals," Community's head reported, "so all those kids who wanted to go to College Prep, they went." He claimed that irate parents had phoned him, screaming, "I'll call my favorite politician and have it changed tomorrow morning!" The high rate of appeals granted to these politically adroit parents could also be attributed to the school's desire not to lose high-achieving students (and their families) to the area's many suburban and private schools (as we discuss further in Chapter 7). One 9th grader admitted that had he not received his first choice of subunit (College Prep), his mother would have enrolled him in a private school. His appeal was successful—Adams clearly wanted to retain such families.

In contrast to more affluent parents, less advantaged Adams families usually accepted subunit placements. Several students and teachers charged that families with certain cultural backgrounds were more acquiescent to the school's decisions than others, and thus less likely to use the appeals process. A Black student we interviewed characterized the students and parents who did and did not pressure the school regarding subunit access:

> It's what your parents are willing to do. I feel that it depends on class and race. If I got my second choice my mom would say, "Oh, just stick with it for a while, they know what's best for you." I don't think she'd bother it anymore. A lot of Haitian parents won't get involved because [they] basically work and give their children what they need to do well in school. Whatever the school decides for that child they feel is best.

CONCLUSION

Advocates of the SWS reform suggest that such schools create subunits whose themes vary so that students can match their interests and future plans to sub-unit offerings. Suggested potential benefits include increased student engagement and the ability to better meet students' needs through focused subunit missions. However, within the five SWS high schools we studied—all of which offered students choice among very different subunits—students' choices often reflected the extent to which they were willing to let high school make demands on their time and effort. The differentiated SWS structures in these five high schools provided options for students who wished to be challenged academically and options for those who simply wanted to be left alone. Students could essentially decide how deeply they would engage the academic content of schooling. Such a laissez-faire approach to students' academic experiences was viewed by most school staff as the means for actualizing a major goal of most public high schools: to accommodate differences in students' social and academic backgrounds. In this sense, stratification was viewed as the natural (even appropriate) outcome of student difference mediated by student choice.

The century-old argument that student learning requires student interest was certainly challenged within these five SWS high schools. Subunit choice itself did not appear to increase student engagement. Motivated students did not require the additional allure of academically oriented subunits; such students (or their parents) were already invested in their educations and sought subunits known for high academic and behavioral standards. Conversely, through differentiated subunit structures, less-motivated students could *reduce* their investment in school. Within each school, students were aware of which subunits placed the fewest demands on their time and effort. This knowledge permitted students to match their willingness to work to subunits' expectations. In short, subunit choice did not appear to influence levels of engagement— *levels of engagement appeared to influence subunit choice.*

Subunits were defined as much by the students they enrolled as by the themes they embraced. Rather than students basing their choices on subunit themes, more often they chose subunits whose members' social and academic backgrounds resembled their own. In several schools we studied, subunit names alone indicated which would be attractive to high-achieving students. That Monroe's Math/Science Magnet or Taylor's Arts/Humanities subunits enrolled higher proportions of motivated students than those schools' Generic or Mechanical subunits is not surprising. Although nothing inherent in Adams's pedagogically based SWS structure would suggest which subunits would appeal to high-achieving students, the subunits in that school were among the most stratified we observed.

Over time, certain subunits had become known for enrolling motivated students and others for enrolling uncommitted students. Particular processes across schools also guided students' choices, including subunit recruitment and enrollment timing. Other procedures were unique to particular schools. A striking example was Adams's appeals process for students whose subunit assignment was not to their liking. Another was the ability of Taylor staff to recruit within the school, as placement and selection into the career-theme subunits did not begin until 10th grade. Such school-based procedures and structures, either shared or idiosyncratic, strengthened the stratification across subunits by students' social and academic backgrounds. In the following chapter we discuss how each school addressed these tensions between personal freedom and the common good.

7

Equity, Access, and the
Schools-Within-Schools Design

PERHAPS MORE THAN any other American social institution, public education faces the daunting obligation of balancing the rights and freedoms of the
individual with the needs of the community and the common good. Balancing this multisided obligation is particularly challenging for comprehensive
high schools. Although their charters are couched in the language of egalitarian ideals and equal opportunity, they are also expected to prepare all students
to succeed within a highly competitive and market-driven society. Cohen and
Neufeld (1981) precisely captured this dilemma: "Schools are public institutions oriented to equality in a society dominated by private institutions oriented to the market" (p. 70). In this sense, our citizens expect public high
schools to use nonstratifying approaches to prepare students to enter a stratified society—an incongruous challenge at best. Indeed, "the inherent paradox
is that American public schools are charged with the task of social selection
and channeling while they are simultaneously expected to fulfill the democratic
mandate of equal opportunity" (Heyns, 1974, p. 1450). In short, U.S. public
high schools are expected to support simultaneously the virtue of *political
equality* and to prepare their students to participate in a nation defined by *economic inequality.*

Historically, social, political, and economic sentiments have influenced how
U.S. schools served these conflicting missions. Importantly, these sentiments
have changed over time. Educational reformers have variously stressed the
social and developmental needs of individual students, the civic requirements
of representative democracy, and the labor demands of a capitalist economy.
Labaree (1997) grouped these competing demands into three broad categories:

democratic equality, social efficiency, and social mobility. "From the perspective of democratic equality, schools should make [good citizens]; from the perspective of social efficiency, they [schools] should make workers; but from the perspective of social mobility, they should make winners" (p. 66). Wells (1993) described three similar adversarial masters that schools are required to serve: the common good, the workforce and the economy, and individual student growth and fulfillment.

At the core of these competing expectations is the reality that schooling is both a public *and* a private good; it serves the wants and desires of individuals, but its aggregate quality benefits (or harms) us all. How, then, can schools—particularly large public high schools—organize themselves to equally honor both their public and private missions? Many scholars have argued that market reforms would naturally resolve these tensions. As competitive free markets, schools would preserve personal freedoms; maximizing individual utility, it is argued, would serve well the aggregate good (see Chubb & Moe, 1990; Friedman, 1962). The contemporary popularity of this logic is not surprising. After 40 years of massive government social programs—viewed by many as both costly and ineffective—solutions to social problems that promise fundamental reform at low cost are welcomed. After decades of legislation and billions of dollars expended, it is argued, both poverty and inferior public schools remain. Don't individual educational consumers understand their own needs better than government bureaucrats? Isn't educational choice more essentially *American* than leaving important educational decisions in the hands of impersonal institutions, however well intended?

In a sense, the SWS reform seeks to reconcile the individual and the collective—to honor personal preference with subunit choice, yet foster more personal social bonds through shared subunit norms, practices, and experiences. Ultimately, the aim is to forge *common* experiences, something that is quite rare in large comprehensive high schools. In this chapter we explore how these five SWS high schools managed the tensions between individual choice and the common good, between freedom and equity. What were the costs or benefits associated with such market-driven structures? To what extent did the reform foster social and academic equality yet acknowledge students' disparate abilities, motivations, and interests?

As we described in Chapter 5, these schools constructed differentiated SWS structures, with subunits organized around themes, career focuses, and pedagogical approaches. Certain subunits were designed to serve students seeking traditional vocational training, whereas others targeted academically motivated, college-bound students. In Chapter 6 we explored students' subunit choices within these free-market organizational structures. In theory, as shown in the left-hand boxes in Figure 3.1, the goal of subunit choice is to match students' interests to subunit offerings. However, in these schools, subunit choices were guided by students' personal characteristics, institutional policies and procedures, and broader socioeconomic forces. Despite the laudable aim of reconciling schooling's private and pubic missions, market-driven mechanisms within these five schools resulted in considerable social and academic stratification. Certain school practices and procedures clearly fomented stratification among subunits. However, student choice was the central mechanism through which student difference led to subunit stratification. Our decision to study only schools that had applied the SWS reform for several years allowed us to see how such stratification develops over time, something that might not be obvious in schools new to this reform.

INFLUENCES ON SUBUNIT SEGREGATION AND STRATIFICATION

The hierarchical nature of these subunit designs resulted from both deliberate and unintended forces. Despite complicated origins, their development can be traced to two primary causes. First, the schools planted the seeds of stratification by implementing subunits that differed—often by design—in terms of prestige and academic rigor. It seems inevitable that differentiated, market-driven, theme-based SWS structures will sort students based on academic background and future educational plans. Second, stratification was exacerbated by social and systemic factors. Over time, students' subunit choices further delineated subunit differences, as high-achieving students tended to select high-status subunits *regardless of subunit themes.* The stratification became a sort of self-fulfilling prophesy.

Race/Ethnicity

Resulting in part from complex relationships between students' social class and their academic achievement, the schools serving racially diverse populations evidenced substantial racial segregation among subunits. Taylor's Mechanical subunit was almost 80% Black, whereas the more academic Arts/Humanities subunit was only 44% Black. Members of other Taylor subunits sometimes referred to Arts/Humanities as "the County," referring to the surrounding suburban district that enrolled fewer minority and low-income students than the city's schools. The modest number of White non-Hispanic students at Monroe disproportionately selected MSM. Staff were uneasy that in a school with a nearly 90% Hispanic enrollment, almost all of the top 10 students were White and from MSM. Even though Adams High School in theory used "controlled choice" to keep subunit racial enrollments within 5% of overall school averages, considerable racial imbalance between subunits persisted; 29% of Alternative's students were Black, compared with over 40% in Community and Core Curriculum.

Minority composition both *reflected* and *influenced* a subunit's status and reputation. Adams and Taylor subunits enrolling more minority students suffered weaker academic and behavioral reputations; such declining reputations further limited their ability to attract high-achieving students. For some students, subunit racial enrollments alone influenced their subunit choice. A White Taylor student told us that he had initially wanted Mechanical because its career focus appealed to him. But he justified his decision to choose another subunit: "I really didn't want to go down there. I'd probably would be the only White boy, and I'd stick out like a sore thumb."

Social Class

Considerable differences in the socioeconomic backgrounds of students were also evident across subunits. About a third of Adams's Vocational and Community subunits' students qualified for free or reduced-priced lunches, compared with only 6% of Alternative's students. "They'll be the neediest kids," is how Community's subunit head described his students. Not coincidentally, almost everyone in the school considered Vocational and Community to be Adams's weakest subunits, whereas Alternative held a high-status reputation. Social class differences among Monroe's subunits were quite apparent, especially between MSM and the Generics. Compared with MSM, twice as many Generic 1 and 2 students qualified for need-based fee waivers for college admissions tests. Many MSM students resided in the expensive housing developments surrounding the school. Conversely, many students in the Generic subunits lived in homes in the surrounding desert, some of which lacked electricity and running water.

Gender

Traditional vocational subunits produced substantial gender enrollment differences between subunits, as males more often selected the vocational programs. One Harrison Science/Technology teacher lamented that his subunit's efforts to recruit more females were unsuccessful: "We've tried everything, but it doesn't make any difference." Subunits enrolling large numbers of low-achieving male students were perceived as having less productive social and behavioral climates. In describing Taylor's Mechanical subunit, whose enrollment was 82% male, an Arts/Humanities student laughingly exclaimed, "It's all one big testosterone-bound place!" Explaining why so few females selected Mechanical, the head of another Taylor subunit claimed that families in the surrounding neighborhoods held traditional "blue-collar" beliefs regarding gender roles: "You're going against a more traditional culture here. This isn't the suburbs, where girls think they can do anything they want." Marked gender differences at Adams reflected both Vocational's substantial male enrollment and an overrepresentation of females in Alternative. The female head of that subunit attributed this phenomenon to Alternative's isolation on the top floor of the building, it's smaller size, and its relatively safe environment: "White girls have tended to pick this subunit more than anybody in the last two years. They feel safe up here in this big school."

Student Behavior

Subunits that enrolled many low-performing students also had reputations for unruly behavior. The head of Taylor's Arts/Humanities subunit—which enrolled higher-achieving students—described her students as generally "easier on teachers" than their counterparts in other subunits. Conversely, Taylor staff described Mechanical students variously as "the real hard core," "the most difficult," and "the largest percentage with probation officers." A Taylor 9th grader told us that he was not going to chose Mechanical because it was "for when you just want to be wild—teachers really don't have control over the kids." Another Taylor Arts/Humanities student agreed that Mechanical was "out of control":

> I don't want to put down Mechanical, but it's one of the more dysfunctional subunits. A lot of people roam the halls, and people in the classes are more disruptive. Up [here] in Arts and Humanities we've got our troublemakers, but it's not as negative-toned as it is in Mechanical.

Similar to Taylor's "dumping ground," Adams staff and students felt that the Community and Vocational subunits were unruly and even dangerous places.

Indeed, student suspension rates were two to three times higher in those sub-units than in College Prep or Alternative. These more negative social climates clearly influenced the types of students Community and Vocational attracted. In explaining her subunit choice, a College Prep student claimed that in eighth grade she was told [about Community], "If you walk down the hallway, all you have to do is look at somebody—you don't even have to look at them the wrong way—and you could get beat up." A Community student remarked, only half jokingly, "Last year we had so many fights in the hallways, if you told a teacher, 'I'm late because there was a fight,' They'd be like, 'Yeah, OK.'"

Special Education Status

Subunits also differed in their special education enrollments. Taylor's and Harrison's vocational subunits enrolled disproportionately large numbers of special education students. Not surprisingly, virtually no special education students selected (or were admitted to) Monroe's MSM subunit. "MSM doesn't have a whole bunch [of special education students] because of the nature of their program," Monroe's principal told us. Over a third of Adams's Community students received special education services, compared to a sixth school-wide. Community was fortunate in having a special education teacher whom parents of special education students regarded highly. "She is wonderful," said one Community staff member, "and every parent of an 8th grader with an IEP knows who she is." Though this teacher clearly benefited the subunit's special education students, her presence amplified Community's reputation for academic weakness.

Language Status

Important decisions face most high schools regarding students with limited English proficiency (LEP); these SWS high schools were no different. In this context, staff must decide whether all LEP students should be enrolled in a single subunit (where perhaps services could be concentrated) or whether LEP students should have their choice of subunits (and thus the responsibility for serving them would be shared). Monroe and Adams, which had the highest proportions of LEP students among these schools, came to opposite conclusions about the issue. Monroe's large numbers of LEP students were allowed subunit choice (although very few selected MSM). Monroe's LEP staff, however, lamented that coordinating classes across multiple subunits limited their ability to serve these students well. During the period of our study, Monroe's LEP coordinator encouraged administrators to consider placing all LEP students into IBM (due to its international theme), thus denying them subunit choice.

Adams's solution was exactly what Monroe's LEP staff recommended. Rather than allowing Adams's LEP students subunit choice, all such students were enrolled in the International/Cooperative Learning (ICL) subunit, where the school's LEP program was centered. Unlike Monroe's overwhelmingly Spanish-speaking LEP population, Adams's LEP program served students from dozens of countries and language groups. Amazingly, ICL offered bilingual classes in Spanish, Portuguese, Haitian Creole, and Chinese; they also created English as a second language (ESL) classes for students who spoke languages other than these. ICL's unusually cohesive LEP staff told us that they would not be able to offer the tailored program they felt was necessary if the school's LEP students were spread across subunits.

Adams's staff and students recognized the social costs of segregating LEP students in one subunit. ICL was also located in a separate building, which further added to the sense that ICL was somehow "different" from the other subunits. But its isolated location also fomented unusually strong subunit cohesiveness (as we mentioned in Chapter 3). Recognizing the many disadvantages of segregation, during our study Adams administrators were negotiating with the LEP department about dividing its students among several subunits in order to limit social and academic isolation.

Academic Background

As we discussed in previous chapters, subunit hierarchies were built on a foundation of student academic difference. For example, every one of Monroe's MSM students passed their state's standardized assessment. At Adams, over half of College Prep and Alternative students achieved Honor Roll status, compared with less than a quarter of students in Vocational, Community, or Core Curriculum. Community students had twice as many course failures as those in College Prep, whereas College Prep students were 2.5 times more likely to take an advanced placement (AP) course than those in Community. Not one Vocational student passed any portion of the state's standardized test in 1998. Its history of low achievement led Adams administrators to close Vocational during the first year of our study. Although Adams continued to offer vocational courses, Vocational was no longer a choice as a stand-alone subunit for students beginning with the 1999–2000 school year. The subunit's weaknesses were so evident that almost no one—not even Vocational staff—protested its closure.

Academic differences among subunits also shaped teachers' beliefs about which subunits were the most desirable workplaces. Although some teachers expressed a special calling to work with their school's weakest students, a larger proportion admitted that they enjoyed teaching successful and motivated students. Recognition that particular subunits enrolled "better kids" influenced teachers' decisions about which subunits they would join. One Harrison teacher's preference for Health/Human Services (HHS) students reflected a general sentiment about the desire to teach students from "good" subunits. Moreover, this teacher made an explicit link between performance and behavior:

> HHS students are the elite—the most desirable to teach. I do like the HHS students better because they're better students. If you have an HHS class, they outperform the other students, as a general rule. And they're just nicer kids. It's a better group of kids that are choosing HHS. A lot of 10th graders in there are top students. And as a teacher, I like that.

DEFINING SUBUNIT QUALITY

Clearly, subunits in these five high schools were qualitatively and quantitatively quite different, with reputations ranging from "full of brains" to "dumping ground." Staff consistently recounted that the major differences between subunits were the types of students each enrolled. As such, subunits' successes and failures were attributable more to student self-selection than to particular subunit attributes or qualities (such as themes, instructional programs, or pedagogical approaches). For example, many of Monroe's non-MSM staff remarked that MSM's success accrued from the fact that it enrolled *already* successful students, not that MSM teachers offered superior instruction. MSM's head admitted, "We need to realize that people who express an interest in math and science are pretty much the stronger kids to begin with." An IBM teacher agreed:

> It's easy to work with those MSM kids because a lot of them just teach themselves. They teach you things, you know? They are self-motivated. They have their parents' backing. They just have so much going for them that a lot of teachers in other subunits don't have in dealing with their kids. So yeah, MSM looks more successful, but it's because of their students.

Grant's Health subunit head acknowledged that her subunit's good reputation was due in part to its ability to attract already-motivated students: "The inherent goof-off isn't going to pick Health, because it sounds harder." Harrison's Health/Human Services (HHS) subunit had a similar reputation. "There is a certain kind of student who gravitates towards health science," claimed a Harrison HHS teacher, "and there is the perception that health science is for the bright kids, the kids who want to be engineers or go into math, science, and all sort of medical things." In these two very different schools, staff across multiple subunits consistently claimed that self-selection drove the superior reputations of the Health subunits.

Explanatory arguments contrasting student self-selection with subunit instructional and programmatic quality were common, especially at Adams. Staff there engaged in continuous and passionate debate about whether Alternative and College Prep were better subunits, or whether they simply attracted better students. "We report achievement by [subunits] as though they had something to do with how the kid is doing," lamented an Adams subunit head, "and I don't think we can prove that, nor do I believe it's the case." An Adams teacher candidly reported on his colleagues' views: "A lot of teachers are aware of all this bullshit that goes on with, 'College Prep is better.' It's crap. But parents have bought into it lock, stock and barrel, and the fact is, a lot of the staff have too." Many Adams staff concurred that subunits' perceived successes were often due to student self-selection, for example:

> When you look at the student data reports, certain subunits look like they're doing well. But maybe they're doing well because these kids would have been doing well anyway, no matter where they were. It's like, "No, duh!" (Adams schoolwide administrator)

> College Prep looks pretty good when you're looking at student data reports. It doesn't really speak to anything that's going on with College Prep. In fact, I can tell you that College Prep has very mediocre teachers. (Adams subunit head)

Several College Prep teachers agreed that their instructional program was no better than those of other subunits. "I think the perception that College Prep attracts talented students is real. Whether or not it gives them any kind of superior education may be myth," a teacher in that subunit acknowledged. College Prep's head conceded that her subunit attracted motivated students largely because it already enrolled such students—a circular relationship from which the subunit benefited greatly. Her denial that her students' successes were due to superior instruction was adamant:

> One of the administrators from another subunit was walking down the corridor and stopped me and said, "You know, as I walk through this floor and I look into these rooms at the teachers that are in here, half of them can't teach themselves out of a wet paper bag, and I can't figure out why you're the subunit of choice." And just this morning, a teacher said to me, "You know, you have some of the worst teachers." And it's true.

However, other College Prep teachers spoke of the value of peers, asserting that high-achieving students benefited from being together. These teachers believed that College Prep students *did* receive a superior education, if for no other reason than the subunit's climate afforded beneficial peer effects. "Because they are together, I think they motivate one another," a College Prep teacher claimed, "and it probably enhances their performance." She added that allowing successful students to *avoid* unmotivated students via subunit choice was valuable, because "when you get into a class where there are not serious students, it's almost impossible to learn." The head of Alternative, Adams's highest-achieving subunit, agreed that peers strongly influenced the learning process: "We all know that you need a critical mass in every class who buys in to make it work. Once you go over the other way, it falls apart."

Other Adams staff expressed concern that the school's subunit choice system had departed from its original purpose: to allow students to select subunits based on learning styles and pedagogical approaches. Instead, high-achieving students simply chose subunits that enrolled other academically similar students. Indeed, Adams staff charged that many middle- and upper-class parents were actually supportive of the academic stratification provided by the SWS structure, in that it allowed their children to experience classes and subunits with other academically motivated students. The Alternative subunit head summed up this attitude:

> The kids want to be with kids who are, quote, "like them." And the parents want their kids with kids who are "like them." They're looking for peer groups—groups of kids who care about school. These families are very sophisticated consumers in this school.

Although quite logical from a student or parent perspective, the organizational implications of free-market choice for subunit segregation and stratification were profound.

THE PRODUCT OF DIFFERENCE

With the notable exception of principal Art Hernandez of Monroe High School, students and staff in the other schools claimed that the competitive atmosphere and social divisions that developed among subunits over time represented a serious and negative aspect of the SWS structure. In one sense, these social divisions could be seen as evidence of a successful SWS structure: committed groups of students and teachers had come together to forge common identities. Although such cohesion surely benefited some students, it created uncomfortable and even counterproductive environments for others.

The presence of MSM at Monroe promoted a divisive and competitive social environment. Non-MSM teachers noticed a sense of superiority among their MSM teacher colleagues. "They are segregated and separate," charged one LEP teacher, "and I've heard teachers say, 'Well, we are MSM. We need to start doing this,' almost directing the rest of the faculty." Monroe's central administrators implemented policies that actually increased this animosity among subunits. One example was that, by design, MSM classes (particularly AP classes) were quite small, which resulted in larger classes elsewhere in the school. Many teachers in other subunits commented on how unfair this was. Another example was that MSM teachers were eligible for an additional 2 weeks' salary per year, as compensation for additional training they received during the summer. "To me, that's the administration saying these teachers are worth more than the rest of us," charged a Generic 2 teacher. "We all work extra days, but the rest of us don't get paid for it like they do." An IBM teacher identified the antagonism among subunits as the least attractive element of the SWS structure:

I like the idea of schools within schools, I really do. And I think it works really well. I love teaching the same kids and knowing the kids so well. But I hate that competition, and I hate that idea that our kids feel like they are disadvantaged because they are in this program as opposed to MSM. I think it's terrible—subunits competing with other subunits.

Beyond the faculty, elitism and privilege also characterized the attitudes of many MSM students. In a focus group composed of only MSM students, one claimed that other students were "afraid to come into MSM because of the challenge; they know that their grades wouldn't be quite as high." In somewhat imperious tones, other MSM students asserted that because they were so clearly superior, comparisons between MSM and other subunits were pointless: "In a way we know the other subunits aren't competition," asserted one focus group member, "so we just compete with each other." His peer added, "It might sound kind of bad, like bragging, but it's true."

Unlike these MSM students, several Generic 1 students asserted that they *did* have something to prove, and that they were in direct competition with MSM. "We're the only ones that give MSM a run for its money," claimed one, "but we're just not up there yet." Resentment of the attention and benefits MSM students received was evident among Generic 1 students, some of whom claimed to have "lost friends" to MSM and its isolated culture.

> You get divided from your friends, and they start getting air-headed like, "Oh I'm better than you. I'm in this subunit, you're in that subunit. You're just idiots." And it's like, "Before, you were my friend, we were all good friends together, and now you're better than me?"

In several interviews, Generic 1 and 2 students vented frustrations about the social distance that separated them from MSM students:

- They always think they're better than everyone.
- MSM [students] hang around with each other.
- It's MSM, and then it's the rest of the school.
- They always want to be by themselves, and they think they are better than everybody else.
- They think, "We're better than you, so we'll sit over here in this section of the lunchroom. You guys just sit over there."
- They go down, get their food and come back to their section. And their section is the opposite of where we are.
- They are, like, stuck-up.
- They have a really bad attitude about how big they think they are.
- MSM thinks it's this high, but I think that every student is equal.

Such tensions erupted in a rather remarkable display of hostility one winter afternoon. At a schoolwide pep rally for an upcoming basketball game, the subunit with the best door decorations was to receive an award. When it was announced that MSM had won, many students from the other subunits loudly "booed" and yelled derogatory remarks. Equally surprising to us, Monroe teachers from other subunits did not intervene. This pep rally behavior was a major focus of conversation throughout Monroe for days afterward. Many teachers told us that they were pleased that schoolwide administrators had witnessed the event, hoping that it would highlight the hierarchies and animosity that had developed in this relatively new school. One teacher remarked, "If this doesn't open [Hernandez's] eyes to how the school feels about MSM, nothing will!"

We also noted unproductive social division at Adams High School. A schoolwide assistant principal worried that each subunit's desire to attract high-achieving students impeded collective, schoolwide efforts to improve teaching and learning:

> We are stratifying the high school in ways that I don't think are healthy. I see a sort of resegregation and warfare because we are competing for the same pool of people. You end up doing kind of a dog and pony show, with "I'm better than the next guy, so come to me." There is some feeling that we ought to be one high school working together, as opposed to six different places.

A schoolwide Adams music teacher invoked an anthropological metaphor to describe the competitive nature of Adams's SWS structure:

> It's tribalism. It's always existed in human society, and it probably will for many centuries more to come. It's, "My country's better than your country." "My state's better than your state," or "My part of the country, my town, my neighborhood, my block, my family's better than your family!" I mean, it just keeps going down to smaller and smaller units and the [SWS structure] is no different.

Such obvious social divisions among subunits troubled some students at Adams and Monroe, several of whom expressed their concerns in student newspaper editorials. An editorial in the Adams newspaper lamented, "With the perception that each subunit attracts a particular group of people, we are reminded that the seemingly wonderful, diverse world of Adams High School is not quite as diverse and integrated as it appears to be." At Monroe, subunits were called "blocks." A student editorial decried that though the SWS structure allowed for closer personal relationships within subunits, relations between subunits were often cold: "Most blocks' students are keeping to their group and have commenced to 'block out' other students; often thinking negatively of the students from other blocks, and even criticizing them."

RESPONSES TO SUBUNIT STRATIFICATION

Even though Monroe and Adams suffered equally severe stratification among subunits, the schools explained and rationalized their inequities quite differently. Although Monroe assistant principals took a laissez-faire approach to subunit disparities, principal Hernandez appeared to prefer and even promote them. Because students were choosing their subunits, he argued, the school could not be faulted for subunit differences; students were self-selecting themselves into different subunits. "*We're* not putting kids into MSM. *We're* not assigning kids to MSM. They are requesting to go into it," Hernandez argued. He viewed the academic and social imbalances between subunits as the natural result of MSM's higher expectations and more demanding curriculum. "That's what can be expected," Hernandez maintained. "A program like that's going to attract some of your brighter kids." He challenged our interviewer: "It's just like saying that you wouldn't expect a kid from the University of Michigan to outperform the kids that are going to some community college in the same area."

Although Monroe was among the most stratified schools we studied, Hernandez was the least willing to acknowledge the disadvantage resulting from inequities that existed among subunits. Despite the recognition among Monroe students and teachers that the Generic subunits were the lowest performing, he refuted the notion that "generic" in any context suggested a mediocre product. "'Generic' does not necessarily equate to 'inferior,'" he argued. "In fact, I will assure you it doesn't." Many teachers mentioned to us that Hernandez's own son was an MSM student. When asked to describe some advantages of choice-driven, free-market SWS structures, he bluntly replied, "It eliminates complacency!" He denied the proposition that such competitive systems invariably produced winners and losers, countering that Monroe's SWS structure was "ripe for a win–win situation." In our exit interview with him, Hernandez went on the offensive, asking rhetorically:

> Who would say that MSM is the winner? Why couldn't IBM, MSM, and Generic 1 and 2, all four of them be winners? They are not all competing for one prize. They are all competing for what? What is their goal? Their

goal is not to win a cup or win a title. Their goal is to try to prepare their kids for success when they get out of high school. Why would that not be a win–win situation?

One could certainly argue that the "cup" or "title" might include status and prestige, material and political resources, and the most talented students and teachers. With such outcomes as prizes in a universe of limited resources, MSM was the clear "winner." Despite Monroe's considerable inequalities, however, we wondered why many administrators were reluctant to admit to differences between subunits. One potential explanation is that unlike social science researchers, who tend to examine average differences between groups, Monroe administrators saw disparities not in terms of means but in terms of absolutes. For example, a schoolwide assistant principal denied that social-class disparities existed between MSM and the other subunits because not *all* MSM students were from affluent families: "I've never really investigated their levels of income, but I know that MSM has students who are very, very poor." Hernandez made a similar remark to dismiss the very clear academic differences between subunits: "Not every single bright kid that we have on this campus is in MSM, because some of them have opted not to go that route." This was certainly the case, but the fact remained that MSM enrolled a disproportionate number of high-achieving students from affluent families.

Adams teachers and administrators seemed less complacent about internal stratification and took steps to ameliorate between-subunit disparities. Adams had engaged the community in a frank, open, and sometimes heated dialogue about social and academic differences among subunits. The most contentious issue was the role of choice in the subunit allocation process, specifically the extent to which choice was the cause of Adams's internal segregation and stratification. Recall from Chapter 2 that Adams City was one of the premier locations for school choice in the nation. Adams staff generally agreed that subunit disparities had been tolerated because they were the result of student and family decisions, not school policies or practices.

As we recounted in Chapter 4, between the first and second year of our study Adams appointed a new, reform-minded principal: Angela Johnson. Very soon after undertaking the position, Johnson publicly questioned the legitimacy of choice and laissez-faire attitudes toward subunit stratification. "I like the idea of choice," Johnson claimed, "but I also think that choice here is a cover for what we don't do well. We say, 'You chose that lousy place, so it's not our fault.'" By providing students the right (and responsibility) of choice, she asserted, schools have often felt relieved of the responsibility to offer only high-quality courses and programs. In her view, choice often hampered school reform, because the impetus to improve is reduced when students willingly select low-quality offerings. For example, despite its obvious shortcomings, students continued to choose Vocational, thus prompting its intentional dismantling. Likewise, Community should have "gone out of business," were Adams's free-market system operating as market advocates suggest.

Teachers in Adams's premier subunits—Alternative and College Prep—were less concerned about stratification than Johnson. Several stated that high-achieving students simply sought and ultimately selected superior "products." An Alternative teacher claimed:

> If you build it, they'll come, but you can't complain if you don't build it. This elitist business drives me insane, because I don't know how elite it is that on our floor there are always people sitting out here working until 5:00 at night, talking with one another and sharing ideas.

Alternative's subunit head echoed this sentiment; she credited her subunit's high status to hard work and what she called "sweat equity." She resented Johnson's assertions that Adams's SWS structure required major restructuring, which she feared would come at Alternative's expense. Because they were "doing their jobs," she argued, Alternative's especially competent teachers would be separated and spread throughout the building to "help [improve] the other subunits." Although she conceded the importance of each subunit having a core of high-quality teachers, she contended, "I'm not convinced that shifting around the dead wood is going to make a change." In a quite prescient moment, she decried: "We're working hard. We're spending tons of hours. We're doing all this stuff. So now what is our prize? Our prize is we get to be divided up and shifted out to be with people who don't want to hear from us."

THE THREAT OF EXIT

The presence of these hierarchical subunit structures was exacerbated by the parents of academically successful students, many of whom appreciated the fact that particular subunits tended to attract academically oriented students. Although such pressures were sometimes viewed as bothersome, administrators recognized the importance of retaining affluent and educated parents within their schools. Ideas found in Hirschman's (1970) seminal book *Exit,*

Voice and Loyalty, are particularly relevant. A middle- or upper-class parent who feels dissatisfied with his or her child's public school has the option to "exit." Exit could take several forms: moving to another school district, transferring the child to another school in the same district (if school choice is available), or enrolling the child in private school. According to Hirschman, a dissatisfied parent may also use "voice" to express discontent through attempts to change the school. For lower income parents, however, exit is less often an option; moving and private schools require fiscal resources. Moreover, disadvantaged families are less likely to exercise voice (recall that it was affluent Adams parents who took advantage of the subunit appeals process). Therefore, less affluent parents' voices are less often heeded (or even heard). The reality is that the parents most likely to exercise voice are also those most likely to exit.

The threat of exit partly explains these schools' desire to offer subunits and programs such parents request. By doing so, however, the schools invariably increase internal stratification. The other high schools in Monroe's school district had developed districtwide magnet subunits similar to MSM and IBM. In a rare effort to justify the internal stratification caused by MSM, Monroe's Principal Hernandez argued that without MSM, high-achieving students would have chosen a selective program in another of the district's high schools. He claimed that the fierce competition for motivated students (and their families) forced the district's high schools to endure a certain degree of within-school stratification to avoid increasing between-school stratification. Hernandez much preferred allowing academically strong students to self-select into one subunit to losing them to another school altogether.

Conversations about within- versus between-school stratification were common at Adams, which was located in an inner-ring suburb that was losing its middle-class families. Although Adams was the district's only public high school, the metropolitan area offered many excellent public and private schools. As a result, district staff were very concerned about exit; they were committed to keeping high-achieving students in the high school and their ambitious parents in the community. Adams staff had evidence that higher-income parents would not hesitate to move their children to private schools if they felt the public high school was not serving them well. This motivation led them to offer subunits that attracted high-achieving students—particularly Alternative and College Prep. In discussing the type of families to which Adams felt it had to appeal, Adams's principal asserted, "We have to serve the elites well! Otherwise we would lose that whole population, because those people can afford to take their kids out—and they will."

Administrators in these five SWS schools were quite aware of the advantages that accrued from having high-achieving students and their parents in their schools. Thus, some of them worried that changing their SWS structures in the direction of more social equity might result in the loss of these families. Many affluent parents viewed schooling as a "zero-sum game," where attempts to create more equitable schools might disadvantage their own children. Schools and subunits that focus too much on equity risk losing middle- and upper-class families, in part because parents of academically successful students often feel that schools already serve their children well. Referring to other school settings, Wells and Oakes (1996) describe a bottom line, where "these powerful parents demand something in return for their commitment to public education—for keeping their children in public schools, as opposed to fleeing to the private schools that many could afford" (p. 139). Unfortunately, the cost of retaining such parents—although an important and worthy goal—is often an increase in social and academic stratification.

Of course, large urban school districts have faced this dilemma for decades. By offering "boutique" schools of choice or magnet schools, urban school districts aim to slow the exodus of high-achieving students. Although magnet schools and those with selective admissions policies may reduce stratification among school districts in a metropolitan area, they generally increase stratification among schools *within* the district. The obvious counterargument is that without access to selective high schools and programs, many high-achieving students and their parents would simply choose not to use urban public schools (and many thousands have already made that choice). It could further be argued, as staff in several of these SWS high schools did, that it is better to suffer internal inequality than to lose high-achieving students (and their politically adroit families) to other schools, districts, or the private sector.

CONCLUSION

Perhaps reflecting the conflicting roles played by public schools—crucibles for democratic equality on the one hand and vehicles for social mobility on the other—we found considerable ambiguity about equity and access in the five SWS high schools we studied. Democratic equality was enacted by all students being members of one subunit in a school, and by allowing choice as the dominant means to determine subunit membership. Social mobility was captured by the different themes around which the subunits were organized and the differential status these subunits were meant to convey. Importantly, the hierarchical natures of these subunit structures were quite apparent. Every informant we spoke with—teachers, administrators, and students—was able to quickly identify which were the strong subunits and which were the "dumping grounds."

Perhaps the hierarchical nature of these subunit structures should be no surprise; subunit career themes reflected the occupational status structure of U.S. society. At one extreme, several schools offered subunits with vocational themes, and these were invariably the ones informants identified as "dumping grounds." At the other extreme, subunits with health and explicit academic themes (e.g., humanities, math and science) invariably carried higher status. Even though many students did not choose their subunits because of an affinity with a particular career theme, the status or reputation the subunit held was a major motivator driving student choice.

Despite the efforts in some schools to create demographic balance across subunits (i.e., an effort toward democratic equality), the fact that schools were anxious to honor students' choices led to considerable stratification by students' race/ethnicity, social class, and gender. These demographic differences also produced quite disparate behavioral environments. Subunits with high minority enrollments or with high male enrollments were invariably locations where student behavior was seen as problematic, at the least, and at worst, "out of control."

Beyond (but perhaps concomitant with) demographic and behavioral stratification, subunits were also quite imbalanced by other student characteristics. Although these public schools served nontrivial numbers of students with special needs or limited English proficiency, the schools chose to carry out these missions quite differently. In some schools, specialized staff trained to serve such students were restricted to only one or two subunits. For example, a well-regarded and talented special education teacher was located in Adams's Community subunit, which resulted in unequal numbers (and consequent burdens) of such students in that subunit. We observed two very different philosophies about serving students with limited English proficiency (LEP) in the two schools enrolling high proportions of such students. At one school (Adams), LEP students had no choice; they were automatically assigned to a particular subunit (ICL), where the school's bilingual specialists were concentrated. At Monroe, LEP students were more equally distributed across three of the four subunits (not MSM). We heard bilingual staff at both of these schools thoughtfully discuss the various advantages and disadvantages of these two arrangements, and they evidenced a healthy understanding of these different approaches although arriving at very different conclusions. Neither approach was ideal, but both were quite rational.

More noticeable, explicit, and troubling to us was the stratification we observed among subunits in each school based on students' academic background and performance. Several subunits were constructed to attract and serve the most able students—Monroe's MSM, Adams's Alternative and College Prep, Arts/Humanities at Taylor, and the Health subunits at Harrison and Grant. Students in these subunits were disproportionately advantaged in obvious and visible ways. Students in other subunits—Monroe's Generic 2, Adams's Vocational and Community, Taylor's Mechanical, Harrison's ST, and Grant's Law/African American Studies—were just as visibly identified as the lowest scoring and the most problematic. Some schools, and some adults in these schools, found this type of stratification and differentiation natural or even desirable. However, many others (including students) found these public displays of privilege or scourge upsetting.

Why would these five schools tolerate, or even structure, such stratification among subunits? We heard many reasons. In one school (Monroe) the principal believed that the stratification in his school was a good thing; he felt that it engendered competition, and that this was a positive force in the school. Other informants believed that the between-subunit stratification in their schools simply reflected natural and inevitable differences in society. As such, the subunit stratification prepared students to participate in a stratified and capitalist adult world.

Especially common among our informants was the view that the schools needed to offer educational options where children of the elite could be well served. The means to accomplish this were to concentrate the best teachers, the most demanding courses, and the most motivated students in subunits enrolling the most elite students. We heard many comments about the value of "the peer effect," but very little mention of a negative peer effect, which would certainly result from concentrating the schools' lowest-performing students. The view in favor of isolating the high-achieving students often reflected educators' fears that their best students (and those students' parents) would select other schools or districts. Every adult with whom we spoke understood the advantages of enrolling high-performing students, and many were frank in their statements about having a preference to teach only such students.

We were not surprised to find some degree of stratification within these SWS high schools, because all of them had diverse student populations and most served relatively large proportions of socially disadvantaged students. However, because this study involved only schools that had not only engaged deeply in a serious reform but had also persisted with the same reform for several years, we were quite surprised by the presence of such a high degree of social stratification. Moreover, we were surprised that these otherwise innovative educational settings were so tolerant of a phenomenon the SWS structure highlighted quite blatantly. Our conclusion in this regard is quite simple: the ability to accommodate socially and academically diverse student populations and also attend to issues of social equity is a challenge for any high school, including those with the SWS structure.

8

Lessons and Recommendations Regarding Schools-Within-Schools High Schools

IT MIGHT SEEM greatly appealing—and now almost commonplace—to recommend that American secondary schools should become smaller in scale. Much of this appeal involves improved relationships—between adults and students, among school-based adults, and among students. If we knew one another better, it is reasonable to assume that we would work together more productively and would more easily coalesce around a set of worthy goals. These appealing ideas stand behind the substantial efforts of more and more U.S. high schools that are working to become smaller. A major means to this end—seemingly requiring very little financial or human cost—is for schools to divide themselves into schools within schools. These ideas not only motivated our research but were also quite common in the schools we studied.

When we undertook this study, so few schools had adopted this organizational form that we chose a deep inquiry into a small number of schools. Such a study design constrains our ability to generalize findings to the growing universe of such schools currently operating across the United States. However, we hope our readers agree with our decision to conduct an intense study of only five such high schools, particularly because these schools had engaged in the reform for many years. Drawing on our relatively deep knowledge of these particular schools, we offer two types of conclusions. First, we present eight lessons from the schools we studied that we hope will both stimulate more general conversations about American secondary school reform and also help school professionals who are considering this reform. Second, we conclude the chapter with four recommendations that we draw from these lessons.

LESSONS DRAWN FROM THE
SCHOOLS-WITHIN-SCHOOLS REFORM

Lesson 1: Subunits Are Socially and Academically Stratified

Despite many differences among the schools-within-schools (SWS) schools we studied, their structures were all organized around two basic elements: (a) subunits designed around themes, and (b) student choice among theme-based subunits. A common purpose across the schools for offering theme-based subunits—predominantly organized around students' future career plans—was to provide easily recognizable differences among them, so that students could make rational choices that were compatible with their current interests and future plans. As intended, the theme-based and career-oriented subunits in these five high schools definitely appealed to different types of students.

However, only a small minority of students reported choosing subunits based on their future career plans. Rather—and unsurprisingly—they chose their subunits in order to be grouped with people like themselves (also very rational). None of the schools we studied reported an intention to introduce social and academic stratification through the SWS design. In fact, many told us that they had moved to this design at least partly to diminish such stratification—at least as it previously had been reflected in curriculum tracking in their schools. However, our observations lead us to conclude that theme-based subunits operating within free-choice contexts lead to rather extreme—and structurally supported—social and academic stratification among subunits. Over the last two decades, a stated and major trend in U.S. secondary education reform has been to consciously move away from curriculum tracking. Nevertheless, we saw the subunits in many of these schools operating as another layer of school-based curriculum differentiation. Even if subunits were not socially stratified when the schools first reorganized into the SWS design, such stratification seemed to increase over time—as students sought out "others like themselves." It seems reasonable, perhaps inevitable, that choice would magnify this trend.

The lesson here is that theme-based subunit structures, particularly organized around future careers, may be inherently stratifying. Some readers may regard such stratification as quite appropriate in that it operates within a social and economic system in which professions and careers are themselves quite stratified. Some of our informants supported this view: they saw schools as necessarily reflecting the society their students would eventually join as adults. This is not our view. Rather, we believe that introducing particular mechanisms into schools that consciously stratify students—intellectually and socially—is inappropriate in U.S. secondary schools.

Recalling the dilemma raised by Cohen and Neufeld (1981) that "schools are public institutions oriented to equality in a society dominated by private institutions oriented to the market" (p. 70), we believe that the equalizing potential of these public institutions should not be subsumed by market forces. Rather, schools, which serve children, should at least in part be beacons of social equity. Thus, schools should move to reduce, rather than to increase, social stratification in educational outcomes. But these SWS schools did not seem to do that.

Lesson 2: Themes Don't Draw Students

The avowed purpose of organizing the schools' subunits around career-based themes was twofold: (a) to be authentically appealing to students with different interests and future plans, and (b) to use such authentic appeal to generate student engagement and commitment to school-based activities. Because the SWS schools we studied enrolled large numbers of students whose commitment to school (at least to the academic purpose of school) was seemingly marginal, the rationale seems reasonable. Moreover, in some instances we did observe students who might otherwise see school as quite marginal to their worlds (e.g., students in Harrison's Arts/Communications or Science/Technology subunits, or in Grant's Health subunit) who were quite engaged in school *because of* the subunits' themes and activities.

Although not absent entirely, matching of students' career interests and subunit themes was actually quite unusual. Particularly for subunits with stronger academic reputations (e.g., Harrison's Health/Human Services subunit, Monroe's Math/Science subunit, or Grant's Business subunit), students seemed to choose these subunits because of their academic reputations rather than their career focus. Moreover, in some subunits the themes were not well integrated into the academic programs. The few students who chose the subunits because of their career themes were often disappointed by not seeing the themes realized within or across courses.

The second lesson is that not only are theme-based subunits inherently stratifying but also the themes seem to be tangential to students' subunit choices. Although vocational themes were appealing to some adolescents who might otherwise be loosely committed to schooling, the costs—in terms of stratification and general lack of attraction to the themes—seem to outweigh the benefits for a few otherwise uncommitted students.

Lesson 3: All Options Are Not Equally Good

The trend toward providing more choice to students and families in the American educational marketplace seems unstoppable. The desire among the SWS schools to provide students with choices—mainly among subunits and also among courses within and across subunits—is quite fundamental. However, we need to remember that even adolescents in high school are still children, and children need some guidance in making good choices. We agree that providing young people with options helps them to develop skills in making and living with choices that will be an increasing part of their lives as adults. However, we observed that not all options provided to the students in the five SWS high schools we studied were good ones, in terms of preparing them for a future that would still be filled with choices. Asking young people to live (for 3 or 4 years) with bad choices is actually damaging. Moreover, some of the choices had potentially negative consequences for their lives after high school (i.e., they weren't preparing students to enter or succeed in college).

Here we refer primarily to choices among subunits. It is hard to argue that in Adams High School, a student would get an equally good education in the Community or Alternative subunits, or that a Monroe student would receive equal educational opportunities in the MSM or Generic 2 subunits. Each school discouraged students from changing subunits. Moreover, it would be practically impossible to move from a less demanding subunit, such as Grant's African American Studies, to a more demanding one, such as the Health subunit. Why? Students in the more academic subunits would have engaged in coursework early in their high school careers that would qualify them for the more demanding upper-level subunit courses (or advanced placement [AP] courses across subunits). Students without the skills acquired in entry-level courses taken early in high school would be less likely to succeed in more advanced and more demanding courses thereafter.

The lesson here is a fundamental issue about educational choice. If students are allowed to make choices within their secondary schooling, all options should be good ones, with equal value. Surely both educational professionals and parents of adolescents might have some disagreements about what constitutes good or bad options. However, we suggest that most adults would agree that allowing students (children, really) to make choices that look like "the easy way out" typically acts to restrict their educational futures. We suggest that structuring subunits around coursework that does not provide students with the skills and knowledge they will need when they face an even more important choice—whether or not to move into higher education, or which institution to shoot for—is unfortunate. We observed this type of low-level coursework in some subunits of all the schools we studied.

Lesson 4: Is Size Really the Issue?

Much of the recent criticism of American public high schools has revolved around their large size. Indeed, a major motivation for the SWS reform movement has been to reduce the actual size of the contexts in which most students experience their secondary education. Descriptions of high schools as large and impersonal institutions, where all but the most able students "fall between the cracks," are endemic in contemporary writings about high schools.

Within this rhetoric, the notion of dividing large high schools into smaller organizational units, where a few teachers get to know a relatively few students well, in course after course and year after year, seems to make sense. However, as we began this study and searched for schools with this organizational structure, we were surprised to find that it was not necessarily the largest high schools that had taken up the SWS design (Lee et al., 2001). Moreover, the SWS high schools in this study were not all large—Harrison and Monroe enrolled fewer than 1,500 students, Adams fewer than 2,000. Only Taylor (2,300) and Grant (2,600) would be seen by most observers as large high schools (see Table 2.1). Although a major stated motivation for dividing high schools into subunits is to reduce their scale, we suggest that enrollment size is as much a socially constructed idea as an actual student count.

When we began our study in 1999, the sizes of subunits also varied considerably (see Table 2.2). Subunit enrollments ranged from about 250 students (Alternative and Vocational at Adams, Science/Technology and Business at Harrison, International Business and Math/Science at Monroe, and Health/Human Services and Mechanical at Taylor) to over 400 students (College Prep and International/Cooperative Learning at Adams, Business at Grant, and Monroe's Generic subunits). Moreover, some subunits serving elite clienteles were allowed to limit their enrollments (Monroe's Math/Science and Adams's Alternative). This required other subunits to enroll more students, ultimately fostering resentment among teachers across subunits. Monroe's size grew substantially as it enrolled students from 9th to 12th grades in the second year of our study. As the school's overall size increased, enrollment in the Generic subunits rose to over 600 students—but the magnet subunits were allowed to remain small.

So far we have mentioned only school and subunit sizes. However, the dimension of size that teachers are most concerned about is class size, and class enrollments varied considerably both among and within these five high schools. Because these schools varied considerably in both their efforts and their desires to keep their subunits "pure," class size was not always a function of subunit size. Although certain elite and purposely small subunits were allowed to offer mostly pure classes (Adams's Alternative and Monroe's Math/Science), their classes (especially their more advanced classes) were quite small. However, such small classes resulted in quite large classes in other subunits. Again, this very visible inequality caused considerable resentment among teachers with larger classes. There was almost inevitable tension between keeping classes pure and having the number of faculty in a school dependent on its total enrollment. These conflicting phenomena led to considerable variation in class size and subunit size.

The lesson here is equivocal—although size was a common motivation for encouraging schools to move to the SWS organizational form, the smaller sizes that were envisioned at the outset were not always realized. The generally smaller subunit sizes did seem to lead to fewer students getting lost in the large variety of classes and activities that constitute high school. Curiously, the construct of "size" was no longer a driving force for the operation of these high schools once they had moved to the SWS form. We were surprised not to hear much discussion about size—of classes and subunits—in our extended conversations with members in these schools, with the exception of a few very vocal complaints about inequalities in class size.

Lesson 5: "Something's Gotta Give" (But It Usually Doesn't)

A few ideas and beliefs have driven U.S. comprehensive public high schools for well over a century. One of the Cardinal Principles laid out in 1918 motivates comprehensive high schools to this day: meeting the needs of different types of students is best accomplished by offering them different types of learning. That is, to serve well the diverse population of American high school students, schools should provide a breadth of instructional approaches and courses with differing levels of demand depending on a student's willingness to engage intellectual work. This would suggest that students could take many different routes—within the same high school—to a common goal: graduation. A common (but unsubstantiated) belief is that the current move to tighten the high school curriculum, which means increasing the number of demanding courses required for graduation, would increase the number of students who would drop out of high school.

The organization of the nation's public comprehensive high schools strongly reflects these fundamental beliefs. Although all five SWS high schools we studied had engaged in fundamental structural reform, they all showed some reticence to back away from major defining elements of the comprehensive high school. In Chapter 5, we described these as "hybrid" school organizations: part small school and part comprehensive high school. In a fundamental way, these SWS schools became even more stratifying after the adoption of the SWS model. With the introduction of stratification among subunits, each school exacerbated the divisions that already separated students based on their academic coursework. To meet what they thought were the needs and desires of their students, these SWS high schools had (a) created a hierarchical subunit structure, (b) retained low-level academic courses (often confined to certain subunits), and (c) permitted choice both among subunits and among courses.

The lesson here is quite simple. The basic ideas driving schools within schools are quite incompatible with the basic ideas that have driven comprehensive high schools for more than a century. Schools need to make some decisions about what elements should go from the comprehensive high schools they supposedly left behind. However, it takes commitment to certain ideas and courage to drop particular attributes of schools that may be compatible with the organizing ideas supported by communities and parents. The tensions inherent in these hybrid structures greatly limited the benefits generally associated with smaller high schools.

Lesson 6: Subunit Autonomy Comes at a Price

One of the fundamental tenets of the SWS reform is that subunits should operate with considerable autonomy, also an important dimension of the high school reform design advocated by the Bill and Melinda Gates Foundation. There was considerable variation in the degree to which the subunits in the schools we studied were able to attain (or desired) autonomy. Certain subunits' autonomy resulted from their offering few courses that were of interest to other students (the subunits with business and vocational themes, for example). The subunits at Grant High School were quite autonomous from the outset, for three reasons. First, autonomy was very important in the context of the SWS design in that school and district. Second, students applied directly to the subunits, rather than to the larger high school. Third, the school was willing to sacrifice honors and advanced (especially AP) courses to achieve this. The same sacrifice of AP courses—also to attain autonomy—was also a feature of Taylor High School. However, these two inner-city high schools both served disadvantaged clienteles, so perhaps student demand (or the necessary prerequisites) was limited. There were many AP courses at Adams, and also great demand for them. Such courses were spread across subunits, which detracted from autonomy. Harrison High School had moved the school's mathematics curriculum completely outside the subunit structure so that the school could differentiate and track math courses in a manner quite standard and well understood in comprehensive high schools. Thus, Harrison subunits no longer offered courses in this core subject.

Each school struggled with how best to operate low-enrollment, specialized, and remedial courses within a subunit structure that favored autonomy. Some schools chose to locate all such courses in a single subunit (e.g., AP math and science courses were concentrated in Monroe's MSM subunit, bilingual education was confined to the International/Cooperative Learning subunit at Adams). However, the usual approach was simply to offer such courses outside of the official subunit structure, to house them in whatever subunit the teacher happened to be affiliated, and to allow students from all subunits to enroll. A general tendency we observed (most overt at Adams) was that as students advanced from lower-grade to upper-grade courses, the autonomy of subunits decreased.

The lesson here echoes Lesson 5: SWS schools simply cannot have it all. As they move from a comprehensive to an SWS design, some hard decisions must be made. Taylor and Grant decided to drop AP courses altogether (to the consternation of some), but most schools decided to keep almost all of the elements of the comprehensive high school (e.g., band, yearbook, AP courses, bilingual education, special education, advanced foreign language courses, different levels of the same courses). Adams considered moving AP courses to early morning before school started, but decided against this because it would disadvantage students who had to expend more time traveling to school. We saw these schools compromise many elements of the SWS organizational structure in order to retain the familiar comprehensive design. Schools need to decide which elements of school design are important and which must be let go. That means they need to attach differential priorities to various design elements. As in most of life, "You can't have it all!"

Lesson 7: State Policy Is Increasingly Affecting the Schools-Within-Schools Curriculum

Our observations here are limited to the five states where our schools were located and to the policy environment in those states during the period of our study (late 1990s, early 2000s). Our discussion here is a bit oblique, in order to honor our promise to avoid revealing the identity of the schools by not describing the states where they are located. During our study of the schools, two of "their" states had enacted new policies that had direct effects on the schools. In both cases, the policies moved to require academic assessments at particular high school grades. Because such policy directives have become even more common since we concluded our study, the lesson here is probably even more widely applicable now than then.

In one state, the policy change was quite profound. Not only did the state introduce high-stakes testing in high school, but the policy also made quite specific requirements about what was taught (and when) in courses in the state's public high schools—particularly in the core subjects of English and mathematics. Within our SWS school in that state, success rates on the state assessment in those subjects varied considerably across subunits. Subunit success rates were quite predictable, based on the type of students each subunit enrolled (e.g., by race and class). In that school, many parents and some faculty publicly proclaimed their opposition to the state assessment (i.e., they were antitesting). Despite the opinion of some parents, the school was unable to ignore either its relatively low overall ranking compared with demographically comparable high schools across the state or the stark differences in success rates across subunits. During our study, many subunit faculty were up in arms about state requirements to create a more common curriculum in 9th and 10th grade in English and mathematics. They recognized that such a move would detract considerably from subunit autonomy.

In the state where another of our SWS schools was located, policy issues took on added importance during our study, but the problem was slightly different. All of the states' high schools were ranked according to average student performance on the state test (this occurred before the more widespread rankings of elementary schools required by the "No Child Left Behind" [NCLB] legislation). Privileges or sanctions flowed to schools based on these rankings. Predictably, in some subunits almost all students achieved the criterion for success on the assessment, whereas in other subunits very few passed. The problem here was that the whole school was ranked—based on average performance—so that cross-subunit differences were externally unimportant. Moreover, lower scoring students were affiliated with the larger subunits, further depressing the average. As this state-level ranking occurred just as we finished our study in that school, we did not learn how the ranking influenced future procedures in the school. However, because between-subunit comparisons were extreme, such questions as "What are those people doing down there?" were asked by faculty in the high-ranking subunit about the low-ranking subunit. Although this would imply that some faculty questioned the instructional effectiveness of their colleagues in other subunits, our observation was that most differences resulted from the types of students in the subunits rather than instructional variation across subunits.

The lesson we draw here is quite general, but it seems important for schools that may be considering the SWS design. Both the states and the federal government seem to be moving in the direction of ascribing more and more importance to school average performance on statewide standardized tests and to comparing subgroups within the schools based on performance. NCLB now includes assessment requirements for high schools, and virtually all states have moved toward more accountability based on student assessments. This strong movement toward schoolwide accountability will surely impinge on the autonomy that subunits seem to have, about the courses they offer, how they teach those courses, and whom they enroll. Moreover, subunit enrollments very often reflect differential demographic compositions, and this kind of stratification would tend to increase (rather than decrease) performance differences by demographic subgroups. We suspect that many SWS advocates see this trend as ominous, and they may be quite justified in this concern. As we make clearer in our recommendations about curriculum later in the chapter, for us this might not be a bad thing.

Lesson 8: The Schools-Within-Schools Reform Doesn't Necessarily Lead to Instructional Improvement

Dividing schools into subunits is, in essence, an organizational or structural reform. In theory, the reform itself has very little to say about the main "business" of schools: teaching and learning. Although we saw some hope that teaching and learning would improve as a result of this rather fundamental structural change, we neither located nor heard many articulated guidelines on how this might proceed. In Chapter 3, we described several subunits that we believed functioned well—where teaching and learning were restructured by smaller groups of teachers with common ideas working closely together as a result of their being located within an SWS school. Moreover, this type of improved instruction was possible in settings that did not enroll the school's students with the strongest academic performance. The subunits we chose to highlight were able to capitalize on their themes (Harrison's Arts/Communications and Adams's International/Cooperative Learning).

The promise of improving teaching and learning within the SWS setting seems similar to the rationale for why charter schools might function well. That is, when a relatively small group of students (and parents) come together with a group of teachers, and all are drawn by a particular theme or approach to teaching and learning, good things often happen. In this sense, it would seem that the SWS structure could serve as a catalyst to improve teaching and learning. However, without any guidelines for doing this, and without a strong and shared purpose or agreement about what direction to move in, it seems unlikely that the SWS reform all by itself would be a catalyst for improved instruction. Even if teachers and/or students are drawn to particular themes— such as Math and Science, Business, Health, or Arts and Humanities—we seldom heard agreement about what might be the best way to actually structure and integrate such courses around these ideas or about the format instruction might take. This issue was raised by Leslie Siskin (1994a) in her description of restructuring of a single California high school.

During our study, we were surprised that we didn't observe more innovative instruction in these schools, which had experienced dramatic restructuring. At first we thought that this relative paucity of innovative teaching was a result of our research design—neither did we use instructional improvement as an factor in selecting the schools nor did we ask the schools to let us observe the most innovative teachers. Rather, in preparation for our first visits we asked schools to direct us to one subunit they thought was particularly strong and another that was struggling in some way. In every case, the subunits recommended as the strongest were those that enrolled the schools' strongest students.

However, instruction in the classes we observed in those "strong" subunits seemed particularly traditional—teachers did almost all the talking, students were expected to supply "the right responses" in class discussions, and there was very little probing of important ideas or disagreement about what the "coda" in these classes was. If we observed innovative teaching—where themes were integrated across courses, where students had a strong role in devising what (and how) to study, where students were encouraged to disagree about fundamental issues, where learning was organized around theme-based projects that extended over several days or weeks—it was generally in the subunits that the schools designated as struggling in some way. Grant's Health subunit, which enrolled some of that school's stronger students, was an exception. Mostly, it seemed to us that schools allowed teachers to "experiment" with innovative teaching only in classrooms enrolling students who were not seen as on the "fast track" to college. It is as though there was less to risk by using innovative teaching methods with such students.

Our final lesson here is multifaceted. Even when teachers are enthusiastic about the SWS design, and even when the design leads to some fundamental changes in their work lives (e.g., closer contact with colleagues, more shared information about students, more interaction with the same students over time), there seems to be little fundamental link between this type of school restructuring and instructional change. It seems logical that teachers would continue to teach as they had before the reform—unless there was some impetus, some professional development, and/or some encouragement to do otherwise. We saw that some teachers, in some subunits, seemed to capitalize on the reform by cooperating more, by being more open about their practice, and by making serious attempts to weave the themes into their courses. But most of the teachers we spoke with and/or observed felt neither obliged nor motivated to do this. Nor did the schools seem to be pushing instructional change.

Over several years, we have had several conversations with James McPartland, the long-term director of the Talent Development High School reform program (TD). He frankly admitted that at the beginning, the major improvements in schools that had adopted the TD model were targeted at improving social control. The schools almost immediately became more orderly and the students more disciplined (and this includes TD member Taylor High School in our study). However, after a few years both the TD developers and the schools that had adopted the TD model began to wonder whether (and how) achievement would improve. The obvious conclusion here—and one that school reformers need to consider seriously—is that students learn what they are taught. That is, the absolute heart and soul of school reform directed at improving learning is the reform of instruction. We restate Lesson 8 in a set of rhetorical questions:

- Is a structural reform enough to improve student performance, or must the reform also involve more fundamental changes to a school's technical core: teaching and learning?
- Even if teachers are enthusiastic about the structural reform, does this mean that they are also enthusiastic about changing their instruction?
- Does organizing a school into a set of theme-based and relatively autonomous subunits mean that the smaller teaching teams will actually come together to work as an instructional team, to open their practice, and to change what they do?

Unfortunately, we must answer each of these rhetorical questions with resounding "no!"

A model that is often invoked by advocates of SWS is Central Park East Secondary School (CPESS), at its outset directed by Deborah Meier. This model small high school, located in the middle of Spanish Harlem in New York City and enrolling disadvantaged students, was a school that surely "worked." However, teachers joined the team (and were selected) at CPESS to work in an environment where everyone was committed to a clear model of teaching and learning; students applied to (and were selected) based on their (and their parents') embrace of this model of teaching and learning. The type of choice that underlined success at CPESS—choice of school by students or teachers—is different from what we observed in the five settings we studied. Instead, the major choice mechanism was subunits. Students overtly chose subunits, as did some teachers. Only a few of those choices were based on pedagogical or career-based themes. Recall that one Adams teacher told us that she chose her subunit based on where it would be physically located in the school—she wanted to stay in the same classroom. Other teachers chose subunits based on their subject-matter expertise; those trained in science or advanced mathematics chose to affiliate with math/science subunits. Business teachers naturally chose to join a business subunit. We heard only a little discussion of teachers choosing to join subunits because they wanted to group with others who held similar ideas about pedagogy. Our highlighted subunits—Harrison's Arts/Communications and Adams's International/Cooperative Learning—were exceptions.

If the SWS model is to instantiate the causal links to improved academic achievement, as we articulated in Figure 3.1, then we suggest that schools need to place more importance on the box that we labeled "Teacher Attitudinal and Behavioral Outcomes." More emphasis must be placed on the elements we labeled "increased collaboration" and "increased collective responsibility for student learning."

RECOMMENDATIONS TO SCHOOLS CONSIDERING THE SCHOOLS-WITHIN-SCHOOLS REFORM

The lessons we have drawn from our research are descriptive, and they are rather closely liked to the empirical evidence from our study. However, in this section we offer recommendations that are more prescriptive than descriptive. Altough they flow from our study of the five SWS high schools, we also base them on our own ideas about education that have developed over our combined years of research, teaching in schools, and broad experience in schools. Our recommendations to high schools considering adopting the SWS structure are in many ways more personal than the lessons described earlier in this chapter. Although they flow from our study of five SWS high schools, they also go somewhat beyond the data from the study.

Recommendation 1: Strive to Reduce, Not Increase, Stratification

Our recommendation here is quite fundamental, in that it would apply to almost any school reform. We base this recommendation on what is, for us, a bottom-line issue: any reform that increases social stratification in educational outcomes is—in and of itself—harmful. We recognize that social stratification is a reality in our society, and that stratification in educational outcomes begins early. Our recent report about race and class disparities in academic achievement as children begin kindergarten documented substantial social disparities in achievement that were not explainable even when we took into account a wide array of demographic, behavioral, and activity differences among children's families (Lee & Burkam, 2002).

Schooling—particularly at the elementary and secondary levels, where all children are required to attend—is one of the very few social interventions that is experienced by virtually all our nation's citizens (and many noncitizens as well). We adhere strongly to the democratic aims of schooling. One of the fundamental aims in this regard is that schools should be vehicles where the strong association between family background and educational outcomes should be weakened rather than magnified. We recognize that schooling is not the only cause of social stratification in educational outcomes. However, we argue that a major responsibility of schools is to ameliorate rather than exacerbate such stratification.

Very few schools consciously create experiences for their students that are associated with race/ethnicity, gender, or socioeconomic status. How our schools are organized—to meet the differing needs of different students—is chiefly meant to address differences in student performance, rather than race, class, or gender. Many educational programs are designed to provide fundamentally different experiences to students based on their performance or their plans for the future. The problem is that students' current performance and future plans are often linked to their social backgrounds. Thus, even without consciously differentiating students' experiences in school by race, class, or gender, allowing substantial differentiation by academic performance or future plans results in stratification by students' social background characteristics.

The enormous race and class differences that exist in student outcomes at the end of high school should not be surprising, simply because of differences in experiences along the way in school—especially in high school. If initial race and class differences in performance increase as children move through school, it seems reasonable to conclude that the schools play an important role in making this happen. We believe that all schools—and surely the nation's public high schools—have a responsibility to take actions that very consciously aim to weaken the links between social background and student outcomes (mostly achievement, even more important—learning, and perhaps graduation). To us, this is a fundamental issue, a bottom-line conclusion.

Thus, the stratification we observed that was so obvious in these SWS high schools is something that SWS schools need to address and change. To identify subunits with themes that reflect the stratification in adult professions and careers—from auto mechanics for some to law, medicine, or humanities for others—will surely sort students by race, class, and gender. This is exactly what we observed. To create an elite subunit such as Math/Science at Monroe High School, and then to relegate other students who either do not understand what this type of sorting is about, have not developed habits where working hard in school is expected or required, or have not accumulated the prerequisite academic or behavioral school records to "generic" subunits is antithetical to what we think our nation's public schools should stand for. This was a particularly egregious example of stratification, but we observed less obvious but equally damaging sorting in other schools. Is it right that one subunit have high academic standards and challenging classes (e.g., College Prep at Adams) while another subunit in the same school has lower standards and aims just to graduate its mostly Black students (Community)? Should these two subunits stand side by side in the same school, and next to another subunit that students openly call "the Haitian station"? We think not. Just because the schools have allowed such differentiation to occur by student choice (even with attempts to balance subunit enrollments by race) does not make it right. We think that it is wrong that such stratification is supported by our most important public institution—the public schools.

Thus, we recommend that SWS high schools consider very carefully the themes around which they organize their subunits and the type of students they allow to enroll in particular subunits—even if the students choose to be there. Throughout the book we have provided evidence that what we have observed— the combination of career-based themes and market-based choices—has increased social stratification in academic outcomes. We are not opposed to choice. However, we recommend that children should be provided with only good options from which they may choose. Although reasonable people may disagree about the value of particular options, it is possible to agree about which choices keep students' future options open. And those options should include a high school preparation that would allow students to matriculate to their state's universities and colleges. Although some subunits may include activities that seem to have a more vocational feel, such as Harrison's Science/ Technology or Arts/Communications, they should also incorporate coursework that is demanding for all students. We recognize that this is not easy—but we hold that it is right.

Recommendation 2: Be Thoughtful About the Curriculum

Subunit autonomy was a theoretical and fundamental aim in all the SWS schools we studied. However, complete autonomy could lead to very different curriculum offerings across subunits. Although the study of curriculum was not a major issue for our study, it was impossible to ignore the considerable variation in curriculum that we saw. Our recommendations about curriculum flow directly from our first recommendation—to reduce rather than magnify social stratification. We wish to be consistent here with our extant writings about curriculum. Our recommendations also draw upon our other empirical work (e.g., Bryk et al., 1993; Lee, 2001; Lee & Bryk, 1988, 1989; Lee et al., 1998), which suggests that students learn more, and that learning is more equitably distributed, if they attend schools that offer a core curriculum that includes mostly academic courses, and that such courses are taken by all students, regardless of their prior school performance or future educational plans.

Although it might seem that the idea of a common academic curriculum and the SWS design would be incompatible, we do not believe that this is necessarily true. We recommend that low-level courses in academic subjects be purged from the high school curriculum—in all subunits. Because subunits are small, reducing the number of courses offered should be both logical and easy. All students should engage in high-level and challenging learning, regardless of which subunit they belong to. Our observations documented in Chapter 3 suggest that in a few subunits, even those that served nonelite students, it was possible to weave themes into academic courses, to integrate courses across subjects, and to still retain rigorous content and solid instruction. It may be the case, for example, that if the Community subunit at Adams or the Mechanical subunit at Taylor were to shift their coursework so that all courses had solid academic content, high expectations, and demanded high-level work from all students, these subunits would not have such high enrollments of Black and male students. If all subunits offered nothing but demanding courses, Black students (especially males) would surely distribute themselves more evenly across subunits. Obviously, making such curricular changes would create quite different subunits—and that would be good.

We recommend that SWS schools (indeed, all secondary schools) move toward a narrower and more common curriculum with mostly academic content. Students who enter high school with academic deficiencies might initially be unable to succeed in such courses. Rather than placing such students in remedial courses, we recommend that they be required to engage in "double doses" of entry-year courses—particularly in math and English—along with taking the demanding courses that are appropriate for their grade levels. This type of curricular "doubling up" is currently in operation in several high school settings; Talent Development high schools do this, all public high schools in Chicago do this, and Catholic high schools have been doing this for decades. There might be some choice in these high schools, but the choice would be between a set of demanding subunits and demanding courses within them. However, there should be no choice for low-performing students to avoid these "double doses" of academic courses. Such students should be required to continue the doubling up only until they function well (i.e., at grade level). There is no reason that the subunit themes could not be woven into all courses, regardless of content or rigor. And there is no reason why currently low-performing students cannot be allowed to engage fully in their high school's or their subunit's curriculum. This type of curriculum, combined with moving away from hierarchical subunit structures, would transform high schools away from stratification and toward an engaging and meaningful academic experience for all students.

Recommendation 3: Monitor Programs and Change Them if Necessary

In Chapter 4, we described a governance structure that seemed to shift many of the functions of high school administrators to the subunit level and away from the typical schoolwide administrators' responsibilities. If curriculum decisions, discipline, and guidance counseling are accomplished within subunits, what responsibilities should be retained by schoolwide administrators? We saw considerable variation in this regard across our schools. Monroe's principal micromanaged every aspect of his school, whereas Grant's principal thought that her main responsibility was to garner resources from the district for the school and move them down to the subunits. Whatever governance structure a SWS high school adopts, the role of the building-level administrative staff must be considered.

We suggest some guidelines. For example, a major responsibility of any building-level administrator—principal, assistant principals, guidance staff, or individuals charged with monitoring such special programs as English as a second language or special education—should be to monitor and regulate the between- and within-subunit stratification we have described throughout this book. Not only should the schoolwide administrative staff be responsible for making sure that subunits are well balanced by race, class, academic perform-ance, and school commitment at the outset, but they must also monitor sub-unit enrollment characteristics over time. If subunits became more balanced (the Epilogue describes how this occurred in Adams High School), then the tendency to magnify differentiation within subunits could increase. Clearly, the appeals process operating in Adams should be abolished. Although it might seem appropriate in some cases for students to move from one subunit to another, such moves should not be outside of the decision-making authority of the school itself and should not upset social and academic subunit balance.

Although we recommend that SWS high schools move toward a core cur-riculum across subunits, decisions about how to infuse the courses with the-matic content should be relegated to the subunits. However, school-level administrators should also monitor these decisions—with the aim of reduc-ing or preventing social stratification. Moreover, school staff may benefit from some explicit professional development about how to do this well. Clearly, such monitoring will be easier, and received more warmly, when the entire administrative team (subunit and central) is working from a common set of guiding principles. Somehow, the role of the school-level administrators should be strengthened from what we observed in several schools. Not only is the principal the building leader (or the head of a leadership team) to garner resources and advise and coordinate subunit administrators, but this person is also the school's intellectual and moral leader. We see educational equity as central to a school's moral responsibilities.

Recommendation 4: Be Willing to Examine All Aspects of High School

As anyone who works in a high school will attest, educating adolescents is hard work. All high schools operate under a rich and dense set of assumptions—the "givens" of U.S. secondary schools. As we have stated repeatedly, but want to repeat as we conclude the book, at least some of these "givens" need revisiting.

As sociologists of education operating in university settings, it may be much easier for us to recognize and confront these "givens" than it is for the hard-working and committed professionals who staff our nation's high schools. A classic question with which we begin our own university-based courses on the sociology of education is "Should our nation's schools simply reflect the society in which they operate and the citizens whom they serve, or should schools be one location that attempts to improve our society?"

School-based professionals clearly feel the pressures of the first part of this question. Public schools are largely locally controlled—run by elected school boards and funded, in large part, with local taxes. Moreover, the parents of children whom the schools serve deserve to make their wishes known and to learn about their children's educational opportunities, experiences, and progress. While recognizing the public pressures on schools to serve the societies in which they operate, we also feel the need to emphasize that schools also have responsibilities to serve the society by enforcing socially accepted behavioral norms, exposing students to important social issues that they may someday play a role in correcting, and recognizing and actively trying to ameliorate social stratification in our society. Those of us who study schools may have the luxury of stepping back (and advocating) that schools have some responsibility to improve our society.

Every school—whether it enrolls very young children or adolescents who are often taller, stronger, and more opinionated than the adults who educate them—should engage themselves in some very fundamental questions. We offer a few for consideration:

- What is the nature of our school's role and responsibility in this society to educate the children we serve?
- What are the guiding principles around which our staff wants to organize this school where we work?
- What should all adolescents learn in this school? Should all students learn the same thing? If not, who should learn what, and who should make those decisions?
- What is the best way to organize instruction in our school to be consistent with our goals and principles about what to teach and to whom to teach it?

It is clear to us that many of the dedicated individuals who work in the five public high schools divided into schools within schools that we studied have deeply engaged such questions. Otherwise, they would not have decided to divide up their schools in the ways that they did (or, in the case of Monroe, design a new school with this form). But it is also obvious that we have been critical of some of the decisions that these individuals either consciously made or less consciously allowed to happen. We recognize that most of these decisions were arrived at in good faith, despite their sometimes unforeseen consequences. Perhaps if the schools had addressed some such set of fundamental questions at the outset, and the staff had engaged in the long and difficult decisions to arrive at solid consensus about these issues, we would have more examples of well-functioning subunits like Harrison's Arts/Communications, Adams's International/Cooperative Learning or Alternative, or Grant's Health subunit. What is startling to us is that these subunits (and others we do not mention here) were able to function well within larger schools where other subunits functioned badly. We end where we began—by stating that unless SWS schools are quite careful, they will magnify rather than weaken social stratification in their students' educational outcomes.

The difficulty in such discussions—and the willingness to engage in actual implementation of reforms that address them—is that virtually every element in the high schools must be "on the table." This reform has the potential to so fundamentally change how high schools function that almost everything needs to be considered. To make it easier to decide which elements to retain and which to change, the people who are considering reform should be willing to discuss some very profound questions such as those we offered earlier in the chapter.

A FEW LAST WORDS

We are somewhat critical of many of the writings about small schools and the SWS organizational form because they seemed to be couched in an advocacy tone. Unlike many of these writers, we came to this topic as agnostics. We have frankly reported a few convictions about schools (particularly about the importance of both excellence and equity) that we both share, and each of us has taught university courses that explicitly focus on issues of educational equity. We also share a firm conclusion about the importance of the organization and structure of schools, and we have published research that documents this importance. One of us (Lee) had devoted considerable research effort to studying the link between high school size and student outcomes (mostly learning). One of those studies concluded that U.S. high schools should be smaller than they are, and that the SWS design could be an economically feasible means to accomplish this aim without tearing down large high school buildings and constructing new small ones (Lee & Smith, 1997).

We began this study with a deep respect for the high schools who engage in this reform, and we maintain that respect to this day. This is a profound reform, in that it requires existing comprehensive high schools to consider and very likely change many aspects of their day-to-day operations. In the schools we studied, we saw (and heard about) school professionals engaging in deep conversations about such important topics as, What courses should we offer? Who should teach what? and How should adolescents' lives be organized? We also heard accounts of even more fundamental conversations of this type when the schools were considering a move to an SWS design. Schools and staff who are willing to discuss such important questions are unusual, and the willingness to engage in the discussions—and invest the time, effort, and soul-searching they require—is laudable. The dialogues in which these schools engaged— both during the period we studied them and, even more important, as they decided to move toward the SWS reform—are valuable in themselves. We suggest that every high school should engage periodically in such discussions— even those that are not considering such changes to address deep problems.

The schools that engage in this reform decided to go beyond talking about these fundamental issues and to actually do something about them. Any educational reform that forces adults to reexamine the "givens" of schools is good, and those who decide to challenge these "givens" are courageous. Thus, we suggest that almost any reform that looks critically at virtually every aspect of the traditional comprehensive high school is valuable. Our final conclusion about the "goodness" of this reform is that it requires that adults engage in reflection about what they do every day with their students. Moreover, the structure of the reform—breaking a big school into many small schools— is generally a good idea.

Hopefully, our deep study of a few secondary schools divided into schools within schools will be helpful to those who are considering engaging in this design, and perhaps will also help schools that have only recently chosen this reform. We do not want our readers to conclude that we think that this ambitious organizational idea is not a good one. Carefully done and closely monitored—with attention to what is taught, to whom it is taught, and how it is taught—we believe that the schools-within-schools high school reform can accomplish wonderful things.

■ ■ ■

Epilogue

IN THIS BOOK we have recounted one calendar year in the lives of five high schools divided into schools within schools. However, we were also interested in how these particular schools have fared since 1999. More broadly, we wanted to know more about the schools-within-schools (SWS) reform's resiliency in the face of institutional change. With these aims, we conducted an additional round of briefer visits to each school in mid-2001, about 18 months after completing our main rounds of data collection. Since these last visits, we have kept track of each school through phone and e-mail conversations, the Internet, and local media. These schools have experienced considerable change; some have confronted substantial turmoil.

All schools have maintained the SWS organizational form, albeit in somewhat different manifestations. One school (Harrison) received a major grant from the Bill and Melinda Gates Foundation to support redesign of its SWS structure, which many of our informants thought was in danger. To create a more equitable SWS structure, another school (Adams) dismantled its subunits, created new nonthemed subunits, and eliminated student subunit choice. Despite the continued presence of the SWS structure, other schools (Taylor, Grant, Monroe) were morphing back into comprehensive high schools, as schoolwide curriculum and the "shopping mall high school" trumped subunit autonomy. In addition to these structural adaptations, changes in leadership were endemic. Only one school (Taylor) had the same principal in 1999 and 2001.

Organizing the Epilogue around these structural and personnel transformations, we asked ourselves several key questions. How adaptable is the SWS structure to changes in leadership, student demographics, and state and district policies? How do tensions between "small" and "comprehensive" play out over time? Perhaps most important, how have equity and equal access been influenced by structural changes in each school's SWS design and by philosophical changes in how they approach the reform?

ADAMS HIGH SCHOOL

Adams experienced the greatest transformation of the five schools; it was a very different school in 2002 than when our study began. Between 1999 and 2002, administrative structures, student assignment processes, and the subunits themselves were entirely dismantled. Events at Adams during this period raise two important issues about school reform: (a) the political dangers inherent in fundamental reform, and (b) the limitations in what reform-minded leaders can accomplish.

Momentous Change in the Schools-Within-Schools Structure

The seeds of change were planted during previous administrations, but Angela Johnson's term as principal catalyzed reform that would affect virtually every aspect of daily life at Adams. Only five months into her tenure, Johnson presented a dramatic restructuring plan to the Adams School Board. The plan's central aim was to reduce the stratification endemic in Adams's existing SWS structure. The plan proposed to replace the existing subunits—several of whose histories dated back a quarter century—with five identical small schools. In a city where support for educational choice approached religious fervor, the plan eliminated subunit choice and randomly assigned students to themeless subunits. To put it mildly, the plan was greeted with suspicion. Johnson later told us, "I knew we were playing with fire."

Stories in the local newspaper suggested that the restructuring plan took the community by surprise. When asked what type of feedback she had received from parents, Johnson laughed and replied, "A lot of crap," particularly from parents of high-achieving students. Adams held several meetings for parents of 8th graders at the end of the 1999–2000 school year to explain (and build support for) the restructuring plan. One teacher reflected that the general sentiment among more educated parents was, "I'm four-square for equity, but I want my kid to be challenged." While nodding toward the need for a more equitable SWS structure, such parents argued that it should not come at the expense of rigorous, college-preparatory education. "The parents wanted reassurance that their kids would be challenged academically," recalled another teacher. Johnson agreed: "I don't want my kid to go someplace where it's all about equity, and they're doing diddly in class." To appease the fears of these vocal parents, Johnson declared publicly, "We're going for equity and we're going for excellence," rather than, "Look, folks, there's a whole group of kids here who aren't getting anything, and this is about them." Despite her efforts, politically adroit parents threatened to remove their children from Adams if subunit choice was eliminated and College Prep or Alternative dismantled. We even received e-mails from several distraught parents searching for guidance, because they knew we had studied the school in the previous year.

In contrast to these parents, another group coalesced in support of the restructuring plan, charging that parents of high-achieving Adams students had disrupted reform efforts for years—especially those that affected the subunits or the subunit choice system. Although the city was well known for its liberal leanings, Johnson was surprised and delighted by this support for her plan among these families, including many affluent parents. At one of the many public meetings about the restructuring plan, an Adams parent declared: "To ignore what is going on in other subunits is like saying, 'My kid is well nourished; where's the hunger?'" A parent who attended one of these meetings wrote a letter to the editor of a local newspaper:

> Some parents act as if Adams is a private school for a select few who have worked the system to their advantage; whose parents have the breathing room to attend every meeting—crossing every T and dotting every I. The parents who raised voices in opposition to change at last week's meeting are still their children's best hope, as are the parents who work three jobs to keep the family afloat and don't have time to attend long, drawn out meetings.

Adams began the 2000–2001 school year by randomly assigning groups of 400 students to five unthemed subunits: "School One" through "School Five." For the first time in over a decade, the district's incoming 9th graders had not been asked to select their subunits the previous spring. According to an Adams publication, the subunit assignment process sought to "achieve a balance of students across the five small schools." For the first time, Angela Johnson proclaimed, each Adams subunit "was a microcosm of the school's population."

The assignment process for entering students was no longer by choice. Rather, students were first sorted by test scores, gender, and neighborhood. In a second step, the distribution of students across subunits resulting from this assignment was examined to ensure subunit balance by race, free/reduced-price lunch status, and feeder elementary school. Step three considered students' foreign language preferences, as not all of the several foreign languages offered at Adams were offered in every subunit. LEP students and faculty were balanced across three subunits. The stratifying subunit "appeals" process that had accompanied Adams's controlled choice plan was eliminated entirely. Johnson argued that the random subunit assignment process assured comparability and thus eliminated questions about the fairness of subunit assignments.

The school's 10th to 12th graders—former members of the disbanded subunits—presented unique problems. Johnson had argued that the previous SWS structure could not be phased out over time, because randomly assigning incoming 9th graders to low-status Community and others to high-status Alternative or College Prep was politically untenable. Instead, individual guidance counselors were assigned to the new subunits, and their existing advisees "followed" them. To avoid stratification, counselors from a low- and high-status subunits were matched.

Administrative structures were also reorganized, and most subunit heads were replaced. Teachers were reassigned to the new subunits, with an effort to balance race, age, gender, former subunit, and subject area. Johnson wanted high-quality teachers balanced across the new subunits, both to eliminate the recurrence of subunit stratification and to convince the community that differences between subunits no longer existed. Although most staff and parents agreed that the new subunits were indeed identical, a few parents and students tried to determine which subunit had the best teachers and administrators. A new subunit head laughed, "Parents have been coming in with their microscopes saying, 'We know you really are different. Help us figure this out.' They're looking for particular teachers and saying, 'Where are they?'"

Dismantling Adams's existing structure outraged many staff members, particularly those from the high-status subunits. An Alternative teacher lamented, "There are many, many teachers who are in despair over this and still mourning what they had and the community that they lost." Others claimed that teacher morale had plummeted, and that Adams's veteran faculty resented having such drastic reform thrust upon them so late in their careers. Johnson recognized the difficulty of reforming schools with experienced faculty. Some teachers told her, "I've been teaching here for 20 years, and *now* we're hearing that this school's not good enough?" A new subunit head summarized these attitudes: "There are people who are openly resistant and angry. There are some people who are so incredibly pissed off at Johnson that she's almost become a phobic object." Less vocally, veteran teachers from the less elite sub-units supported the new SWS structure, especially the opportunity to teach different types of students. A former Community teacher claimed, "I've got more smart kids, and I've got more White kids. Before my classes were all Black kids, and mostly low achievers."

The Ghost of Choice Returns

Recall that the Adams school district was one of the birthplaces of school choice in the country. Agreeing to suspend choice only for the 2000–2001 school year, the Board insisted that Adams reinstate subunit choice with the 2001–2002 school year. The superintendent convinced the Board that Adams's new plan should mention that "choice" would be reinstated, but not necessarily "subunit choice." Local newspapers reported the planning process in detail; telephones buzzed and e-mail flew among parents and community leaders. In February of 2000, the School Board approved the plan, which we noted was implemented with the 2000–2001 school year. Johnson's acquiescence about retaining the word "choice" in the plan would come back to haunt her.

In January 2001, four months into the new SWS structure, Johnson and the superintendent submitted (as required) an updated plan for 2001–2002 to the School Board. That the updated plan did not explicitly include subunit choice led the Board to inquire about its absence. The superintendent and Johnson—feigning a misunderstanding—responded that *they* had interpreted "choice" as curricular choice, which was indeed part of the plan. They reminded the Board that the phrase "subunit choice" had been removed. Irate Board members, in a secret midnight meeting, voted 4–3 to reject the plan and reinstate subunit choice. "This administration knew [subunit choice] was the policy," claimed one Board member. "Why would they wait until the very last minute to try to change it?" Another asserted that certain subunits had already emerged as "better than others," which justified reinstating choice. Interviewed by the local newspaper, one Board member claimed that subunit choice "had been unfairly blamed for all kinds of ills." However, the Board president, himself an Adams graduate and quite aware of Adams's internal stratification, "moved to reconsideration," requiring the Board to vote again on the issue at its next regular meeting.

The next morning, as news of the vote became public, hundreds of students, parents, and teachers congregated at Adams to protest against the return of subunit choice. Local newspapers displayed photos of protestors carrying signs reading, "Big decision made while we were sleeping. Thanks!" and "End segregation at Adams High School." An article stated that Johnson, the superintendent, and several administrators would not renew their contracts if the Board ratified their midnight vote to reinstate subunit choice. Another article quoted an Adams graduate as lamenting, "If this goes through, Alternative was lost for nothing!" As the new structure had been in place only six months, many argued against implementing yet another structure so quickly.

In the weeks before the Board meeting at which subunit choice would be reconsidered, the superintendent and Johnson lobbied Board members, stressing that with five identical small schools, student choice was meaningless. Several members offered the puzzling argument that this was the ideal time to reinstate choice, as there was nothing to choose; students and families would have little on which to base their choices—so stratification would not occur. Johnson countered that in a structure with choice and identical subunits, families of higher socioeconomic status were even more likely to flock to the same subunits, basing their choices simply on the subunits chosen by children from families like their own.

Hundreds of students and parents packed the School Board meeting, which included over six hours of testimony. The overwhelming majority of speakers opposed the return of subunit choice. Even those originally against the restructuring plan argued that the Board should allow it more time to work. Many recognized that eliminating the desirable subunits—Alternative and College Prep—had also eliminated the *need* for choice among many families. At 2:15 A.M., the Board agreed that student assignment to subunits "may" include choice as a factor beginning in the 2003–2004 school year. Johnson had won the battle, but the war was far from over.

The Political Limits of Reform

Adams High School exemplifies the volatility, unpredictability, and barriers that often surround high school restructuring. A few months after her victory in reorganizing the school, Johnson shocked the school and community by resigning as principal. She told us several months later that she was simply "too exhausted to keep fighting the same battles." The Board had pressured the superintendent to find some reason to release Johnson from her contract. Under the guise of a minor contract disagreement, Johnson and the superintendent arrived at an impasse. Soon after resigning, she assumed the leadership of a nearby public high school. Although many in the Adams community supported Johnson's efforts to create a more equitable social and academic climate, the resulting aftershocks were extremely disruptive for many stakeholders. "They had no idea who they were getting when they hired me," Johnson lamented during our last conversation.

Johnson's departure foreshadowed an unstable period for Adams and its district. A "no-confidence" vote by the School Board forced the resignation of the district's superintendent in 2003. Shortly thereafter, a regional school accreditation association placed Adams on probation, citing an "incoherent mission" and "fragmented leadership." A new principal, hired in 2002, brought a measure of stability and assisted Adams in gaining reaccreditation. Adams continued to build on Angela Johnson's reform efforts. Although gradual declines in enrollment forced the closure of one additional subunit, four randomly composed subunits remained in operation during the 2005–2006 school year. However, midway though the 2005–2006 school year Adams's principal—the fifth in eight years—announced her resignation. Adams has once again initiated a nationwide search for leadership.

GRANT HIGH SCHOOL

After steady improvement in school climate, student performance, and community reputation over the previous decade, by 2001 Grant High School again had become shrouded in anxiety and uncertainty. Among our five schools, Grant staff were the most disheartened during our last visit. A guidance counselor asserted, "We're just overwhelmed and discouraged!" Several teachers we knew from previous visits recounted that Grant was heading in the wrong direction and students were again "out of control." "Kids are screwing up left and right," lamented one teacher. During the 2000–2001 school year, half of Grant's students missed more than 37 days of school (i.e., more than 20% of the 180-day year). We were told that the district was once again "dumping" unwanted students on Grant. A subunit head asserted that the principal's office "looked like a police station."

Reasons for a Downward Slide

Two important events precipitated this downturn. First, the district retired its superintendent, a man with a national reputation who had been a major supporter of the SWS design throughout the district. The second reason was internal to the school: staff pointed to the retirement of Principal Lincoln during the Summer of 1999 (between our first and second visits). Recall from

Chapter 4 that Lincoln was widely credited as the force behind Grant's renaissance during the 1990s. One teacher sighed, "We miss her enormously!" Staff lauded her skills at consensus-building, her modesty in claiming that she was "simply one vote" in school decisions, and her ability to leverage the district bureaucracy to Grant's benefit. As another teacher put it, "She came to the school with 25 years of administrative experience, so she didn't kowtow to anybody." Under Lincoln's leadership, district teachers requested transfers to Grant from other high schools. When she retired, Grant had reverted to a "school of last resort" for district teachers. The mathematics department chair was especially troubled by the loss of veteran faculty:

> I've watched some wonderful things that were in place just fizzle away. Lots of people are putting in for transfers, and the old veteran people here are not happy campers. I wanted to offer statistics and trigonometry in the fall, but the two teachers who would teach it are trying to get out of here. It's a little scary.

In addition to Lincoln's departure, staff attributed their sense of uncertainty to the exodus of three of four assistant principals during the subsequent (2000–2001) school year. One left education altogether; one entered an administrative licensure program; and the third—who had been charged with student discipline—left Grant on a stretcher after suffering a heart attack. These departures left Grant with only one assistant principal and the common opinion that the school was adrift.

Changes in Enrollment and Staff

Assuming the principalship in the 1999–2000 school year, Todd Anderson implemented numerous structural and procedural changes. During the 1990s, several Grant subunits had attracted students from across the city. Despite the (relatively) advanced skills of these citywide admits, Anderson questioned Grant's ability to serve 900 entering 9th graders. He proposed reducing 9th-grade admissions to 500 per year, and instructed subunit heads to admit only 35–50 students from middle schools outside of Grant's feeder system (they were obliged to admit all neighborhood applicants).

Down from the 900 ninth graders it enrolled in 1999, Grant admitted 751 in 2001, and only 588 for the 2002–2003 academic year. Grant's enrollment thus dropped from almost 2,300 students during the late 1990s, when our study began, to only 1,897 by the 2002–2003 school year. Staff realized that fewer students meant fewer subunits. Several teachers speculated that the African American Studies subunit would be the first casualty, because it attracted lower achieving students and was widely considered the least effective. Moreover, Anderson had reportedly come to view the subunit's head as an "obstacle," due to her public challenges of his leadership and policies. Indeed, the African American Studies subunit was dismantled in 2002, and its dynamic head left Grant.

Considering Grant's academic and behavioral challenges, reducing 9th-grade admissions may seem logical. But the process of doing so also reduced the number of academically motivated students and weakened Grant's reputation and ability to attract talented faculty. Due to a combination of factors, including Anderson's efforts and the city's changing demographics, Grant's enrollment had continued to decline. With the 2005–2006 academic year, enrollment dropped below 1,250 students—a full 1,000 fewer students than when our study began. Ironically, according to the standards of many large urban school districts, Grant has finally become a "small school" through avenues unrelated to the SWS reform.

Outside Assistance

During the 2000–2001 school year, Anderson negotiated with the university-based Talent Development reform organization about adopting its SWS model (the group had earlier helped Taylor implement its SWS structure). The SWS model Grant was considering was identical to Taylor's, especially the separate 9th-grade subunits. The partnership had the potential to provide much-needed support, particularly staff development and curricular guidance. Grant teachers, however, strongly opposed this particular SWS model, especially its requirement of block scheduling into 90-minute class periods. Although Talent Development sought a minimum of 75–80% teacher buy-in to the model (which they had obtained at Taylor), Principal Anderson was reportedly prepared to adopt the model regardless of staff sentiment. "If he wanted it, it was going to be done," was how one teacher put it.

Through several faculty votes, teachers rejected the full Talent Development model but agreed to implement 9th-grade subunits. That decision proved to be irrelevant. Interpreted by many as another indicator of Grant's disarray, Talent Development staff abruptly ceased negotiations with the school. Several staff members claimed that the group became frustrated with the lack of support among teachers and said, according to one teacher, "Come back to us when you're serious!" Another teacher added: "I just think they walked away and said, 'We can't waste our time over there anymore.'" Despite the severed relationship with Talent Development, on its own Grant implemented 9th-grade subunits. Similar to Taylor, beginning in the 2003–2004 school year, Grant's 9th graders were assigned to a themeless 9th-grade subunit. Grant continued to operate the 9th-grade subunit and the four upper-grade career-oriented subunits through the 2005–2006 school year.

HARRISON HIGH SCHOOL

Change between the original study and our return visit to Harrison was both extreme and modest. Between 1999 and 2001 Harrison had experienced the least change in terms of size, curriculum, demographics, and SWS structure. However, several factors would fundamentally transform Harrison by the 2005–2006 school year. Foremost among the earlier changes was the replacement of Ben Miller with Greg Jenkins as principal. By our last visit to Harrison, Jenkins had garnered considerable staff support. "Having him here has been the best thing that's happened to us in nine years!" asserted one teacher. Miller's retirement received equal acclaim, particularly among those who had decried his apathy toward the SWS reform. In his first month as principal, Jenkins created two teacher-led "design teams" charged with deciding whether to drop Harrison's SWS structure—which most agreed had become "watered down"—or to revitalize it with meaningful subunit themes and missions. Jenkins had privately expressed to several staff members his own ambivalence about the SWS structure.

A Major Restructuring Grant

A second transformative factor came from outside the school. Soon after Jenkins's arrival, the Bill and Melinda Gates Foundation announced a major national grants program for schools interested in implementing autonomous schools within schools. Although the school had adopted the SWS structure a decade earlier, its subunits were far from autonomous. Teachers joked that Jenkins's indifference to the SWS model evaporated quickly upon hearing about the grant possibility. The principal and a district administrator declared publicly that such a grant would further the work of the design teams. Harrison quickly crafted a proposal to the Gates Foundation. One design team member summed up the proposal:

It was to create four or more autonomous schools within schools. We would take what we were doing already and just take it that next step. Instead of having these jumbled up schools within schools, they would be autonomous schools: all students would take all of their courses within their school within school.

The proposal was successful; Harrison was awarded a grant of close to a million dollars over three years. Interestingly, staff feared that the community would perceive the grant as yet another indicator that Harrison was in trouble and in need of outside assistance, rather than as an honor. As they planned the new SWS structure, Harrison staff cautioned against creating subunits with traditional career themes, which they feared would further Harrison's reputation as the district's vocational high school. One subunit head commented on the types of schools that normally implemented the SWS structure, the nature of the themes around which subunits were typically organized, and the supposed appeal of the reform:

> Let's face it. If you look at the research, most schools that have gone to the schools-within-schools concept are schools that are failing. And so, in trying to create something that works well for their students, they're picking something that they think is "appropriate" for their students— they're going to give them skills to go to work.

Tensions Between Subunit Autonomy and Differentiation

Although Harrison hoped that the grant would allow them to replace its "compromised SWS structure" with more autonomous small schools, staff discovered the challenges of implementing autonomous subunits within a comprehensive high school. For example, Jenkins noted that the need to staff multiple levels of the same course within each subunit limited the ability to create "pure" subunits. Indeed, Harrison's 2001–2002 course catalogue listed 16 different mathematics courses, ranging in rigor from "Applied Math" to AP Calculus. In addition to the clash between a comprehensive curriculum and subunit autonomy, Jenkins recognized that Harrison's broad curriculum produced stratified learning opportunities. However, he hoped to reduce student academic difference by requiring struggling students to "double up" on math and English courses. Closing the skills gap would permit a more constrained curriculum, which would in turn simultaneously allow for subunit autonomy and result in weakening the relationship between students' backgrounds and their subunit choices:

If kids all have the appropriate skill levels, they will make good subunit choices for themselves. If they don't have that, they're going to make choices based upon friends; they're going to make choices based upon other things. That's a hell of a leap of faith [that increased skills will lead to good choices], and I don't know if it's true or not.

Tension between the SWS structure and the comprehensive high school was stated as a central theme of Harrison's Gates Foundation proposal:

[Harrison] has two conflicting missions: (1) comprehensive high school with 13 departments all operating independently of each other, plus more than 20 co-curricular activities also operating independently; and (2) four schools-within-a-schools attempting to integrate all subject areas into a school mission. The original design of the SWS concept was to provide strong student–faculty relationships, but due to a comprehensive high school structure, SWS have not met the original objectives.

Staff also questioned other fundamental issues. For example, how could honors and advanced placement (AP) courses be scheduled within autonomous subunits? Harrison had dismantled its honors program when it adopted the SWS structure in the early 1990s, reinforcing the belief among many high-achieving students (and their families) that Harrison could not serve them well. Harrison's Gates proposal stated that it "wants desperately to create a new image: one that parents and students alike recognize as the 'place to go' due to its high standards, strong relationships, and impressive results." Staff felt that achieving this goal required honors and AP courses. Again, however, the obstacle was the inability to schedule pure sections of honors and AP courses due to low numbers in each subunit. Harrison staff who supported the renewal of the reform feared that subunit autonomy would again be sacrificed in order to attract (and retain) high-achieving students and their families.

Image and Reputation

Harrison's reputation as the weakest high school in its district has remained. "There's still that feeling that if you've got the worst test scores, it must be because you've got horrible teachers," one teacher lamented. Staff feared that their efforts to reform Harrison's SWS structure would be evaluated solely in terms of test scores. "The district is tired of the same song and dance," claimed one teacher, "and the bottom line is that you've got to get your test scores up!" Several teachers noted that the SWS model facilitated—but did not automatically produce—innovative approaches to teaching and learning (our major conclusion in Chapter 3). They feared that Harrison's latest reforms would continue to focus on the SWS structure, rather than on improving practice. "On its own [the SWS structure] is not going to raise student achievement. After ten years we're still at the bottom of the barrel," claimed one teacher. "What we need to do is change what's happening inside of the classroom," asserted another. Others questioned why professional development associated with the Gates grant was targeted for meetings about schools within schools rather than improving teaching and learning. A district-level administrator worried that Harrison's restructuring efforts would "focus too much on relationships. It's not the structure only; it's what happens inside the structure that needs to change." Her sentiments echoed the findings from the national Gates Foundation evaluation of SWS "conversion" high schools described in Chapter 1 (AIR & SRI, 2005).

In addition to augmenting its honors and AP offerings, Harrison hoped to improve its public image by implementing a districtwide International Baccalaureate (IB) program. One way to raise test scores was to attract better students in this district where choice existed between schools. However, the potential for increased stratification between subunits led staff to question whether the IB program should be a separate subunit—as had originally been discussed. "I think what it does is it creates a class system," Principal Jenkins noted. Harrison staff were aware that neither the IB organization nor small-schools advocates recommend subunits designed for elite groups of students. "I think the majority of us feel that we don't want that elitism in the ways that we obviously know that it could exist," claimed a district administrator. Instead, students would leave their subunits to take IB classes in whatever subunit a particular IB class was offered. However, Harrison was caught in a dilemma. The Gates Foundation cautioned Harrison not to create a separate IB subunit, yet simultaneously called for autonomous subunits. Ultimately, Harrison did not implement a separate IB subunit, but decided to offer IB courses that students select from across subunits.

Structural Change

Harrison experienced further transformations beginning in 2004. First, the school began admitting 9th graders, whereas it had previously enrolled only grades 10–12. One result was that Harrison's enrollment immediately increased from 1,300 to over 1,800 students. Second, Harrison implemented its re-designed (and Gates-funded) SWS structure. Similar to the dramatic restruc-turing at Adams, after 15 years in operation, Harrison completely dismantled each of its four subunits. However, unlike Adams, which created nondescript and randomly composed subunits, Harrison created five themed subunits and continued to allow student subunit choice. These new subunits are organized around rather loosely defined themes reminiscent of those we described in Harrison's AC subunit in Chapter 3, such as "change," "relationships," and "breaking down ideas." It seems unclear exactly what students would be choos-ing between as they select their subunits.

The Burdens of Reform

Several Harrison teachers remarked that they were weary from implementing multiple top-down reforms simultaneously. In addition to the International Baccalaureate discussions and the Gates-funded redesigns, Harrison had recently adopted a new reading program for 10th graders and was consider-ing a new mathematics program as well. As one teacher put it, "There comes a time when it doesn't make any difference whether you give teachers a mil-lion dollars or you give them a dime, there's no more time in their day! How do you keep reform going when teachers are exhausted?" At a school that had suffered years of intense community criticism, some teachers feared that despite their concerted efforts and a substantial influx of outside funds, Harrison's reputation would continue to languish, and measurable improvement would remain elusive.

MONROE HIGH SCHOOL

Shortly after our year-long study, Monroe had also experienced substantial change—starting with administrators. Beginning in early 2000, in only 14 months Monroe had lost its principal, half of its assistant principals and guid-ance counselors, and had changed three of its four subunit heads. These staff changes were precipitated by the unexpected departure of Principal Arthur Hernandez, the original impetus for the new Monroe High School and its SWS structure. Without warning and in the middle of the 2000–2001 school year, the superintendent "rotated" principals among the district's three high schools. Rumors, ranging from mundane issues to criminal malfeasance, circulated about the cause of the "principal swap."

Regardless of the actual catalyst, Art Hernandez's departure and Ron Lewis's hasty appointment as principal ultimately resulted in greater equity and a healthier school climate at Monroe. As principal at another district high school, Lewis was aware of the "tremendous animosity between MSM and the other subunits," and the "elitist view of the people who were in MSM." In the late 1990s Lewis had also visited Monroe as a member of a state evaluation team. The report noted "tension and downright anger among teachers. They were angry at MSM, because MSM got everything they wanted and did whatever they wanted to do." Upon arrival at Monroe, Lewis publicly declared two goals: (a) repair damaged subunit relations, and (b) reduce subunit stratification.

Increasing Equity

Accomplishing Lewis's aims required the elimination of MSM's privileged status. Since the departure of Hernandez—who would soon become a district-level administrator, as many had predicted—staff had learned that state funds targeted for schoolwide programs had been funneled to MSM. Ending this practice, Lewis told us, "What was supposed to be spread throughout the entire population of the school went to one subunit—which is completely inequitable!" Lewis also eliminated MSM teachers' two additional weeks of salary.

Lewis's most sweeping decision was to permit non-MSM students to enroll in MSM courses. This quickly reduced the animosity aimed at MSM. Unsurprisingly, MSM teachers, students, and parents resented Lewis and his policies. Protests erupted in front of Monroe and in the cafeteria, where MSM students carried signs reading "Help Save MSM!" Newspaper reporters called Lewis to inquire whether he planned to dismantle MSM. Adding fuel to these tensions, Lewis decided that subunit heads could not also serve as department chairs. MSM's head, who was also science department chair, chose to remain department chair and relinquished control of MSM. She eventually transferred to the high school where Art Hernandez briefly served as the new principal. Several Monroe teachers asserted that this was no coincidence: Hernandez sought to replicate MSM at his new school. The new MSM head supported Lewis's efforts to reduce stratification and constrain MSM's "elitist ethos":

> If kids in another subunit cannot take AP Biology because it's not offered anywhere, who am I to tell their parents they cannot have the class? I think some of that flexibility really helps with the morale and rapport with the other subunits, because they don't feel like their kids are getting the short end of the stick.

Despite these efforts to reduce stratification, subunit and class size disparities persisted. By design, Monroe's enrollment had grown by several hundred
students each year since it opened, as it added new classes to become a school
enrolling grades 9–12. Because MSM and IBM were subunits of choice, students were not required to enroll in them. However, as student interest in MSM
and IBM was not keeping pace, Generic 1 and 2 had to differentially absorb
Monroe's burgeoning enrollment. By the Spring of 2001, each Generic subunit
enrolled over 800 students; MSM and IBM each served fewer than 350. Moreover, the Generic subunits were required to admit students who had left MSM
and IBM, as well as those who transferred into Monroe after 9th grade. These
conditions led to growing class size disparities between subunits. Keeping
courses in MSM and IBM pure required multiple offerings of the same course,
with the resulting small class sizes. However, because the Generics had each
grown to the size of many traditional high schools, their classes enrolled up to
38 students.

A Changing Subunit Hierarchy

As reported in earlier chapters, by 1999 Generic 2 had the reputation as Monroe's weakest subunit—in terms of leadership, instruction, and students. It was
"lowest on the food chain," Lewis noted, a "de facto vocational subunit." Lewis
hoped that the redistribution of high-achieving students across subunits would
equalize their reputations, as all students gained access to advanced courses.
Due partly to increased curricular access, even fewer students were selecting
MSM. Simultaneously, Generic 1's reputation improved; some academically
oriented students selected it over MSM. "The kids were thrilled that they
wouldn't have to go into an oppressive subunit and be beat over the head every
day," Lewis told us.

MSM may have become what it was intended to be: a subunit that enrolled
students interested in math and science. As Lewis claimed, "MSM is becoming in effect a much purer subunit, because it's not getting the [future]
lawyers." However, the subunit's enrollment decline precipitated a crisis.
Although many students wanted some AP and honors courses, few students
wanted only advanced courses—and MSM offered only advanced coursework. Blamed largely on the increase in schoolwide curricular choice, in
2001–2002 only twenty 8th graders initially selected MSM, compared with
about ninety who had normally applied. This drop in applications forced
MSM teachers to recruit heavily at the district's middle schools and to dispel

rumors about MSM's demise. Through these last-minute efforts, MSM eventually enrolled 74 students that year—still fewer than they had hoped for or were staffed to accommodate.

Unsurprisingly, few teachers in the other subunits expressed dismay over MSM's predicaments. Generic 1's head, long concerned about MSM's elitism, seemed delighted about MSM's struggles: "It was nice to see them put in their place; nobody feels sorry for them." As MSM's reputation in the school and district weakened, relationships between MSM students and teachers and those from other subunits improved. Allowing outside students to take MSM classes reduced MSM's exclusivity and perceptions of its students as arrogant. Eliminating MSM teachers' extra income and guaranteed access to Monroe's most academically motivated students also began to mend years of damaged relations.

The Comprehensive High School Returns?

Similar to what we reported about Taylor and Harrison, several teachers sensed that Monroe was devolving into a traditional comprehensive high school. Although pleased that students now had more freedom to take courses in other subunits, staff recognized that a more permeable (albeit more equitable) SWS structure would likely weaken subunit cohesion and the ability to foster unique subunit identities. "It's crumbling by the wayside, and I don't see [the SWS structure] lasting for much longer," predicted a doubtful teacher. Others noted that with each passing year, fewer teachers present at Monroe's creation remained. New teachers and administrators had been hired who were unfamiliar with (and relatively uncommitted to) the school's founding philosophy. As a result, overall staff interest in schools within schools was declining.

Although Monroe's efforts at fostering equity among subunits represented a positive development, these moves could also result in a traditional comprehensive high school. Monroe's new administration showed little inclination to implement a constrained curriculum with mostly academic courses. Rather, it sought to equalize access to the sort of choice-driven differentiated curriculum that typifies comprehensive high schools. As we have discussed throughout this book, such choices are strongly related to students' social and academic backgrounds. Monroe may well replace one type of stratification (among subunits) with another (among courses). Although Lewis's equity considerations focused only on between-subunit inequality, they also initiated broader conversations about equity and access that had been stifled since Monroe opened.

Structural Change

Monroe experienced another period of change beginning in 2003, when Ron Lewis departed as Monroe's principal. The new principal furthered Lewis's reforms, including a dramatic reconfiguring of Monroe's subunit structure. Although the MSM and IBM subunits remained (the latter with an added focus on law), the Generic 1 and 2 subunits were dismantled. Monroe created three new subunits with themes organized around the arts, teaching careers, and technology. The move to five subunits was motivated by Monroe's (and the district's) continued enrollment increases. Monroe enrolled almost 3,000 students by the 2005–2006 school year, and growth in the surrounding areas led the school district to open yet another high school in 2003. Interestingly, this new school is not organized around the SWS design.

TAYLOR HIGH SCHOOL

Among these five high schools, in some ways Taylor had enjoyed the greatest substantive improvement and achieved the most stability in the years since our research began. This is extraordinary, considering its designation as the second worst high school in its state only a decade earlier. Subunit leadership had remained quite stable, and Taylor was the only school to retain the same principal throughout the length of our study. Although still an academically struggling school, in 2001 Taylor staff were generally optimistic about their school's direction since our original study in 1999. In terms of measurable outcomes, student attendance had improved almost 40% between 1998 and 2001, and test scores had modestly but steadily increased. Taylor was attracting stronger faculty, and it was no longer the school on which the district "dumped" unwanted teachers. Veteran burned-out teachers were retiring, and according to several staff members, younger and more energetic teachers were "revitalizing" Taylor.

Explaining Taylor's Turnaround

Most informants attributed these improvements to the arrival of Diana D'Angelo as principal in 1998. Staff appreciated her hard work, her high expectations, the fact that she "fought" for the school, and that she had remained at the school for the last 6 years. "She's probably the best principal I've seen since I've been here," claimed a veteran subunit head. Staff credited two D'Angelo policies for Taylor's improved social climate. The first was her decision to "clean the rolls" of students with sporadic school attendance. "You have to weed the garden," D'Angelo told us, "because we don't want adults in here masquerading as students." She had reportedly told students, "You're either going to be a student, or you're going to go." Many had gone. The second policy involved her aggressive approach to student discipline. During Angelo's tenure, "weeding the garden" included substantial increases in suspensions, expulsions, and the number of problem students sent to district alternative high schools. One subunit head remarked, "The message went out to the kids about what would and would not be tolerated."

D'Angelo also implemented a student uniform policy. Beginning in 2001, 9th graders were required to wear black golf shirts with the First-Year 1 and 2 emblem, and 10th through 12th graders wore blue oxford shirts with their subunit's emblem. Teachers asserted that the uniforms permitted them to identify outsiders roaming the building. "Somebody's not going to go out and buy a uniform just so they could walk around Taylor High School," noted one teacher. Many staff professed a link between student dress and behavior. "Girls were coming to school dressed so inappropriately," claimed one subunit head, "and boys were dressed like thugs." Staff, especially D'Angelo, took the uniforms seriously. During morning announcements one day, we heard D'Angelo scold students who had not worn their uniforms: "We expect nothing but the best of you at all times. This is not a beach. This is a place of business."

Declining Enrollment

Taylor's student enrollment has declined considerably, due to forces both within and beyond its control. At the beginning of the 1998–1999 school year (when our study began), Taylor enrolled over 2,300 students. Enrollment declined to 1,900 by 2002, and 1,600 by the 2005–2006 school year. Projections suggested that Taylor would lose an additional 30 students per year through the end of the decade. Moreover, Taylor has also lost a disproportionate number of White students: by 2005, White enrollment was only 15% at Taylor. These declines reflected several trends: (a) the city's aging population, (b) the continued phenomenon of middle-class flight from the city to the suburbs, (c) D'Angelo's removal of nonattending students from the rolls, and (d) local housing patterns. Following national trends, the city had demolished several large public housing projects, including one located in Taylor's catchment area. Declining enrollment may present a future challenge to the school. Because schools are funded on a per-pupil basis, Taylor's declining enrollment may require staff reductions. Staff recognized the quandary. Had Taylor continued to enroll nonattending students, it would have maintained its funding and full teaching staff. However, in keeping marginal students, Taylor's test scores, attendance and graduation rates suffered, threatening a return to the state's list of reconstitution-eligible schools. "It's a no-win situation," concluded one subunit head.

As at Grant, enrollment declines may reduce the number of Taylor subunits. Enrollments in several subunits had slipped below 300. Several teachers suggested that First-Year 1 and 2 be dismantled and 9th graders be permitted to choose from among the regular subunits. Despite the original enthusiasm for this innovation, staff came to agree that the First-Year subunits did not address 9th graders' needs and were the "weakest link" in Taylor's SWS structure; the lack of contact with older students left 9th graders with few positive social or academic role models. "They're down there with a whole group of kids who are horrors," claimed one upper-grade subunit head. However, staff admitted that organizing 9th graders into separate subunits helped to isolate the worst behavior problems.

Toward Differentiation

Since assuming leadership in 1998, D'Angelo has gradually moved Taylor away from the SWS structure toward a more traditional comprehensive high school. Quite early in her administration, academic departments were reinstated and Taylor's curriculum was expanded at both the lower and upper levels. At the upper end, Taylor restored the honors and AP courses it had eliminated when it converted to the SWS structure in 1994. At the opposite end, D'Angelo introduced a series of career "pathways" and "completer programs" in the 2000–2001 school year. The programs entailed a four- to six-course sequence, after which students were eligible for a state-recognized "certificate of completion." Taylor had offered several state-certified vocational programs in the 1970s and 1980s that had been dismantled by previous principals. D'Angelo asserted that the demise of these vocational programs was unfortunate for school and students alike. Many programs were eligible for state and federal funds, and their return meant an influx of fiscal resources. D'Angelo further argued that Taylor graduates rarely completed college (or even left the neighborhood), meaning Taylor's career pathways should prepare students for employment in the local economy.

Some staff did not support the completer programs. Practically, they noted the challenges of requiring highly mobile students to complete 3-year course sequences; students who missed even one course were denied the completer certificate. Philosophically, others questioned the appropriateness of career and vocational education in the 21st century, and also the ability of 14-year-olds to make decisions about their occupational futures. In particular, these staff members questioned whether the career pathways led students away from higher education and toward low-level occupations. Others claimed that the additional career pathways courses hindered students' ability to take high-level academic courses, further qualifying them only for low-paying, low-skill jobs.

A Return to "Normal"

Despite some qualms, Taylor staff saw themselves on a positive trajectory. School climate, staff morale, and student outcomes were steadily improving. However, Taylor's slow devolution into a traditional comprehensive high school suggests that the long-term viability of its small-school structure is uncertain. Talent Development, the very successful university-based reform group that had helped Taylor implement its SWS structure, has subsequently distanced itself from the school. Contrary to early claims, they no longer used Taylor as an example of schools within schools "done right." Although Taylor's support for the structure continued, several teachers and administrators wondered whether the SWS model served as an "emergency configuration" more appropriate for schools in disarray. Now that they had achieved some stability, a few teachers believed that Taylor should return to a more "natural" state—the traditional comprehensive high school. Despite these ruminations and dramatic enrollment declines, Taylor's SWS structure remained virtually unchanged through the 2005–2006 school year.

Instability from Outside

To underscore yet again the instability that haunts many large urban school districts, Taylor's future is again in jeopardy. Citing budget concerns and declining district enrollments, early in 2006 the school district unveiled a plan to close Taylor High School. However, after considerable community outrage—including walkout protests by Taylor students and much newspaper publicity—the district reversed its decision and declared that Taylor would be spared. Ironically, a school that adopted the SWS structure to ameliorate the negative effects of large size may fall victim to district concerns that its school is too small.

In addition to these pressures from within the district, Taylor again faced serious outside threats from the state. Early in 2006, the State Board of Education voted to transfer control of roughly one dozen low-achieving district middle and high schools to third-party organizations. One school slated for takeover is Taylor High School. The state superintendent, the governor, and a sizable group of state legislators all supported the plan. The issue remained unresolved as we completed this book, with multiple parties threatening litigation. After a decade's experience with the SWS reform, Taylor finds itself exactly where it started—threatened by state takeover due to low student achievement.

■ ■ ■

APPENDIX A:
Research Procedures

IN THE SOCIOLOGY OF EDUCATION, there is a long and distinguished tradition of intensive ethnographic study of single high schools (e.g., Coleman, 1961; Eckert, 1989; Fine, 1991; Grant, 1988; Hollingshead, 1975; MacLeod, 1995; Willis, 1977). These seminal single-site case studies explored associations between students' social and academic backgrounds and the organization of the schools they attended. Although this labor- and time-intensive methodological approach certainly produces a rich tapestry of information, its advantages are accompanied by a serious limitation: a lack of comparative groups of students, teachers, schools, and communities.

In contrast to single-site ethnography, some exemplary and more contemporary studies have collected data through field research in multiple sites. Many studies at the center of research on high school social and academic organization make use of the multisite case study approach (see, for example, Bryk et al., 1993; Cusick, 1983, Lightfoot, 1983; Newmann & Associates, 1996; Powell et al., 1985). In addition to their sociological outlooks, these cross-site investigations share some characteristics that we found relevant to our study. In particular, they depart from classic ethnography on at least two important dimensions. First, the authors spend less time in each site, and rarely (if ever) come to be seen as "insiders" or participant observers by the schools under study. Second—and especially appealing to us— is that compared with classic ethnography, which is often unconcerned with applicability, this work generally seeks to influence both policy and practice beyond telling an interesting story. Thus, the cross-site case study tradition represents an important grounding for our work. In this appendix we provide more detail about how we selected the schools and how we analyzed the data we collected in our multiyear, multisite study of five high schools divided into schools within schools.

THE MAIN STUDY

Our initial task was to recruit a team of researchers to conduct the field-based study. The full research team of 11 members included both faculty members and doctoral students, from the Universities of Michigan, Maryland, Oregon, and Ohio State; however, the majority of members were affiliated with the School of Education at the University of Michigan. We created two-person teams—a team leader more experienced with field-based research and/or knowledgeable about the schools-within-schools (SWS) reform and an assistant with less experience and knowledge—and assigned teams to schools.

Each team devoted two week-long visits to "their" schools in the spring and fall of the 1999 calendar year (i.e., over two different academic years). These visits consisted of interviews (with school-level, subunit-level, and district-level administrators; teachers; guidance counselors; and other special staff); focus groups (separately with teachers and students by subunit); shadowing a few students for a day; observations of interactions in hallways and other public locations; attendance at any special events (including athletics) that occurred during our visit; mapping each building's physical layout; collecting papers and documents pertinent to school life; and learning about the larger context in which each school operated. Almost all interviews were audiotaped, transcribed verbatim, and verified. Unrecorded interviews were described in fieldnotes. Transcribed interviews, which comprised the majority of data from the study, were augmented by other data sources, including detailed fieldnotes each researcher prepared about his or her observations and impressions, and extensive sets of documents collected from each school.

The research teams generally used the first data collection round to familiarize themselves with the processes and contexts of "their" school's SWS structure. As few members were familiar with schools within schools at the outset of our work, gaining an understanding of the structures and processes that constituted the SWS model was an important first step. After the first data collection round, teams prepared school-specific case studies, organized around a common outline. We included issues unique to each school in the case studies, as well as information obtained from the five sites. We convened a teamwide retreat where we discussed findings and themes that were both unique and common across schools. We then revised the data collection designs based on our increased knowledge about the schools.

During the second round of data collection, teams focused on social relations within each school and how the SWS structure influenced those relations. Each team updated, expanded, and refined its initial case study, organized around the same outline. They revised and enriched the original case studies, which were again exchanged in another retreat. The methodological approach of the "collective case study" helped us to refine our conceptual framework and provided us insight in isolating constructs around which to organize our data analysis. Stake (1994) suggests that a collective case study is "not a study of the collective, but [rather] an instrumental study extended to several cases" (p. 237). Teams based their first case study drafts on the initial wave of data, then filled evidentiary gaps with data from the second wave for the final drafts (see Yin, 1994). Although the case studies were important analytic tools upon which we relied heavily, we returned to the raw data for many of the analyses reported in this book. Especially useful were the thousands of pages of documents and interview transcripts.

Analytic Approach

Our analytic approach involved several iterative steps, where we moved back and forth between the data and emerging themes and conclusions. Although we began coding with a theoretical framework in mind, we did not begin with predetermined analytic codes or categories. Rather, the analysis was "free-flowing" and not "structured or rigid" (Strauss & Corbin, 1998, p. 58). The codes themselves emerged from the data (Merriam, 1998) and were generated inductively through the coding process (Maxwell, 1998). This approach was meant to assure that the themes and analytic categories that progressively materialized during our analyses were empirically grounded and well aligned with the data (Miles & Huberman, 1994).

Our first step was to read through the entire body of data, noting potential patterns and regularities that might eventually become codes (Goetz & LeCompte, 1984; Marshall & Rossman, 1999; Merriam, 1998). In the second step we again read the data, this time combing them more thoroughly and coding relevant text using the preliminary codes created in the first step. An important component of this step was recognizing disconfirming evidence in informants' words and documents (Bogdan & Biklen, 1997). We did not ignore such data; rather, we coded and analyzed them.

In the third step we organized the coded text into categories and subcategories based on the codes created in the first two steps. Guba and Lincoln (1981) note that this third step is both divergent and convergent, in that some categories are refined and fleshed out, whereas other subcategories or categories that "stick together" are combined. At this stage, we eliminated several categories because the volume of data was insufficient to support them; some categories "just didn't work." Conversely, new categories and ideas emerged that we had not recognized during earlier stages; subtle nuances suggested that certain categories be broken down further into subcategories.

This iterative process, where we moved between data and emerging codes and categories, can be conceptualized as "comparative analysis." We contrasted the quotes and themes with one another to uncover differences and similarities (Strauss & Corbin, 1998). The goal of such "pattern coding" is to identify broader meanings by grouping codes into themes and constructs (Miles & Huberman, 1994). We concluded this process when sufficient numbers of "regularities" emerged (Lincoln & Guba, 1985). Indeed, the categories and themes resulting from this process "often turn out to be the conceptual hooks on which the analyst hangs the meatiest part of the analysis" (Miles & Huberman, 1994, p. 72).

SUBSEQUENT VISITS

The fact that this work extended over multiple school years allowed us to observe between-year changes that would not have been evident if our data collection had been confined to a single academic year. We hope, as readers have become familiar with these five SWS schools, it has become evident that few of them were problem-free. Even though we selected the five schools based partly on the maturity of their SWS designs, we found that in some schools the basic design was under "stress." Thus, we decided that it would be useful to revisit each school almost two years after our second data collection round. Fortunately, the Spencer Foundation agreed with us about the value of these return visits and provided further financial support.

In the Spring of 2001, we returned to each of the original five schools. These visits were shorter and more targeted. Our major aim was to investigate the stability of the SWS reform, particularly in one or two schools where we had suspected that the long-term viability of the model was in doubt. Remarkably, we found the SWS structure still operating in each school. However, four of the five schools were led by new principals since our first visits in 1998–1999. At two schools, we spoke with both the current and the former principals (who had assumed positions in other area schools). As with the first two rounds of data collection, all interviews were taped and transcribed verbatim. After this third round of visits, we have continued to augment our knowledge about the schools through e-mail, phone exchanges with the original informants, and an additional visit to one especially turbulent site (Adams High School).

■ ■ ■

APPENDIX B:
Subunit Descriptions

ADAMS'S SUBUNITS (LISTED ALPHABETICALLY)

Alternative. Conceived almost three decades ago by faculty at a local university, Alternative's social and academic environments were quite different from a traditional high school. It offered courses in African American literature and women's studies. Progressive pedagogical techniques—including self-directed learning activities—dominated many classrooms. Students called teachers by their first names, and few teachers assigned detention or issued passes to enter or exit class. Such policies lent Alternative a reputation as a home for "slackers," although it actually enrolled a disproportionate number of high-achieving students. Alternative limited enrollment, making it much smaller than other Adams subunits.

College Prep. This subunit focused on traditional academic achievement and boasted of its internally tracked curriculum. College Prep's reputation became quite strong, based on its students' successes in gaining admission to selective colleges and on standardized tests. This reputation attracted more students to College Prep than there were places, requiring it, along with Alternative, to turn away half the students who applied each year. College Prep appealed to serious students (and their parents) and was proud of its reputation in the Adams community as the most traditional academic subunit.

Community. Although Community began as a generic subunit within Adams, later it adopted a "leadership" theme to distinguish itself and to attract students. However, this theme was never fully developed. The subunit once mandated community service, but beginning in the late 1990s students were only *encouraged* to engage in such activities. A seemingly weak theme contributed to a lack of distinctive identity; most Adams faculty and students considered Community among the weaker subunits. Community's low status was furthered by the fact that it enrolled a disproportionate number of minority and low-income students.

Core Curriculum. This subunit began in the mid-1970s as an option for students and parents who wanted a more traditional and structured high school education than was provided by either of the district's regular high schools or by the Alternative subunit (at the time the district's only other small school of choice). Originally housed in a former Catholic school, the Core Curriculum subunit came to the main campus over 20 years ago, although it tried to maintain its tight-knit community and its reputation for academic rigor. Other subunits, however, overtook it in terms of academic reputation.

International/Cooperative Learning (ICL). The ICL subunit incorporated such progressive pedagogies as cooperative teaching and an integrated curriculum into its multicultural approach. This subunit enrolled all students in the English as a Second Language (ESL) program; thus ICL was the automatic "choice" for students who entered Adams with little or no English (including the unusually high proportion of Adams's foreign students). Despite its reputation as the subunit for foreigners, ICL enjoyed a relatively high application rate from students who sought an unconventional approach to learning and a chance to broaden their cultural perspectives.

Vocational. This was the only subunit at Adams that resembled a traditional vocational education program. Its students were able to select from several different programs, including culinary arts, auto mechanics, and child care. For a decade, Vocational was known for its low test scores and its socially and academically unmotivated students. As our research at Adams began, rumors surfaced that Vocational would not be a choice for students for the 1999–2000 school year and would soon be dismantled. In fact, this occurred.

GRANT'S SUBUNITS

African American Studies (AAS). This subunit, which had recently added Law to its focus, used African American history, literature, culture, and values to foster a tight-knit learning collective in which self-esteem, responsibility, and leadership skills were developed. AAS students were trained (in theory) to enter either work or college after graduation. This subunit experienced high staff turnover and difficulty implementing curricular innovations, in part because of its high proportion of low-achieving students. These difficulties constrained the subunit from realizing many program goals. Its classroom environments were thought throughout the school to be the least conducive to teaching and learning.

Arts. Although Arts claimed to prepare students for college, students seemed interested in other postsecondary opportunities besides higher education. Arts traditionally enrolled large numbers of low-achieving students, and its reputation thus suffered within the larger school community. Arts students engaged in the visual, graphic, and performing arts and pursued courses in music appreciation, architecture, and theater. Students also participated in dance and theatrical productions as culminating projects.

Business. Business faculty and students boasted of a community spirit, which was perhaps tied to the subunit's high application rate. The curricular and physical integration with the business department, together with its positive reputation in the district, contributed to high staff stability and student attendance. Students prided themselves on the practical life skills they learned from the subunit's focus on finance, computer applications, and a general orientation toward business professions. Business faculty actively recruited students from a large number of middle schools outside Grant's catchment area.

Communications. Communications began as a district-level magnet program before the other Grant subunits were established. Like Business, this subunit formerly received special funds from the district but was later required to access these from the school's operating budget. The curriculum included journalism, mass communications, drama, graphic technology, a school TV studio, and computer applications. Students prepared presentations, engaged in original research, and refined writing skills. Although Communications's stated intentions were to prepare students for both work and higher education, subunit staff encouraged students to pursue college. Like Business, Communications staff recruited students from middle schools in the city at large.

Health. Health claimed to prepare its students for either work experience or postsecondary education, but the subunit strongly emphasized college as a goal for its students. Its curriculum was mostly problem-based, focused on math and science, and linked to public health and medicine fields. Students had the opportunity to learn about diverse career opportunities in the health industry through working with professionals at local universities and through shadowing experiences, guest lectures, and internships. These experiences were available mostly in the upper grades. Along with Business, members of Grant's community viewed Health as one of its strongest subunits, based on high application rates, student grades, and college acceptances.

HARRISON'S SUBUNITS

Arts/Communications (AC). This subunit emphasized the integration of English, social studies, and the arts and was known for its emphasis on artistic and aesthetic values. Although staff used traditional subject-specific curriculum and assessment methods, the subunit was quite innovative along these dimensions: (a) the staff wove themes across subjects, (b) students were involved in developing their own assessment criteria, and (c) students engaged in project-based learning. Students wrote poetry and essays, produced a wide variety of artwork, and had the reputation of being nonconformists. AC faculty used themes to cultivate interpersonal sensitivity, respect, and collaboration among students. Faculty in this subunit were particularly strong supporters of interdisciplinary collaboration and Harrison's schools-within-schools structure.

Business. This subunit offered students a program of applied business practices in an international context. Students learned how to use the Internet and were encouraged to study other languages and cultures. Along with Health/ Human Services, Business was considered by its students and faculty as the college preparatory subunit, although its graduates were equipped to enter either the workplace or postsecondary education. Faculty and students shared strong interests in practical business skills and preparation for employment.

Health/Human Services (HHS). The HHS subunit claimed to prepare students for careers in health and human services, but the claim was not realized; very little in the curriculum reflected the career component and theme. The HHS program, which emphasized traditional courses in math and science, was viewed as the subunit most resembling a traditional college-preparatory track. In the past, HHS staff participated in interdisciplinary collaboration through authentic learning opportunities and projects with health and environmental themes. However, as faculty found it difficult to sustain curriculum integration and project work, much of this disappeared.

Science/Technology (ST). The Science/Technology subunit attracted students interested in mechanical and technological activities. Within Harrison, ST was the program closest to a traditional vocational education program. Subunit faculty worked hard to create an integrated learning experience for the subunit's students. English and science teachers worked quite closely with vocational teachers to integrate their courses. Students produced go-carts, paddle-boats, and rockets as culminating activities over the years we studied Harrison's ST, which enrolled a disproportionate number of males and low-achieving students, still managed to retain a student cohort interested in college.

MONROE'S SUBUNITS

Generic 1. Students who did not select one of Monroe's magnet programs were randomly assigned to Generic 1 or Generic 2. Although Generic 1 started without a specific theme during the year of our study, students and faculty developed a theme representing their ability and drive to attain success, both in school and in their postgraduation plans, which may have involved work or college. The newly conceived theme did not resonate with many faculty and students (most could not remember what the theme was), and it still retained a generic character. The subunit's curriculum reflected a basic high school program with few advanced placement courses.

Generic 2. The principal characterized this subunit as "still struggling"; its members had not developed a theme nor established an identity within the school at the time of our study. No special curriculum or orientation toward college preparation or school-to-work transition existed. Similar to Generic 1, Generic 2 offered a standard high school program. The two generic programs were defaults for students not interested in business or math/science. Generic 2 also employed the majority of Monroe's athletic coaches, which some teachers attributed to the lack of dedication and cohesion among Generic 2's faculty.

International Business Magnet (IBM). Students applied directly to this subunit (IBM) from across the school district. Although IBM was not selective, the program was developed before Monroe opened (as had MSM). Thus, IBM had a preestablished reputation when Monroe opened. The subunit's core curriculum consisted of traditional courses in English and math as well as tailored courses in multicultural issues and business designed to instruct students about world cultures and the importance of Hispanic cultures to business. IBM's mission was to prepare students to enter either college or the workforce after graduation.

Math/Science Magnet (MSM). The MSM program was established at another district high school about five years before Monroe opened; thus, its reputation for rigorous college preparation in math and science was well known. Once students were accepted into MSM, subunit faculty claimed they worked tirelessly to retain the students. MSM offered only honors courses and recruited high-achieving students from the entire district. It enjoyed disproportionately smaller class sizes than the other subunits and enrolled more White and affluent students. Non-MSM students and faculty at Monroe felt that MSM had many special privileges in terms of resources and teacher hiring, resulting in considerable resentment.

TAYLOR'S SUBUNITS

First-Year 1 and First-Year 2. All of Taylor's incoming 9th graders were randomly assigned to either First-Year 1 or First-Year 2. Following a team-oriented middle school organizational model, these two subunits attempted to provide incoming students with a supportive environment in which to develop academic skills and adjust to disciplinary expectations. During the 9th grade, students completed surveys to identify career interests and assist them in selecting one of the four upper-grade career academies. Teachers were divided into interdisciplinary teams from whom students took the majority of their classes. Each team also had primary responsibility for students' attendance and disciplinary problems. When Taylor adopted the SWS structure in 1995, an effort was made to staff the First-Year subunits with experienced middle school teachers. Soon thereafter, however, many original faculty members moved to upper-grade subunits, where students' academic and discipline problems were believed to be less troublesome (because many Taylor students dropped out after 9th grade). New subunit faculty were less experienced, further compounding the problems with daily operation of the First-Year subunits.

Arts/Humanities (AH). Of Taylor's four upper-grade subunits, Arts/Humanities (AH) had a reputation for the most productive academic and behavioral climate. Students who transferred to Taylor from academically selective citywide schools were usually placed in AH. The subunit offered four career pathways: computer science, law, visual arts, and cosmetic services. AH teachers reportedly were among Taylor's most traditional. Compared with Taylor's other subunits, a disproportionate number of female and White students selected AH.

Business. Faculty described the business subunit as tantamount to a "general" track. Along with a college preparatory curriculum, the subunit offered three career pathways: administrative technology (primarily clerical work), marketing, and consumer services or retailing. Many business students participated in apprentice programs sponsored by local merchants as part of their career training. Flags from countries across the world decorated the Business corridor to remind students of the growing importance of the global economy.

Health/Human Services (HHS). The HHS subunit offered four career pathways: sports training, pharmaceutical technology, emergency medical technician, and child care. This subunit was characterized as a home for "jocks," although the subunit head was anxious to change this reputation through the introduction of stronger career pathways. Perceptions among younger students at Taylor reflected the subunit head's goal; they considered HHS academically rigorous and disciplined. HHS enjoyed relatively high attendance in a school where student attendance was an ongoing problem.

Mechanical. Mechanical offered four career pathways: Air Force ROTC, automotive technology, manufacturing, and drafting. Taylor's ROTC program was citywide, and students enrolled in ROTC were the most academically oriented students in the subunit. Students in the automotive technology pathway participated in apprenticeships with local mechanics (Taylor had few automotive facilities). The atmosphere in this subunit was suggestive of a traditional high school vocational program. Faculty and students not associated with Mechanical characterized its students as undisciplined and academically less skilled. The hands-on curriculum attracted a disproportionate number of males and students with academic difficulties.

References

AIR & SRI [American Institutes for Research & SRI International]. (2004). *The National School District and Network Grants Program: Year 2 evaluation report.* Washington, DC: American Institutes for Research.

AIR & SRI [American Institutes for Research & SRI International]. (2005). *Getting to results: Student outcomes in new and redesigned high schools.* Washington, DC: American Institutes for Research.

Allen, L. (2001). *Wall to wall: Implementing small learning communities in five Boston high schools.* Providence, RI: Northeast and Islands Regional Educational Laboratory (Lab Working Paper No. 3).

Angus, D., & Mirel, J. (1999). *The failed promise of the American high school, 1890–1995.* New York: Teachers College Press.

Ayres, L. P. (1909). *Laggards in our schools: A study of retardation and elimination in city school systems.* New York: Charities Publication Committee.

Barker, R., & Gump, R. (1964). *Big school, small school: High school size and student behavior.* Stanford, CA: Stanford University Press.

Bidwell, C. E. (1965). The school as formal organization. In J. G. March (Ed.), *Handbook of organizations* (pp. 972–1022). Chicago: Rand McNally.

Bobbitt, J. F. (1924). *How to make a curriculum.* Boston, MA: Houghton Mifflin.

Bogdan, R., & Biklen, S. (1997). *Qualitative research for education.* Boston: Allyn & Bacon.

Boyer, E. L. (1983). *High school: A report on secondary education in America.* New York: Harper & Row.

Bryk, A. S., & Driscoll, M. E. (1988). *The school as community: Theoretical foundations, contextual influences, and consequences for students and teachers.* Madison: University of Wisconsin, Center on Effective Secondary Schools.

Bryk, A. S., Lee, V. E., & Holland, P. B. (1993). *Catholic schools and the common good.* Cambridge, MA: Harvard University Press.

Buchanan, C. M., Eccles, J. S., & Becker, J. B. (1992). Are adolescents the victims of raging hormones? Evidence for the activational effects of hormones on moods and behavior in adolescence. *Psychological Bulletin, 111,* 62–107.

Chubb, J. E., & Moe, T. M. (1990). *Politics, markets, and America's schools.* Washington, DC: Brookings Institution.

Clark, B. R. (1962). *Educating the expert society.* San Francisco: Chandler Publishing.

Cohen, D. K., & Neufeld, B. (1981). The failure of high schools and the progress of education. *Daedalus, 110*(3), 69–89.

Coleman, J. S. (1961). *The adolescent society.* New York: Cromwell-Collier.

Conant, J. B. (1959). *The American high school today: A first report to interested citizens.* New York: McGraw-Hill.

Cook, A. (2000). The transformation of one large urban high school: The Julia Richman Education Complex. In E. Clinchy (Ed.), *Creating new schools: How small schools are changing American education* (pp. 101–120). New York: Teachers College Press.

Cremin, L. A. (1961). *The transformation of the school: Progressivism in American education.* New York: Knopf.

Cuban, L. (1988). *The managerial imperative and the practice of leadership in schools.* Albany: State University of New York Press.

Cusick, P. A. (1983). *The egalitarian ideal and the American high school: Studies of three schools.* New York: Longman.

Eccles, J. S., & Midgley, C. M. (1989). Stage/environment fit: Developmentally appropriate classrooms for young adolescents. In C. Ames & R. E. Ames (Eds.), *Research on motivation in education* (Vol. 3, pp. 139–186). New York: Academic Press.

Eccles, J. S., Midgley, C., Wigfield, A., Buchanan, C. M., Reuman, D., Flanagan, C., & MacIver, D. (1993). Development during adolescence: The impact of stage–environment fit on young adolescents' experiences in schools and in families. *American Psychologist, 48*(2), 90–101.

Eckert, P. (1989). *Jocks and burnouts: Social categories and identity in the high school.* New York: Teachers College Press.

Elmore, R. F. (2004). *School reform from the inside out.* Cambridge, MA: Harvard Education Press.

Fine, M. (1991). *Framing dropouts: Notes on the politics of an urban pubic high school.* Albany, NY: SUNY Press.

Fine, M. (1994). *Chartering urban school reform: Reflections on public high schools in the midst of change.* New York: Teachers College Press.

Fox, W. F. (1981). Reviewing economics of size in education. *Journal of Education Finance, 6,* 273–296.

Friedman, M. (1962). *Capitalism and freedom.* Chicago: University of Chicago Press.

Gewertz, C. (2001, May 2). The breakup: Suburbs try smaller high schools. *Education Week, 20*(33), 1, 16, 18–19.

Goetz, J., & LeCompte, M. (1984). *Ethnography and qualitative design in education research.* Orlando, FL: Academic Press.

Goodlad, J. I. (1984). *A place called school.* New York: McGraw Hill.

Grant, G. (1988). *The world we created at Hamilton High.* Cambridge, MA: Harvard University Press.

Guba, E., & Lincoln, Y. (1981). *Effective evaluation: Improving the usefulness of evaluation results through responsive and naturalistic approaches.* San Francisco: Jossey-Bass.

Hammack, F. M. (2004). *The comprehensive high school today.* New York: Teachers College Press.

Heyns, B. (1974). Social selection and stratification within schools. *American Journal of Sociology, 79,* 1434–1451.

Herszenhorn, D. M. (2005, November 18). Mayor plans new education measures, including reshaping 8 troubled high schools. *New York Times,* A1.

Hirschman, A. O. (1970). *Exit, voice, and loyalty: Responses to decline in firms, organizations, and states.* Cambridge, MA: Harvard University Press.

Holland, N. E. (2002). Small schools: Transforming teacher and student experiences in urban high schools. In V. E. Lee (Ed.), *Reforming Chicago's high schools: Research perspectives on school and system level change* (pp. 89–124). Chicago: Consortium on Chicago School Research, University of Chicago.

Hollingshead, A. B. (1975). *Elmtown's youth and Elmtown revisited.* New York: John Wiley and Sons.

Institute for Research and Reform in Education [IRRE]. (2006). *Small learning communities.* Retrieved October 23, 2006, from http://www.irre.org/ftf/slc.asp

Jordan, W. J., McPartland, J. M., Letgers, N. E., & Balfanz, R. (2000). Creating a comprehensive school reform model: The Talent Development High School with career academies. *Journal of Education for Students Placed at Risk, 5,* 159–181.

Kemple, J. J., & Herlihy, C. M. (2004). *The Talent Development High School model: Context, components, and initial impacts on ninth-grade students' engagement and performance.* New York: Manpower Demonstration Research Corporation (MDRC).

Kemple, J. J., Herlihy, C. M., & Smith, T. J. (2005). *Making progress toward graduation: Evidence from the Talent Development High School model.* New York: Manpower Demonstration Research Corporation (MDRC).

Kemple, J. J., & Rock, J. L. (1996). *Career academies: Early implementation lessons from a 10-site evaluation.* New York: Manpower Demonstration Research Corporation (MDRC).

Kemple, J. J., & Snipes, J. (2000). *Career academies: Impacts on students' engagement and performance in high school.* New York: Manpower Demonstration Research Corporation (MDRC).

Kliebard, H. M. (1995). *The struggle for the American curriculum 1893–1958.* New York: Routledge.

Labaree, D. F. (1997). Public goods, private goods: The American struggle over educational goods. *American Educational Research Journal, 34*(1), 39–81.

Lee, V. E. (2000). School size and the organization of secondary schools. In M. T. Hallinan (Ed.), *Handbook of the sociology of education* (pp. 327–344). New York: Kluwer Academic/Plenum Publishers.

Lee, V. E. (2001). *Restructuring high schools for equity and excellence: What works.* New York: Teachers College Press.

Lee, V. E., & Bryk, A. S. (1988). A multilevel model of the social distribution of high school achievement. *Sociology of Education, 61,* 78–94.

Lee, V. E., & Bryk, A. S. (1989). Curriculum tracking as mediating the social distribution of high school achievement. *Sociology of Education, 62,* 172–192.

Lee, V. E., & Burkam, D. T. (2002). *Inequality at the starting gate. Social background differences in achievement as children begin school.* Washington, DC: Economic Policy Institute.

Lee, V. E., Burkam, D. T., Chow-Hoy, T. K., Smerdon, B. A., & Geverdt, D. (1998). *High school curriculum structure: Effects on coursetaking and achievement in mathematics for high school graduates* (Working Paper 98-09). Washington, DC: U.S. Department of Education, National Center for Education Statistics.

Lee, V. E., Ready, D. D., & Johnson, D. J. (2001). The difficulty of identifying rare samples to study: The case of high schools divided into schools-within-schools. *Educational Evaluation and Policy Analysis, 23*(4), 365–379.

Lee, V. E., Smerdon, B. A., Alfeld-Liro, C., & Brown, S. L. (2000). Inside small and large high schools: Curriculum and social relations. *Educational Evaluation and Policy Analysis, 22*(2), 147–171.

Lee, V. E., & Smith, J. B. (1995). Effects of high school restructuring and size on gains in achievement and engagement for early secondary school students. *Sociology of Education, 68*(4), 241–270.

Lee, V. E., & Smith, J. B. (1997). High school size: Which works best, and for whom? *Educational Evaluation and Policy Analysis, 19*(3), 205–227.

Lee, V. E., & Smith, J. B. (1999). Social support and achievement for young adolescents in Chicago: The role of social academic press. *American Educational Research Journal, 36*(4), 907–945.

Lightfoot, S. L. (1983). *The good high school: Portraits of character and culture.* New York: Basic Books.

Lincoln, Y., & Guba, E. (1985). *Naturalistic inquiry.* Beverly Hills, CA: Sage.

Lortie, D. (1975). *Schoolteacher: A sociological study.* Chicago: University of Chicago Press.

Louis, K. S., Marks, H. M., & Kruse, S. (1996). Teachers' professional community in restructured schools. *American Educational Research Journal, 33,* 757–798.

MacLeod, J. (1995). *Ain't no makin' it: Aspirations & attainment in a low-income neighborhood.* Boulder, CO: Westview Press.

Marshall, C., & Rossman, G. (1999). *Designing qualitative research.* Thousand Oaks, CA: Sage.

Maxwell, J. A. (1998). Designing a qualitative study. In L. Bickman & D. Rog (Eds.), *Handbook of applied social research methods* (pp. 69–100). Thousand Oaks, CA: Sage.

McMullan, B. J. (1994). Charters and restructuring. In M. Fine (Ed.), *Chartering urban school reform: Reflections on public high schools in the midst of change* (pp. 63–77). New York: Teachers College Press.

McPartland, J. M., Legters, N., Jordan, W., & McDill, E. L. (1996). *The Talent Development high school: Early evidence of impact on school climate, attendance, and student promotion.* Baltimore, MD: Johns Hopkins University, Center for Research on the Education of Students Placed at Risk.

McQuillan, P. (2004). *Three years down the road: Small school reform at the Manual Educational Complex.* Chestnut Hill, MA: Boston College, Lynch School of Education.

Meier, D. (1995). *The power of their ideas: Lessons for American from a small school in Harlem.* Boston: Beacon Press.

Merriam, S. B. (1998). *Qualitative research and case study applications in education.* San Francisco: Jossey-Bass.

Miles, M. B., & Huberman, A. M. (1994). *Qualitative data analysis.* Thousand Oaks, CA: Sage.

Muncie, D. E., & McQuillan, P. J. (1996). *Reform and resistance in schools and classrooms: An ethnographic view of the Coalition of Essential Schools.* New Haven, CT: Yale University Press.

National Association of Secondary School Principals [NASSP]. (1996). *Breaking ranks: Changing an American institution.* Reston, VA: Author.

National Center for Education Statistics [NCES]. (2001). *Digest of education statistics.* Washington, DC: U.S. Department of Education. Retrieved October 23, 2006, from http://nces.ed.gov/programs/digest/d01/dt151.asp

National Center for Education Statistics [NCES]. (2002). *Digest of education statistics.* Washington, DC: U.S. Department of Education. Retrieved October 23, 2006, from http://nces.ed.gov/programs/digest/d02/dt087.asp

National Center for Education Statistics [NCES]. (2004). *Digest of education statistics.* Washington, DC: U.S. Department of Education. Retrieved October 23, 2006, from http://nces.ed.gov/programs/digest/d04/tables/dt04_005.asp

National Commission on Excellence in Education. (1983). *A nation at risk: The imperative for educational reform.* Washington, DC: U.S. Government Printing Office.

National Education Association. (1893). *Report on the Committee of Secondary School Studies.* Washington, DC: U.S. Government Printing Office.

National Education Association. (1918). *Cardinal principles of secondary education: A report of the Commission on the Reorganization of Secondary Education.* Washington, DC: U.S. Government Printing Office.

Newmann, F. M. (1981). Reducing student alienation in high schools: Implications of theory. *Harvard Educational Review, 51*(4), 546–564.

Newmann, F. M., & Associates. (1996). *Authentic achievement: Restructuring school intellectual quality.* San Francisco: Jossey-Bass.

Oakes, J. (1985). *Keeping track: How schools structure inequality.* New Haven, CT: Yale University Press.

Oxley, D. (1989, Spring). Smaller is better. *American Educator, 13,* 28–31, 51–52.

Oxley, D. (1993). *Organizing schools into smaller units: A planning guide* (CRDHE Publication Series 93-1). Philadelphia: Temple University, Center for Research in Human Development and Education.

Oxley, D. (1994). Organizing for responsiveness: The heterogeneous school community. In M. Wang & E. Gordon (Eds.), *Educational resilience in inner-city America: Challenges and prospects* (pp. 179–190). Hillsdale, NJ: Lawrence Erlbaum Associates.

Patton, M. Q. (2002). *Qualitative evaluation and research methods* (3rd ed.). Newbury Park, CA: Sage.

Powell, A. G., Farrar, E., & Cohen, D. K. (1985). *The shopping mall high school: Winners and losers in the educational market place.* Boston: Houghton Mifflin Company.

Quint, J., Bloom, H. S., Black, A. R., & Stephens, L. (2005). *The challenge of scaling up educational reform: Findings and lessons from First Things First.* New York: Manpower Demonstration Research Corporation (MDRC).

Raywid, M. A. (1996). *The subschools/small schools movement: Taking stock.* Madison, WI: University of Wisconsin, Center on the Organization and Restructuring of Schools.

Raywid, M. A., & Schmerler, G. (2003). *Not so easy going: The policy environments of small urban schools and schools-within-schools.* Charleston, WV: ERIC Clearinghouse on Rural Education and Small Schools.

Rowan, B. (1990). Commitment and control: Alternative strategies for the organizational design of schools. *Review of Educational Research, 16,* 353–389.

Schoggen, P., & Schoggen, M. (1988). Student voluntary participation and high school size. *Journal of Educational Research, 81*(5), 288–293.

Sedlak, M. W., Wheeler, C. W., Pullin, D. C., & Cusick, P. A. (1986). *Selling students short: Classroom bargains and academic reform in the American high school.* New York: Teachers College Press.

Siskin, L. S. (1994a). Is the school the unit of change? Internal and external contexts of restructuring. In P. Grimmett & J. Neufeld (Eds.), *The struggle for authenticity: Teacher development in a context of educational change* (pp. 121–140). New York: Teachers College Press.

Siskin, L. S. (1994b). *Realms of knowledge: Academic departments in secondary schools.* Washington, DC: Falmer Press.

Sizer, T. R. (1984). *Horace's compromise: The dilemma of the American high school.* Boston: Houghton Mifflin.

Sizer, T. R. (1992). *Horace's school: Redesigning the American high school.* Boston: Houghton Mifflin.

Smylie, M. A., & Hart, A. W. (1999). School leadership for teacher learning and change: A human and social capital development perspective. In J. Murphy & K. S. Louis (Eds.), *Handbook of research on educational administration* (2nd ed., pp. 421–441). San Francisco: Jossey-Bass.

Spillane, J. P., Halverson, R., & Diamond, J. B. (2001). Investigating school leadership practice: A distributed perspective. *Educational Researcher, 30*(3), 23–28.

Sporte, S. E., Correa, M., & Kahne, J. (2003). *Chicago High School Redesign Initiative: A snapshot of the first year of implementation.* Chicago: University of Chicago, Consortium on Chicago School Research.

Stake, R. E. (1994). Case studies. In N. K. Denzin & Y. S. Lincoln (Eds.), *Handbook of qualitative research* (pp. 236–247). Thousand Oaks, CA: Sage.

Steinberg, L. (1990). Interdependence in the family: Autonomy, conflict and harmony in the parent adolescent relationship. In S. S. Feldman & G. R. Elliot (Eds.), *At the threshold: The developing adolescent* (pp. 255–276). Cambridge, MA: Harvard University Press.

Stern, D., Raby, M., & Dayton, C. (1992). *Career academies: Partnerships for reconstructing American high schools.* San Francisco: Jossey-Bass.

Stevenson, D. L., & Barker, D. P. (1987). The family-school relationship and the child's school performance. *Child Development, 58,* 1348–1357.

Strauss, A., & Corbin, J. (1998). *Basics of qualitative research: Techniques and procedures for developing grounded theory.* Thousand Oaks, CA: Sage.

Thorndike, E. L. (1906, October). The opportunity of the high schools. *The Bookman, 24,* 180–184.

Tyack, D. (1974). *The one best system: A history of American urban education.* Cambridge, MA: Harvard University Press.

Tyson, K., Darity, W., & Castellino, D. (2005). Black adolescents and the dilemmas of high achievement. *American Sociological Review, 70*(4), 582–605.

U.S. Department of Education. (2006a). *School size.* Retrieved October 23, 2006, from http://www.ed.gov/about/offices/list/ovae/pi/hs/schoolsize.html

U.S. Department of Education. (2006b). *Smaller learning communities program.* Retrieved October 23, 2006, from http://www.ed.gov/programs/slcp/index.html

Useem, E. L. (1992, October). Middle school and math groups: Parents' involvement in children's placement. *Sociology of Education, 65,* 263–279.

Wallach, C. A., & Lear, R. (2005). *A foot in two worlds: The second report on comprehensive high school conversions.* Seattle: Small Schools Project.

Warner, W. L., Havighurst, R. J., & Loeb, M. B. (1944). *Who shall be educated? The challenge of unequal opportunities.* New York: Harper & Brothers.

Weber, M. ([1922] 1978). *Economy and society.* Berkeley: University of California Press.

Weick, K. E. (1976). Educational organizations as loosely coupled systems. *Administrative Science Quarterly, 21,* 1–19.

Wells, A. S. (1993). *Time to choose: America at the crossroads of school choice policy.* New York: Hill and Wang.

Wells, A. S., & Crain, R. L. (1997). *Stepping over the color line: African-American students in White suburban schools.* New Haven, CT: Yale University Press.

Wells, A. S., & Oakes, J. (1996). Potential pitfalls of systemic reform: Early lessons from detracking research. *Sociology of Education, Extra Issue,* 135–143.

Willis, P. (1977). *Learning to labor: How working class kids get working class jobs.* New York: Columbia University Press.

Yin, R. K. (1994). *Case study research: Design and methods* (2nd ed.). *Applied Social Research Methods Series: Vol. 5.* Newbury Park, CA: Sage.

Yonezawa, S., Wells, A. S., & Serna, I. (2002). Choosing tracks: "Freedom of choice" in detracking schools. *American Educational Research Journal, 39*(1), 37–67.

Index

Page numbers followed by italic letter *f* refer to figures; those followed by *t* refer to tables.

■ ■ ■

About the Authors

VALERIE E. LEE is a Professor of Education in the University of Michigan's School of Education and a Faculty Associate at the University's Institute for Social Research. She has conducted a large body of research about the social and academic organization of high schools and how these organizational character-istics influence how much students learn over their high school years. A partic-ular focus of her work has been the equitable distribution of learning by race/ethnicity and socioeconomic status. More recently, her research has shifted to learning in younger children, including a book, *Inequality at the Starting Gate* (2002), coauthored with David T. Burkam. Many of her studies of high schools were summarized in *Restructuring High Schools for Equity and Excellence: What Works* (Teachers College Press, 2002). She was also a coauthor (with Anthony S. Bryk and Peter Holland) of *Catholic Schools and the Common Good* (1993). She teaches courses on quantitative research methods, program evaluation, and the sociology of education.

DOUGLAS D. READY is an Assistant Professor of Education at Teachers Col-lege, Columbia University. A sociologist of education, his research examines the influence of educational policies and practices on educational equity and access. In addition to writing on high school reform, his research also examines race and social class disparities in young children's cognitive growth. Work represen-tative of these two strands—and his broader interest in educational equity—has appeared in *Educational Evaluation and Policy Analysis, American Journal of Education, Sociology of Education, Teachers College Record, Elementary School Journal,* and the *Brookings Institution's Papers on Education Policy.* He teaches courses in research methodology, and the sociology and politics of education.